Foreign Cultures

An Introduction to Ethnology for Development Aid Workers and Church Workers Abroad

Lothar Käser

/VTR
Publications

Bibliographic Information Published by the Deutsche Nationalbibliothek
The Deutsche Nationalbibliothek lists this publication in the Deutsche
Nationalbibliografie; detailed bibliographic data are available in the Internet
at http://dnb.d-nb.de.

ISBN 978-3-95776-113-2

VTR Publications
Gogolstr. 33, 90475 Nürnberg, Germany, http://www.vtr-online.com

© 2014 by Lothar Käser

Translated from German by Geoffrey Sutton

Printed by Lightning Source

For Klaus and Ulrike Müller,
friends from our years together on Chuuk, Micronesia

Contents

Preface to the First German Edition

In September 1969 I accepted a teaching post on Toon, one of the islands of Chuuk Atoll in Micronesia. There I began a period of completely new, diverse, interesting and often difficult experiences which I distilled over the years into preparing and writing FOREIGN CULTURES.

The organization *Dienste in Übersee* (Service Overseas) eased me and my family through the *Liebenzeller Mission* in Bad Liebenzell (Black Forest) to the *Evangelical Church of Truk*. The organization (then based near Stuttgart) is a grouping of Protestant churches which recruit and prepare staff for development aid projects on behalf of Third-World partner churches. The planning, organization and overseeing of the project was remarkably free of bureaucracy, yet thorough and careful. On the induction course before we flew out we learned a lot about the culture and about the forthcoming changes to our way of life: the unfamiliar tropical and cultural environment, and the notably different mind-set that we would need to tune ourselves to and deal with. In the reality of a South Sea Island where we soon found ourselves it quickly became clear that, despite our varied course of preparation, we were still ignorant about essential things. These things are the contents of this book.

Foreign cultures have structures a foreigner must understand as quickly as possible for him to be effective in working within them. This is much easier said than done! Most of these structures elude direct scrutiny and assessment because they are cognitive in essence and are rooted deep in the thinking of the collective indigenous mind. Much would have been simpler for me if I had known that there are categories, concepts and coping strategies which highlight foreign social structures and trains of thought and help to explain them; and – a later revelation of even greater priority – which are open to one's own exploration. The discovery that the study of *ethnology* opens up these categories, concepts and coping strategies was one that I only made when I was in the foreign culture. I was confronting problems of my own making because my knowledge of ethnology – not to mention my general experience – was lacking.

The feature that gave me the greatest difficulty – because it was so unfamiliar to me – was that the youngsters and adults I taught had a super-ego orientation towards the collective. This orientation towards the collective is among the most important features that European workers need to embrace if they wish to be effective in a community-minded environment in Asia, Africa and Latin America, whether they are teachers, doctors, agriculturists, craftsmen or church workers (see chap. 10). On our induction course these problems had been alluded to only in passing – vague references which I only appreciated afterwards when confronted by reality.

It seems to me particularly striking that the many institutions involved in training development aid workers, and even church workers and overseas mission workers, include in their programmes virtually nothing about ethnology (or at most only the bare essentials) even these days. The effect of such ignorance on how my own colleagues in Micronesia (staff from the Liebenzeller Mission, Bad Liebenzell) were responding to the Islanders and their behaviour was only too obvious. I want to emphasize strongly that, with a very few exceptions, they themselves recognized this as a serious lack; much of what I myself had to learn stems from their willingness to discuss issues and their great readiness to deal with their own ignorance.

My experience convinced me that a knowledge of ethnology is a great benefit to the worker operating in a foreign culture – without it he cannot be well-integrated and effective. This led me after my eventual return from Micronesia to becoming intensively involved with ethnology as a professional. For more than twenty years of teaching university students ethnology, missiology, and general linguistics on courses preparing them to be medical staff in the Third World – and on lecture tours and field trips to South Asia, Africa and South America – I have been refining the following introduction to ethnology, choosing the contents according to the needs of the target groups mentioned in the book's subtitle and arranging them into a teaching scheme.

Many of the ideas, arguments and examples used here stem from my reading of hundreds of publications in ethnology. Regrettably, and despite great efforts, I have often been unable to pinpoint references. I apologize to authors for my oversight. Because **FOREIGN CULTURES** has been conceived as a *textbook*, and to avoid overburdening the text, I have deliberately dispensed with (ample) references in the form of footnotes and other attributions usual in academic publications. Where a note was unavoidable I have placed it in brackets in the main text.

To all those who in whatever way have contributed to the success of the difficult and arduous process of this project I wish to convey my heartfelt thanks, but particularly to my wife Gisela for her thoughtful and motivating support throughout, and Gisela Bücking and Hanna Robisch for their proofreading of the manuscript. But for their attention to detail, I would have overlooked a whole number of infelicities of style and argument, and mistakes.

Schallstadt, Summer 1997
Lothar Käser

Preface to the Expanded, Second German Edition

After its first publication the book was blessed with recognition, which came as a pleasant surprise for the author; it won the "George W. Peters Prize" awarded by AEM (Association of Evangelical Missions). The book has stimulated a number of research projects for Master's and Doctoral theses. Many organizations working overseas have been including it on their induction programmes. Meanwhile it has not only been found useful for those it was originally intended: some museums of ethnology recommend it for their visitors as an introduction to the subject.

In 2004 the book was published in Portuguese, and in 2008 in French. The bibliographical details are as follows:

Käser, Lothar: Diferentes culturas. Uma introdução à etnologia. Londrina 2004, (ISBN 85-8714390-5).

Käser, Lothar: Voyage en culture étrangère. Guide d'ethnologie appliquée. Charols/France 2008, (ISBN 978-2-7550-0085-6).

It is now time to undertake a second edition, not a thorough revision but an expanded version, justified by the recent publication of a number of recent studies whose contents need to be incorporated.

Thanks are due to my reviewers who have sometimes taken great trouble to share their judgements, indeed to all those who have offered their thoughts, hopes and encouragements. With their help a number of factual errors have been avoided.

Schallstadt, Winter 2012
Lothar Käser

Chapter 1
Introduction

This chapter explains how Europeans and others from Western backgrounds came to be present in foreign lands; what work they did there and still do; and what impact they had; and the reason why in the framework of a foreign culture one needs the particular areas of expertise described in the subsequent chapters.

If one looks at the world from the perspective of our modern transport options, one's impression is that the world has shrunk considerably in recent times. In the first half of the twentieth century it still took several weeks to travel by boat from Europe to South-East Asia. These days an aeroplane does the same journey in less than twenty hours. Foreign landscapes, peoples and cultures are thus no longer accessible merely to a few but to anybody with enough money set aside. That number has been growing.

It is an open secret that foreign societies and their cultures hold a fascination for us. Nowadays tourists from the so-called developed (rich) industrial countries of the Northern hemisphere flock to the so-called under-developed (poor) non-industrial countries of the Southern hemisphere to experience as foreign tourists the *adventure* of contacting real and accessible alien cultures.

Of course, foreigners had been there before. Yet their interest tended not to focus on tourism. They were *pioneers, slave merchants, businessmen, plantation owners, soldiers and officials on colonial service*. All of them pursued, among other things, tangible political and commercial interests on public or private assignment. Contrary to popular belief, Christian *missionaries* were very seldom the first arrivals in non-European societies. Generally they came after the above-mentioned categories, and with quite different aims (see chap. 18). Nevertheless, however nuanced the intentions of all these pioneers were, there was one common feature: their presence triggered *changes* in the cultures they moved into.

If from today's standpoint we look back at the changes they caused we can easily *misjudge the issue*. We tend to see it as deviation from an ideal which the cultures originally embodied. Looking at it this way, we tend to suppose that the issue is not one of change but of destruction, sheer outright destruction. However, matters are not so simple; to simplify in this way portrays a false and hasty reflection of the real situation. Of course, the peoples of indigenous foreign cultures had much taken from them by the foreign arrivals. Nevertheless at the same time they had much given to them. Thus it is more appropriate to speak here not of cultural destruction but of *cultural change*. Calling it thus allows us to label destruction where it did occur by its due name.

Until roughly the mid-twentieth century the activity of those who changed the foreign culture was compromised by their impaired thinking: they were seldom clear about the meaning of the term *culture* and the significance of a particular culture for the people establishing their lives within it. The consequences of this knowledge deficiency were considerable. The agents of change acted with no responsible conscious awareness of the inevitable outcomes, outcomes which neither the indigenous people nor the agents of change anticipated. The criteria guiding the changes stemmed from the value systems of the newcomers and not – or very seldom – of the locals. This misjudgement should never have occurred.

To avoid repeating the mistakes incurred by the agents of change of what I term the old type, people began to conceive of a new type of (European and Western) foreigner who was expected to create change without destruction. The new type of foreigner was expected both to ascertain whether what foreign cultures held dear would stand the test of time and to *develop* new cultural elements.

After the Second World War, in the wake of decolonization, many of the overseas old type agents of change disappeared from what became known as the Third World. The slave trade had been brought to an end in the second half of the nineteenth century. Yet Christian missionaries continued to work in not insignificant numbers. They were joined by a new phenomenon, the *development worker* and – where mission activity led to an indigenous church – the *church worker*. The missionary had of course always been involved in development work whether as a doctor, teacher, technician, craftsman or agriculturist, which is why to this day the distinction between a missionary and a development worker has remained slight. But the new foreigner, particularly the development worker, was – it was assumed – able to pursue his activity in many nuanced and less destructive ways, for two reasons: because prior to his work he had been made aware of the foreign nature of his own home background, and because he was an acknowledged *specialist* in his field. (It was not unusual for the media to call him a "development expert", a phrase that Third-World NGO representatives rightly felt was arrogant, as they still do.) This contrasted generally with attitudes towards a team member working in Christian mission and missiology, the only realm where expertise was acknowledged.

The increasing arrival of development workers to the Third World brought with it two new viewpoints to the consciousness of the First World from which mission workers and development workers came. The First World became convinced that Third-World poverty arose essentially from inherent structural faults and could be overcome by changing these indigenous structures. It was taken for granted that these changes were beneficial because they underpinned a good purpose whose aim was acknowledged; from this same perspective it was assumed that the people being served also intended making the necessary changes.

Indeed European and Western opinion saw development aid during the euphoria of its early years until well into the 1970s as a kind of new gospel for the recipient countries. Against this backdrop the work of Christian missions and churches lost its profile, at the same time as the limelight given to development organizations increased. The image of the mission worker suffered a singular decline in the esteem of the general public. In some media the image was distorted to a caricature. Whatever the missionary had done and continued to do, he was thereafter seen as the prototype destroyer of cultures, an accusation whose tone diminished somewhat in the 1990s but which surfaced continually in public debate. By contrast the development worker (without any specific input of his own) gained the aura of a benefactor and long-term philanthropist. This public evaluation failed in large degree to do justice to the actual circumstances, as we have since come to recognize.

But there is a plus in all this. From this controversial situation there grew an ever clearer imperative for more information about the *intrinsic value of cultures* and about the benefits they bring for those who use them to inform and manage their own lives. Both groups – the churches or missions and the development aid organizations – made (tentative) efforts to appropriate attitudes drawn from *ethnology* and *cultural anthropology* and include them in their courses and training programmes. There were difficulties along the way, and one cannot yet say that the concepts satisfy all partners. However, the fabled first step has been taken in the right direction.

For the edification of future *theorists* involved with foreign cultures, such as ethnologists and cultural anthropologists etc. there are already a host of brilliant introductions dealing with the thought-processes and methods pertaining to culture as an object for theoretical research. For the *practitioner* involved in church contexts or secular development aid these introductions are too full of material and details; their comprehensive treatment makes them difficult to understand and apply. What the practitioner has been missing until now is a *simplified introduction* to fundamental issues whose mastery will enable him to undertake a number of things: find his bearings in the literature of ethnology for his specific area of activity; recognize these basic concepts in the cultural reality he is immersed in; apply them; and do *his own research.*

FOREIGN CULTURES is a simplified introduction with this aim.

Not all specialisms within ethnology are equally important for European and Western experts to work successfully in a foreign context. This explains why ethnological research into *issues of justice*, and the ethnology pertaining to *art, cities or museums* are not covered. On the other hand the *processes of enculturation, ethnopsychology* and particular aspects of *medical practice and religions* in foreign cultures receive especially full treatment, because this knowledge has proved vital for fieldworkers.

Chapter 2
Ethnology as an Academic Discipline

This chapter explains how ethnology can be defined, what its area of research and that of its allied disciplines cover, in Germany and America, and what type of links exist to these allied disciplines.

2.1   Ethnology and Its Object of Research

Ethnology is the *study of people's way of life* (the totality of all people of a kind living in a specified area) insofar as they form separate groups and differ from one another in their ways of life (according to Fischer 1983:11). The phrase "ways of life" in this regard means everything which is required and used for *shaping life and coping with it*. Instead of ways of life, as I shall be demonstrating, one can use the simple term *cultures* (cf. chap. 4).

Basically all cultures could be the object of the academic discipline called ethnology, cultures *surviving into the present* or *archaic* ones known to us only from archaeological finds or from other historic evidence. However in reality ethnology confines itself to the research of current cultures having particular *features*, as it were, taking account of specific cultures in a particular way. Such features are principally the *absence of any writing* and the *very limited control over nature*. Many publications mention *non-industrialized* or *pre-industrial, non-state, pre-state* or *tribal societies;* others address the issue that in cultures without writing systems special significance is accorded to oral transmission of knowledge and values, calling these *tribal cultures*. Nowadays in ethnology the use of terms such as *underdeveloped* or *primitive cultures* is rightly frowned upon.

2.2   The Term "Primitive Culture"

In many older ethnographies (descriptions of cultures) the term *primitive people* or *primitive culture* is used. This terminology is quite problematic. In the past primitive cultures were considered the opposite of so-called civilized cultures. This was a false contrast, since – without exception – primitive peoples also have a culture. The use of this term is problematic in another respect.

Such peoples are indeed more dependent on their living environment than people of industrial societies, and they are often very well adapted to it. But one should not suppose from this unreservedly that they live in "harmony with nature" or even "in one of the few remaining paradises" as is often said in a sentimental and idealizing way. One must also reckon that these societies are characterized by their inner tensions and contradictions. Like everywhere else, women are the target of prejudice, animals are mistreated, children abused and nature exploited. The fact that this was already happening back in prehistoric times (deforestation with irreversible consequences, the extinction of the moa bird – a flightless bird perhaps related to the emu), is known from the Polynesian Maori of New Zealand (Anderson in Martin/Klein 1984:723-740; McGlone 1983:11-25). We also know this from the North American Indians who – in a drastic distortion of reality – have been happily considered the "first Greens". If such societies are not causing damage and stress to their own environment it is certainly because they are relatively small groups.

The potential extent of these cultural deficits even among so-called primitive peoples has been thoroughly documented in Edgerton 1992 (German 1994). Illius (2003:92) has references to articles in the periodicals "Human Organization" and "Journal of Contemporary Ethnography" which of recent times increasingly "publish field studies on abortions, alcoholism, AIDS, child abuse, corruption, Satanism,... and sex-for-crack deals".

2.3   Ethnic Societies and the Ethnologist's Field of Study

All cultures can be studied in terms of how they function and what they mean for those endeavouring to take charge of their lives. Cultures of pre-literate peoples (or where literacy is a recent phenomenon) are particularly suited by virtue of their simpler structure. It is of great benefit to ethnology that it has concentrated and confined its interest to pre-literate cultures.

The relatively simple structure of cultures, enabling ethnic groups to shape their lives and manage them, is one of their signal features. The scope of their components is generally so straightforward that even a single researcher can take in its full extent. This is not achievable in studying European-Western cultures, or indeed Far Eastern ones, because of their complexity. Our formulating what postmen actually need to know and do is only slightly more involved than our merely observing that they bring the post – which might justify postmen taking us for simpletons! The fact that we non-postmen have only the vaguest of notions about their work shows that cultures needing postmen are complex and difficult to comprehend. Even the members themselves of a society are familiar with an ever smaller aspect of it; and they can no longer give an outside enquirer sufficient information about it.

So for ethnologists the field of study – the laboratory almost – involves pre-literate, ethnic societies. The chapters that follow will describe the details of many of their cultures. This is for two reasons: Firstly, as a member of the association of ethnologists and an author, I have had my most significant experiences among foreign cultures of various ethnic groups. Secondly: most development aid workers and church and mission workers from European-Western cultural backgrounds operate largely in an ethnological context and do so even when the mainstream culture of the country where they work is regarded as "civilized and advanced". In fact they nearly always interact with non-urban peoples, "simpler folk" on the land who have not generally had any schooling; who can scarcely read and write (if at all); and who thus have a very straightforward view of life. These circumstances are very similar to those in a pre-literate ethnic society. The fact that I am concentrating on them does not mean that I am excluding other more complex cultures with bolder structures. Observations about pre-literate societies can be carried over and applied without difficulty to other so-called advanced cultures, including European cultures.

2.4   Academic Disciplines Surrounding Ethnology

Like any academic discipline, ethnology is often not clearly distinguishable from its *neighbouring disciplines*. Its boundaries are particularly fluid where they touch disciplines – like ethnology – whose focal point is man himself (Greek: *anthropos*) or one of his countless aspects.

Anthropology deals with the biological aspects of the (normal, healthy) individual and his body. It describes *the races of mankind*; mankind's anatomy (the academic study of the body's structure); physiology (the study of how the body's cells and organs function) and psychology; mankind's development and relation to advanced animals (primates). It is often also called *physical* or – for some years now – *biological anthropology* (Gadamer/Vogler 1972). One of its many branches, which is enjoying at the moment significant and controversial growth is *human genetic research* (recent introductions to this topic are Knußmann 1980 and Henke/Rothe 1994). *Philosophical anthropology*, mentioned occasionally, is not so much a discipline as the attempt to understand man's thinking as he reflects upon himself. To put it more clearly: philosophical anthropology is about finding why and how man thinks, especially when he reflects on his own existence.

Cultural anthropology is in direct contrast to physical/biological anthropology; but at the same time it is the full counterpart and complement. The object of its research is man: a living being with a unique culture he owns and uses (and needs to use!) in order to shape and control his life. In this respect cultural anthropology and ethnology coincide. However, they do indeed differ – even if the difference is slight.

The object of cultural anthropology is mankind's *culture* in general, something that does not exist specifically. Humankind has very many actual cultures; it is these individual cultures that are open to scrutiny, description and analysis. Yet because they are all built on the same principles and all function similarly they constitute "human culture" – if one analyses the commonly held structures of a sufficient number of cultures. It needs to be clearly understood that the general culture derived from this analysis is only a model (albeit a complete one taking account of all possibilities): a researcher's construct of the mind, having no existence in the real world.

To put it more simply: it is this ideal cultural model that forms the object of studies in anthropology. Anthropology is, of all cultural disciplines, the one with the least specific orientation. It therefore shares some aspects in common with philosophy. In this it is distinct from ethnology, whose particular bias is the study of non-literate cultures. (Girtler 1979 and Stagl 1981 are both very readable introductions to the subject-matter proper to cultural anthropology and its relation to ethnology).

The links between anthropology, physical/biological anthropology, cultural anthropology, cultural studies and ethnology have grown and established themselves rather differently in the U.S.A., where *anthropology* is the umbrella term embracing all the disciplines which study (normal, healthy) humans in their physical and cultural manifestation. Subordinate to this are *physical/biological anthropology* and *cultural anthropology*. Topics which are studied by American physical/biological anthropology are fully equivalent to those studied by German physical/biological anthropology.

It is not quite the same for cultural anthropology, which equates broadly with German "Völkerkunde", but differs in that German-speaking researchers arrange the components differently. *Cultural anthropology* consists of *archaeology*, the discipline relating to past (archaic) cultures; of *ethnology*, the discipline relating to current cultures; and *general linguistics*. This American academic model (from Fischer 1983:32) is as follows:

anthropology

physical/biological   cultural
anthropology   anthropology

archaeology   ethnology   linguistics

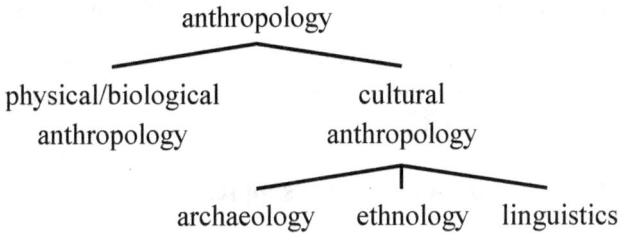

The above structure for cultural anthropology is a much clearer one than its German counterpart. Furthermore, man and culture as its focus for study is rather more central than in the structure for cultural studies, in that with cultural anthropology both literate and pre-literate cultures are viewed even-handedly as proper fields for research. "Culture, finally, also includes civilization. No modern anthropologist regards civilization as qualitatively different from culture, nor does he make a distinction between the civilized and the uncivilized. All civilizations, including the great ones of today and ancient times, are but special instances of culture, distinctive in the quantity of their content and the complexity of their patterning, but not qualitatively different from cultures of so-called uncivilized peoples" (Beals/Hoijer 1959:226-227). More than ever, German ethnology is currently recognizing the aspect of language and its role as an implement of knowledge for researching cultures. In future it will probably relate to the structures of American cultural anthropology more and more closely.

It is noteworthy that in the English-speaking world it is enough to introduce oneself as an ***anthropologist*** to mean one is an ethnologist (or researcher in cultural studies). The message is conveyed properly despite the absence of the adjective ***cultural***. This has seen a new meaning for the term anthropology steadily emerge in Germany over the last few years. Those missions and development aid organizations which have begun to include insights from ethnology in their training procedures and induction courses (especially the more evangelical ones) are calling the discipline "anthropology" instead of ethnology, cultural studies or cultural anthropology.

As we have seen, there is a real linguistic confusion whose Babel-like impact is inhibiting progress. The fault lies with these research disciplines and their historical development, but we need to learn to live with it if we wish to engage with foreign cultures and read and understand the literature.

Additional, more Detailed Introductions to this Chapter's Topic

A clear survey of ethnology as a discipline and its associated fields is given in Fischer 2003. He includes a manageable bibliography with additional publications of merit.

Additional material on this chapter's topic:

Anderson, Atholl: The extinction of moa in southern New Zealand. In: Martin/Klein 1984:723-740.

Beals, Ralph L.; Hoijer, Harry: An introduction to anthropology. New York ²1959.

Beer, Bettina; Fischer, Hans (ed.): Ethnologie. Einführung und Überblick. Berlin 2003. (This is the 5th ed., revised, of Fischer 1983).

Edgerton, Robert B.: Sick societies. Challenging the myth of primitive harmony. Toronto et al. 1992. [German ed.: Trügerische Paradiese. Der Mythos von den glücklichen Naturvölkern. Hamburg (Kabel) 1994.]

Fischer, Hans (ed.): Ethnologie. Eine Einführung. Berlin 1983.

Fischer, Hans: Ethnologie als wissenschaftliche Disziplin. In: Beer/Fischer 2003:13-31.

Gadamer, Hans-Georg; Vogler, Paul (ed.): Neue Anthropologie. N. p.1972.

Girtler, Roland: Kulturanthropologie. München (dtv) 1979.

Harris, Marvin: Kulturanthropologie. Ein Lehrbuch. Frankfurt et al. (Campus) 1989. (Detailed, readable, highly recommended).

Henke, Winfried; Rothe, Hartmut (ed.): Paläoanthropologie. Berlin. (Springer) 1994.

Hirschberg, Walter (ed.): Neues Wörterbuch der Völkerkunde. Berlin 1988.

Illius, Bruno: Feldforschung. In: Beer/Fischer 2003:73-98.

Keesing, Roger M.; Keesing, Felix M.: New perspectives in cultural anthropology. New York 1971. (Manageable and fluently written introduction to American ethnology.)

Knußmann, Rainer: Vergleichende Biologie des Menschen. Lehrbuch der Anthropologie und Humangenetik. Stuttgart (Fischer) 1980.

Kohl, Karl-Heinz: Ethnologie – die Wissenschaft vom kulturell Fremden. Eine Einführung. München (Beck) 1993.

Martin, P. S.; Klein, R. G. (eds.): Quaternary extinctions. Tucson, Arizona 1984.

McGlone, M. S.: Polynesian deforestation of New Zealand: a preliminary synthesis. Archaeology in Oceania 18.1983:11-25.

Stagl, Justin: Kulturanthropologie und Gesellschaft. Eine wissenschaftssoziologische Darstellung der Kulturanthropologie und Ethnologie. Berlin ²1981.

Thiel, Josef Franz: Grundbegriffe der Ethnologie. Vorlesungen zur Einführung. St. Augustin 1977. (An easier read than Fischer 1983)

Trimborn, Hermann (ed.): Lehrbuch der Völkerkunde. Stuttgart 1971. (An older introduction; not so up to dates in parts, but with important chapters on issues not mentioned in Fischer 1983 und Thiel 1977, e.g. music ethnology, linguistics and ethnology)

Vivelo, Frank R.: Handbuch der Kulturanthropologie. Eine Einführung. Stuttgart 1981 (Highly recommended).

Chapter 3
A Short History of Ethnology

> In this chapter I explain where the origins of ethnology are to be found; how eth-
> nology developed in the various circumstances of cultural history from ancient
> times to the Middle Ages and on to recent times; who the most important re-
> searchers have been in shaping modern ethnology; and what the most important
> research trends are in ethnology.

3.0   Introduction

We do not have an exact date for the *start of ethnology*. A joker once
quipped that primitive forms of ethnology existed even in the Old Stone
Age or *Palaeolithic* Period. Itinerant humans living in small interrelated
groups and roaming across the land as hunter-gatherers are said to have
sat around the camp fire at night discussing their neighbours, and laugh-
ing at their unusual behaviour and their speech and manners. Thus began
the first accounts about "the others", and "foreign cultures" came into being. If indeed something like this happened then ethnology took off with
a classic case of *ethnocentrism*! (Ethnocentrism is the habit of judging
foreign cultures according to one's own viewpoint and values.)

3.1   Greeks and Romans

Among the written documents of ancient civilizations (China and the
Middle East) there are numerous references to pre-literate peoples and
their customs. But scholars agree that the actual history of ethnology –
like the history of Western culture in general – begins with the *ancient
Greeks* and *Romans*.

The Greeks held that in their known world there were only two types
of people: native *Hellenes* on the one hand, and *Barbarians* on the other.
They were called Barbarians from their supposed babble, their various
languages, which the Greeks considered "inarticulate".

What we find with the Greeks and their preoccupation with unfamiliar
cultures nevertheless does not amount to a systematic discipline akin to
ethnology. Yet it is *ethnography*: the description of foreign ethnic
groups, their life-style, manners and morals.

Herodotus (c. 490-430 B.C.) is the acknowledged founder of ethnography. In his writings about the Persians, Scythians, Egyptians etc. he ex-

plains, among other things, the characteristic variations among ethnic groups by mentioning their differing environments and climates. Herodotus is also interesting for his tendency to idealize foreign cultures. This leads him to claim that people in the *earliest settings* of human cultures had been imbued with a *general virtuousness*. Gradually over the course of cultural history their original virtue had waned. In this light Herodotus sees *nature* and *culture* as contrasting concepts, and the change from a *state of nature* to one of *culture* as a kind of *degeneration*. In the modern era his thinking has been repeated in various contexts by particular "schools" of ethnology to explain away certain cultural features as resulting from historical developments. Herodotus himself argued that mankind was to work back towards the state of nature.

A similar *theory of degeneration* – meaning that mankind must have left behind an existing "golden age" – is to be found in the works of the Greek philosopher *Plato* (c. 427-347 B.C.).

Herodotus' understanding of nature and culture is even more evident in the writings of *Posidonius* (c. 135-51 B.C.). This Greek, born in Syria, was the first writer of history to use the term *indigenous people* for the various ethnic groups that had come over the Greeks' horizon as a result of Alexander the Great's conquests. Posidonius knew of these groups from his own experiences as a scholar travelling from the Middle East through North Africa and Southern Gaul to Spain. He also emphasized the effect of environment on the development of cultural differences between the ethnic groups known about at that time. In his view the environment shaped not merely people's physical make-up but their *mental-moral* one. He claimed that Barbarians were dominated by their emotions (thymos), whereas the Romans tended to be bound by their intellect (logos).

From the first century A.D. we have *Tacitus* (c. 55-116 A.D.) and his *Germania*, a very significant book of ethnography. In it he praises the Germanic peoples to his Roman contemporaries as examples to imitate, whilst not failing to mention that they also had less worthy habits which would eventually lead to their being conquered by the Romans.

3.2   The Middle Ages

When the Roman Empire adopted Christianity as the official religion it was the start of a trend to equate being a person with being a Christian. The distinction in antiquity between Greeks and Barbarians changed to being *Christian* and being *heathen*. In the Middle Ages heathens essentially were seen as belonging to Satan's realm. Academic involvement with them was virtually nil and was even considered life-threatening. Anybody seriously interested in heathens would have been suspected of being in league with the Devil. After the fall of the Roman Empire, from the period of the great migrations until quite late into the Middle Ages, there were therefore hardly any descriptions of ethnic groups comparable with those from Antiquity.

As the Church's official doctrine, Christian theology formed the basis for the developing Mediaeval world picture. Accordingly, all that could be known was in the Bible. People tried to solve by *speculation* any questions that remained unanswered; in other words, it was not seen as necessary to investigate any theoretically elaborated hypotheses by checking their validity against reality.

Speculations on the issue of what lay at or even beyond the confines of the *oekumene* (the original Greek term for the known inhabited world) led to people believing that these regions were the haunts of all manner of *ill-shaped monsters*, hound-headed mongrels with tails, or freaks with faces full in their chests. Notoriety surrounded the mythical monopodal creature native to South America; it supposedly lay on its back and stretched its giant foot up and out like a parasol against the sun.

Traditions from Antiquity were followed by tales recounted by Arab scholars journeying to India, Ceylon (Sri Lanka) and East Asia who compiled their findings. *Marco Polo* (1254-1323) famously described his travels to Asia.

3.3   Renaissance and Early Modern Period

The next significant period for European ethnology was not until the *Age of Discoveries* beginning gradually in the 13th century, reaching its climax in the 16th and 17th centuries and only waning towards the middle of the 19th century. The onset of this Age saw a very large increase in the number of ethnographical reports.

In 1400 or thereabouts scholars in Italy rediscovered manuscripts of Classical Greek and Roman authors, heralding a *Renaissance*, a renewed preoccupation with the ethnographical descriptions contained in them. At the same time scholars received news of foreign ethnic groups in reports back to Europe from large-scale expeditions; the material stirred up a lively interest.

The *Portuguese* and *Spanish* expeditions in particular yielded impressive findings. The Portuguese prince *Henry* ("the Navigator"; 1394-1460), founder of a nautical academy, received the commission to explore the west coast of Africa southwards. *Vasco da Gama* (c. 1468-

1524) discovered the sea passage to India around Cape of Good Hope. The monopoly that the Portuguese claimed for this route on to its territories in East Asia impelled the Spanish to send *Christopher Columbus* (1451-1506) on an expedition across the Atlantic to find the Western sea route to Asia. In doing so he discovered America (1492). Only a few years later in 1513 *Vasco Nuñez de Balboa* (1475-1517) discovered the Pacific Ocean, which *Ferdinand Magellan* (1480-1521) crossed in 1521.

These discoveries led to numerous other expeditions in the centuries following. There were various reasons for this, chief among them being the *quest for valuable goods* like silk, gold and spices. Their riches, together with their territories, were seized. Furthermore, the European rulers felt duty-bound to Christianize the indigenous "heathen". Unlike nowadays, this did not generally occur by missionary mentoring with the consent of the people. The outworking of zeal still took the form of a crusade against unbelievers, backed up – where necessary – by force.

This was accompanied by the fateful notion that the culture of the discoverer and conqueror was the best and most humane. From this crass *ethnocentric position* it is not difficult to justify even acts of violence as salvific acts for the supposed good of the "natives".

The reports which arrived back to Europe with the returning explorers were full of basic errors: only a small minority of their compilers had a scientific education or an interest of that kind. They were interested in writing *sensationalist reports* overblown with distortions. These wild creatures were characterized as barbaric savages, more like animals than people.

The strongly negative flavour of reports into foreign cultures prompted European social philosophers to *formulate theories about mankind's original, primal, state*. One theory, that of *Thomas Hobbes* (1588-1679), states that originally man (without culture) confronted his counterpart as a wolf to a wolf ("homo homini lupus"), antagonizing all. Only what he termed a "social contract" brought any security.

Over this period the attitude to the question raised in the Middle Ages, namely whether "savages" could be considered human beings or not, underwent a fundamental shift. A papal bull of 1537 answered the question in the affirmative. This meant on the one hand that enforced conversion to Christianity was deemed legitimate. It meant, however, that *missionaries* having no agenda for power politics nor for riches began to side with the "savages", and denounced the conquerors' acts of abuse and brutality. Most significantly of all, they collected and published information about foreign cultures based on *long-term observation and experience*; in their writings a more positive picture of foreign cultures and societies came to the fore.

3.4   Enlightenment

Above all, a significant role in bringing about this change of attitude was played by Jesuit missionaries. They worked as ethnographers and ethnologists; that is, they were involved in gathering data about foreign cultures and formulating theories from this base through *participant observation*. One of the most influential was *Joseph-François Lafitau* (1681-1746). He spent seven years among the Iroquois Indians in Canada, publishing articles comparing their culture with those mentioned by ancient authors. Through his method of recognizing common features and differences across very varied social systems he managed to formulate ethnological categories such as *initiation rites*, *matriarchy*, *customs relating to purchasing a bride*, and so on.

Lafitau lived at a period of confident *Enlightenment* thinking when sciences were gradually freed from the embrace of theology. The Enlightenment was virtually known as the *age of the travelogue*. The accumulated information was published in contemporary multi-volume *encyclopaedias* written with an eye to making the current state of knowledge widely accessible. The sources on which the writings about foreign cultures relied were, however, rarely subjected to critical scrutiny.

This fact was one of the reasons for a new view of humankind which emerged in the Enlightenment: the concept of the *Noble Savage*. Whereas Thomas Hobbes had envisaged even in earliest society a wolf-against-wolf struggle, *Jean Jacques Rousseau* (1712-1778) supposed that man in his natural state – free from social ties and maintaining the simplest forms of culture – led a carefree and truly fulfilled life. This ideal state, Rousseau said, began its decline when more elaborate forms of culture appeared: division of labour and private ownership.

Evaluating travelogues to support Rousseau's theory resulted in early examples of what today is dismissed as *armchair anthropology*, namely theoretical studies on foreign cultures by desk-bound pundits who fail to test their findings against reality. Voyages of ethnological reality were undertaken with the cherished aim of showing that theoretical results were indeed matched by actual reality. The Frenchman *Louis-Antoine de Bougainville* (1729-1811) sailed the Pacific on behalf of the French crown from 1766 to 1769 and was the second European to discover the Polynesian island of Tahiti. In his descriptions the islanders are identified with the "Noble Savages" in ways that still reverberate with Europeans dreaming of the South Pacific paradise.

The Enlightenment is the period when ethnology in its modern form, indeed when all sciences, began to develop. The emphasis was on the role of *reason as the instrument of cognition* and on the *laws of nature* which had been investigated in the meanwhile and which were being gradually devolved upon humankind and their societies.

Enlightenment ideas on the development of ethnology began to take effect in the second half of the 18th century. This period is known as the *classical age* of ethnology. Its related publications used the terms *ethnography* (in Germany also called *Völkerkunde*), influenced by the term "Erdkunde" (geography). The development of ethnology was boosted by the fact that the purpose of explorations had since changed fundamentally in one respect: the primary aim was no longer to find sea routes to rumoured riches. *Expeditions* now had closely defined *scientific objectives*. They included appropriately qualified scholars. Three expeditions under the leadership of *Captain James Cook* (1728-1779) were of great significance.

In Germany the University of Göttingen played the lead in introducing Enlightenment ideas for the development of the new knowledge. *Johann Reinhold Forster* (1729-1798) and his son *Georg Forster* (1754-1794) had both been on Captain Cook's second voyage to the South Pacific (1772-1775). Göttingen was also the centre for *physical (biological) anthropology* and its ground-breaking studies in human races. One of its leading researchers of racial types was *Johann Friedrich Blumenbach* (1752-1840).

Significant for a later development in a specialism of ethnology were ideas in the history of language proposed by the philosopher and linguist *Wilhelm von Humboldt* (1767-1835). He challenged the view that there were so-called primitive languages, and demonstrated that each human language contained a characteristic view of reality proposed by its speakers. With these ideas Humboldt became the pioneer of what in the second half of the 20th century was called *ethnoscience*, then *cognitive anthropology* (cf. chaps. 12 and 19).

3.5 Developments in the 19th Century

In the *Romantic period* after the French Revolution and the ensuing political upheavals, scientific interest chiefly centred on the individual nation or ethnic group. Political theories developed as *historicism, national studies in linguistics*, and research into *Indo-European languages* were established. From these developments grew the so-called *philologies*, the specialist disciplines which dealt with foreign cultures possessing a script (Chinese and Japanese studies and many others). In this period ethnology's interest in pre-literate culture stagnated.

During the Enlightenment intellectual concerns had tended away from theology and the Bible; now they began to assume the foreground. People in pre-literate societies, supposedly "primitives", were no longer valued as "Noble Savages", but as people whose original culture after the events of the tower of Babel had *degenerated* from this exalted level into their current circumstances. The inference was that only peoples whose cultures reached the level of *civilization* have the wherewithal to achieve a *higher development*.

3.6   Charles Darwin

In this intellectual milieu around the mid-19th century a new scientific model became evident; it had been foreshadowed for quite some time in the field of natural sciences. Its fulfilment came in the person of *Charles Darwin* (1809-1882) whose ideas on the origins of life and species precipitated the breakthrough for biological *evolution*, one that enveloped all the sciences like a landslide and determined the course for ethnology in particular from 1860 to 1900.

Pre-literate cultures in this period were viewed as remnants of early forms of contemporary high culture and civilizations. With the help of the *comparative method*, ethnologists – just like biologists – apparently could determine coherent *sequences of development* from cultural structures, for example from an acquaintance with possessions the move from communal property to private property; or in the context of religious practices the move from worshipping one's own ancestors via fetishism (belief that objects of any kind have a potency which is released through their being offered to achieve personal aims), idol worship and polytheism (belief in the existence of several gods with similar potential), right through to monotheism (belief in a single God). One of the main representatives of evolutionism in ethnology is the Englishman *Edward Burnett Tylor* (1832-1917). He also introduced the term *animism* to designate the religions of "primitive" cultures. The American *Lewis Henry Morgan* (1818-1881) applied evolutionary principles to research into kinship structures.

The academics researching these principles did so furthermore from their desks. They pored over reports of "explorers", looking for statements (even random ones) about specific phenomena of cultures; they evaluated them and drew their own conclusions. Considering all the deficiencies of this process, evolutionism must be seen as the first phase of ethnology with closed, theoretical thinking. Its outworking in the 20th century was the *social ideology of Marxism* and the *racial ideology of National Socialism*.

3.7   Specializations in the Modern Period

Europe, America and East Asia in the mid-19th century witnessed the first societies and museums devoted to ethnology. Ethnology as a discipline was established at universities, with the first German, *Adolf Bastian* (1826-1905), lecturing in Berlin. Like many of his colleagues he was a medical doctor, and cofounded with *Rudolf Virchow* (1821-1902) the Berlin Society for Anthropology, Ethnology and Prehistory (Berliner Gesellschaft für Anthropologie, Ethnologie und Urgeschichte).

At the beginning of the 20th century, evolutionism was superseded by a series of *schools of ethnology* each with its own theoretical tendency. In Germany, *study of cultural history* was inaugurated by *Friedrich Ratzel* (1844-1904) and his student *Leo Frobenius* (1873-1938), who was a researcher in the history of pre-literate cultures, developing methods – in the absence of written sources – for studying the *spread and influence of cultural elements*. The *Vienna School of Ethnology* (Wiener Schule der Völkerkunde) expounded its doctrine of "Kulturkreise" (individual cultural circles or entities), which interpreted cultural elements evident in different ethnic groups not – as in evolutionism – as a simultaneous phase of development, but as a *transmission* from one culture to another. For this reason, the research called this tendency *diffusion*.

In England evolutionism gave way to methods which mostly stem from French sociology, which is why ethnology there is also called *social anthropology*. One of its main proponents is *Bronislaw Malinowski* (1884-1942). He researched cultural elements and their functions for satisfying human needs, and from this grew *functionalism*. Moreover, he is known as the founder of *on-the-spot field research*; in contrast to the procedures of "armchair ethnology", Malinowski's research data – collected in the indigenous groups themselves – established the preconditions for drawing well-founded and verifiable theories.

Franz Boas (1858-1942), a German scientist and student of Adolf Bastian, emigrated to The United States, where he ensured through his activities as a researcher and teacher that *general linguistics* became integrated as a vital partner discipline into cultural anthropology and contributed to an exceptionally fruitful combination of methods. In contrast to Europe, this was easier to achieve because of the ethnic groups of American Indians, whose prolific languages had such different structures than Indo-European languages. Over the course of the second half of the 20th century this combination involving *linguistics* developed into *cognitive anthropology*.

3.8   The Present

In more recent times a number of specialisms within ethnology have emerged: regional ones (studies of American Indian and of Pacific Island cultures, for example) and theoretical ones (political ethnology, music ethnology, etc.). It is not easy to predict how the future will direct these studies. There are practically no more pre-literate groups living in isolation. The children of those who only a generation ago still survived by planting yams or by hunting and gathering nowadays organize cooperatives, work with computers, and watch television in the evening. It is unclear how long ethnology in its original sense can be maintained. Perhaps, after the disappearance of the last few pre-literate societies and their absorption into a highly technical world culture, ethnology will become one with cultural anthropology. That may take some time. Ethnology's *raison d'être* will surely endure for the first half of this new 21st century.

More detailed introductions to this chapter's topic:

An intelligible account of the history of ethnology is Stagl 2003. He also gives a manageable bibliography with further significant publications. Detailed books on the history of ethnology are Mühlmann 1968 and (exhaustive in detail and scope) Petermann 2004.

Additional material on this chapter's topic:

Beer, Bettina; Fischer, Hans (ed.): Ethnologie. Einführung und Überblick. Berlin 2003 (This is Fischer's 5th ed. of 1983 in a new version).

Fischer, Hans: Anfänge, Abgrenzungen, Anwendungen. In: Fischer 1983: 11-46. (short and precise)

Fischer, Hans (Hg.): Ethnologie. Eine Einführung. Berlin 1983.

Harris, Marvin: The rise of anthropological theory. A history of theories of culture. London 1968.

Mühlmann, Wilhelm Emil: Geschichte der Anthropologie. Frankfurt/M. et al. [2]1968 (extraordinary in its detail and scope, but needs revision in places).

Petermann, Werner: Die Geschichte der Ethnologie. Wuppertal 2004.

Stagl, Justin: Die Entwicklung der Ethnologie. In: Beer/Fischer 2003:34-52.

Chapter 4
The Concept of Culture

This chapter explains the various meanings behind the use of the word culture, how ethnology and allied disciplines use the word, what effects culture has on human behaviour, and what consequences there are for those in contact with foreign cultures.

4.0   Introduction

It is almost impossible to define the concept of *culture* in a few words and bring out its meaning. This is why there have been numerous attempts at a definition. A child once solved the problem from his perspective as follows. Somehow he was correctly aware that the words *culture* and *nature* formed a pair of opposites. (Herodotus and Posidonius had had this thought and discussed it, as we have seen from the previous chapter). Because children simply love vivid thinking, he used an example. His argument was that a wood, by the fact that it grew by itself, was a very appropriate embodiment of the concept of nature: culture was what a person put into the wood. By that the child meant paths and benches.

The child's explanation is undoubtedly useful. The term culture is related to agriculture and plantations in that we speak of cultivating vegetable patches or acres of fir-trees. A similar concept is at work when biologists breed cultures of bacteria on incubator trays. But this meaning is not the heart of the matter.

In a quality newspaper the "Culture" section comprises theatre and concert reviews, museum opening times and much else. It is clear from this context that we are linking culture to something intellectual, and particularly so given that vegetable patches and bacteria incubation are not the first things that come to mind when we are defining culture. By associating culture with intellect we are dealing with the *common* or *general* understanding of the word.

In our dealing with foreign cultures this meaning can only be partially useful, designating only a small and diminishing proportion of what ethnologists (and other cultural specialists) understand by it. In our common or general usage we don't do justice to its meaning. As an instrument for acknowledging the phenomenon of culture the term is too rough and ready, just as unsuitable for the task as a hammer is for repairing a watch mechanism. Indeed, cultures can be compared with watch mechanisms: complicated, having components that are variously interdependent, each one functioning like a gear train of the utmost technical precision.

The question as to what culture comprises is actually so difficult to answer that even specialists fail to give straight responses. This is obvious when one considers that by 1950 some 164 definitions of culture had been formulated and published (Kroeber/Kluckhohn 1952). Understanding the idea of culture is made easier when some of its impact is seen in the specifics of our European-Western lifestyle. Here is an example from my experience:

4.1   Culture and Behaviour

When I was a student on a journey to Switzerland via Geneva I found myself outside the local synagogue. Because I had never before seen inside one, and because the door was open, I ventured in. I had taken off my cap out of reverence for a place of worship. I had scarcely stepped into the building when a bearded figure with a broad-rimmed hat advanced towards me from the shadows, swearing loudly. He must have been the sacristan. Because his swear words rained down on me in furious French I could only understand the barest essentials. He bellowed words about respect (which he patently supposed I lacked) and barked at me to put my cap on again quickly or to leave the synagogue at once. I was so shocked that I did both.

From this unforgettable experience I derived some essential aspects of what culture is, how it works, and what it does for those who know and cherish a particular culture. The cap incident shows particularly that culture has to do with how people *behave* under certain circumstances. When people behave, they do so in a characteristic way according to the culture cueing their actions.

In order to understand the link between culture and human behaviour we first need to be clear that a person's behaviour is always subject to an underlying cause, an *intention*, which he or she – at least in an incident like the one above – could identify if asked to do so. If the irate sacristan had enquired why I had entered without my cap on, I could naturally have said that out of respect for a holy place any "decent fellow" should take his hat off.

Coupling my intention of showing respect with my specific act of removing my cap seemed in the circumstances so self-evident that I had no doubts about whether the link was appropriate or not. I did what I had to because it seemed reasonable and necessary. But how had the sacristan acted? He too intended to show respect through very specific behaviour. His behaviour deviated from mine significantly, in that he had put his hat on. What would he have said if I had asked him for his reasoning? His answer would assuredly been that any "decent" person shows respect for a holy place by covering his head.

It is noteworthy that both individuals can have the **same intention** but express it through **different behaviour**. The cap incident seems to bring the principles of the matter to a head! Both express an intention not only through differing behaviour but through completely contrasting actions; which leads to the thought that between an intention and an action there is no natural, pre-defined link to help one make an intention unambiguous and communicate one's intention clearly to others.

In most cases we have several options available for this, at least in theory. Indeed there are people who show respect for a holy place by removing their shoes. The link between intention and behaviour is in fact so loose that one could equally well express respect by rolling the eyes or placing the left leg on the right knee.

This is the important reason for the great number and variety of cultures known to us. From all the many ways of signalling an intention each culture has selected one in particular and set it up as the **norm**. This explains why in European-Western culture a man shows respect through baring his head and in Jewish culture through covering his head.

Rarely if ever is it worth answering the question why in any particular culture a specific intention is allied to its corresponding behaviour. The matter is further complicated because in both cultures mentioned the respect shown here with the help of caps and hats is only appropriate for men, and not for women. In this case, for women there are other rules.

On the other hand, the question about why in any particular culture a specific behaviour has become the norm is easier to answer with regard to **ergology** (the study of the shape and use of products) or **technology** (the study of how tools and equipment are made) (see chap. 7). Both areas involve tangible things and workers' use of them. Tools are generally so determined by their purpose that significant variations in their shape and use are not possible; the norm is here determined by the environment of the ethnic group. But even in ergology and technology variations from the norm make for a range of practice which cannot be explained away satisfactorily. Just from a purely technical standpoint there are a number of different ways of lighting a fire. For example, one can place the wood in layers or like a cone by arranging the pieces at a slant and touching at the top. It can depend on the type of wood available, but not exclusively so. Somehow and at some time each culture settled upon one of many ways of lighting a fire without it being plausibly stated why one way was deemed right and no other.

One of the most important functions carried out in cultures is ensuring that they determine the actions of their members by means of rule-bound links between intentions and behaviour, rather in the way the **grammar** of a language gives structure to a message conveyed by a speaker. This means that I as a European follow the rule for taking my hat off to express respect just as I would follow the rules for expressing the thought in speech or writing, according to which the subject, predicate and object have their proper place. The culture of an ethnic group is thus essentially nothing more than the grammar made by their members as a yardstick for their behaviour. Because in formulating the grammar of a language one needs to consider all the rules that have to be applied in order to speak "properly", one can see in the culture of a people group the **entirety of all rules** to follow when wishing to behave "properly".

For comparison's sake we shall look at a second example of how, in a different way, linking may occur between intention and particular behaviour. People celebrating want to express their joy. They do so by talking to other people, and by their facial expressions and gestures displaying their joy. Sometimes joy is vociferous, e.g. from spectators in a football stadium when a goal is scored. A farmer from Southern Italy may show his joy by singing at the top of his voice. In many societies when people are glad they start dancing; this is very common behaviour throughout Africa.

We are seeing that there is a range of options to express joy, only some of which – perhaps just a few – are typical of a particular region or society. This is the only range considered "normal" for somebody wishing to express joy. If one analyses this phenomenon it becomes clear that behaviour is underpinned and triggered by a set of rules, like data in a computer programme. These rules are, of course, only valid when followed by the majority of people within the culture for which the rules are the **behavioural norm.**

Such rules exist for situations where we don't particularly want to voice respect or joy, but rather our wishes and – most importantly – our needs. We humans are set on satisfying our needs throughout life. To these essential needs belong principally eating and drinking. Because normal folk the world over are filled with a desire to survive, they develop elaborate strategies to help secure their physical existence. In this drive to secure an existence we recognize an intention (in the above sense of the word); to fulfil this requires particular behaviour.

To this end, behaviour requires actions of the most varied kind imaginable, according to circumstances. To secure their livelihood indigenous groups inhabiting the Arctic regions (Alaska, Siberia) behave quite unlike the Bataks of North Sumatra, for example, since climatic conditions in the Arctic Circle differ from those at the Equator. Thus the first groups live essentially from hunting (and from breeding reindeer), the others from cultivating rice. Despite the fundamental differences, both groups follow rules shaping their behaviour so comprehensively that they manage to get enough food for themselves and their families.

The ways people behave in securing their livelihood can differ enormously even within a particular culture. In Europe an architect who needs to ensure enough to eat behaves quite differently from a farmer, though they have the same aim. The architect works in an office, drawing plans for the construction of houses. For this work he gets money to enable him to buy what he needs in a grocer's. The farmer on the other hand works in the fields, produces directly from his effort all kinds of foods and ensures his existence in that way. Both are pursuing the same aim, both are fulfilling an identical intention, and yet they behave fundamentally differently. However each is guided in his action by quite distinct behaviour governed by rules permitting others to recognize one as an architect, the other as a farmer.

Rules like this operate in all areas of life within a human community, regardless of whether they apply to people's livelihood, entertainment or religion. They guide their members' behaviour in every single instance, just like the grammar of their language giving shape to sequences of sounds and words. The entirety of all these rules being followed by people while their lives are being shaped gives rise to that typical behaviour recognized by an observer as their over-arching culture.

The ethnologist Wolfgang Rudolph has defined this matter more generally in a very readable contribution (1971:54-55): Culture is "the totality of the (directly and indirectly, consciously and subconsciously) accepted social phenomena relating to humans as they shape their existence". This is the definition of cultural anthropology, a discipline which deals with the universal – universal only in theory – culture of mankind. The definition of ethnology, a discipline which – unlike cultural anthropology – deals with the real-life cultures of peoples, is in Rudolph's terms: Culture is "the totality of accepted social phenomena relating to humans as they shape their existence in a way characteristic of a particular ethnic entity".

4.2   Culture as a Strategy

These definitions of culture as a concept are still too complicated for the worker living in a foreign culture. Even contemplating these definitions is arduous. However, there is an even simpler definition which describes cultures as the totality of rules applied by a society to shape its existence. This definition can be gently introduced with a simple example from an everyday situation.

Picture a crossroads. There are no signs to indicate special priority. So priority is given to the traffic on the right. Three drivers reach the crossroads at the same time. All three intend proceeding straight ahead. So each has an issue to solve which forms an important element of their life and their life-habit. To carry out their intention each driver needs to reveal particular behaviour. Several options are open. All three could, for example, drive straight on. The solution is not practicable, because that would create a further problem involving considerable expense, to say nothing of trouble with the police. Wisdom dictates that the three drive on in turn, one after the other. This could be achieved by the one with the biggest car continuing ahead first, leaving the one with the smallest car last. Or one could settle the matter according to the prestige of the makes of car: first the Rolls Royce, then the Mercedes, and finally the Volkswagen. (In Africa, I was told, priority goes to the car with the greatest horsepower). Another feasibility would be for the drivers to discuss who should go first, second and last. Whatever the solution, the matter needs deciding.

Because there are crossroads like this every hundred yards and because this life-issue needs solving by a driver every minute or so, the rules have been set out in advance. Individual deals would be too time-consuming. Furthermore, so that our three drivers have these rules in mind for each occasion, they need to learn them by heart. Because each of them knows which rules are applicable at crossroads the problem is solved very quickly, to the satisfaction of all three drivers without further discussion. All three know that the driver "furthest to the right" or not turning off can continue straight on ….

With this string of rules all three drivers have a workable *strategy* for coping with unexpected traffic situations involving more than one driver. (If there were only one lone person on the planet that person could do what he wanted at crossroads and elsewhere, and would not need to follow any rule!)

Other situations demand quite different strategies for solving the issues arising. If I need to phone somebody I only get through if I know the specific procedure, which involves me knowing, for example, what a phone box looks like and where I can find one. I also have to know what coins I need and where to insert them. I need to know my friend's code and number by heart, or failing that where to look; and so on.

Even fun leisure activities require a person to be familiar with strategies so as to be in a position to take part. Somebody wanting to play the accordion or sing in a choir can only do this if they have learnt about notes, appreciate the significance of musical beat and understand the conductor's gestures, etc. The extent of the rules which need mastering just to allow that is wide-ranging. Consequently, one can justifiably say we are dealing with finding strategies to solve one of life's issues, since a person needs leisure to maintain his or her mental and emotional poise.

Taking all these communal strategies as a whole amounts to a description of what a culture consists of. Armed with these, we are guided to a simple definition of what cultures in their entirety represent: *Cultures are strategies for giving shape to human existence.* And because life in an actual cultural setting often has to be built under difficult circumstances it is true to say:

Cultures are strategies for getting to grips with living.

Animals also have strategies for overcoming the trials of living. It is just that their strategies are much less complex than a human's. Animals probably have far fewer, or no, distinctive mental structures. These are triggered by a stimulus setting off a reaction whose impact an animal can rarely, if ever, intentionally change. An animal is conditioned by instincts, and these function *without needing to be learnt.* Animals control their existence using their instincts via a fixed *pattern of stimulus and response*, with scarcely any flexibility.

Because humans do not have a comparable stimulus-response tendency (or at best only a faint trace of one), they require a cultural dimension to help them take charge of their life; and a cultural dimension needs to be *learnt.* Without it, humans would fall prey to life's perils.

4.3   Culture as a Precondition for Survival

A computer experiment once demonstrated the extent of the reliance of human communities on their culture. American ethnologists developed a programme to give them answers to two questions. The answer to the first was meant to show what would happen if humanity was denied its cultures but allowed to preserve the memory of them. The answer was as follows: people would immediately set about rebuilding their cultures along such fixed lines that after only a few generations they would regain their former way of life.

The second question was meant to elicit what would happen if human-ity was denied its cultures, and all memory of them was erased. The an-swer was as follows: most of those affected would die very soon after be-cause with no memory of vital strategies for overcoming life's problems and with no recourse to the simplest survival ploys they would fall prey to the sink-or-swim vagaries of their environment. Even in the temperate zones of the North and South hemispheres people cannot survive without knowing how to grow crops. Furthermore, given the current population density here in Europe, if people knew nothing about medicines a flu epi-demic here would have devastating consequences.

Computer simulations are of course prone to many imponderables that make for less than confident pronouncements, but they do serve to show how important cultures are for the societies which need them to shape ex-istence; and they further serve to light the blind alleys that could threaten death, even if only a single element were to change or to be missing. For example, Western Europe at present would only be able to feed a fraction of its population if suddenly there were no more oil supplies – indeed starvation would just be one of numerous other consequences.

4.4   Culture and Ethics

Unlike instincts, cultures are made up of flexible strategic tendencies each permitting a high degree of nuanced behaviour, adaptations, opinions and interventions as a result of deliberate decision-making. The result is that cultures also have an *ethical dimension* for the purpose of giving life its shape, whereas discerning good and evil is not an issue for animals.

In this respect the distinction between human behaviour and animal behaviour is illustrated by the fact that a chimpanzee can learn to start crossing the road when the light goes green, but he stays stranded in the road if the light meanwhile changes from green to red. The process that compels a person to continue crossing requires insights and decisions that a chimpanzee responsive merely to stimuli and reactions cannot compre-hend. However, for a (normal) human being a decision like this is second nature.

Because everything people need to shape their lives inevitably links to their culture, our own European-Western culture involves not only be-longing to choirs and visiting local museums and so on but also knowing about ordinary things like matches, mathematical expansions such as $(a+b)^2=a^2+2ab+b^2$, and the Medieval proofs for the existence of God – to say nothing of trivialities such as board-rubber fights in the classroom or the right way to blow one's nose in polite company!

Regarding the latter, Europeans use a handkerchief. That at least is the expectation. However, South Sea Islanders are repulsed if they see a European scrumpling their handkerchief and stuffing it back into their trouser pocket. The Islanders block one nostril with the thumb and blow air vigorously through the other, a habit that Europeans consider crude. (We pupils used to call it the "horse and cart driver's greeting"!)

4.5   Culture as Value System

These examples illustrate that cultures have strategies for *assessing the value* of things, actions, characteristics and forms of behaviour. For us Europeans the theft of grocery items is a much less serious offence than killing somebody by careless driving. In cultures where food is scarce and the birth-rate is very high the opposite can apply, even in law. Such differences in value systems are particularly unpleasant sources of conflict when partners from different cultures are involved in the same project. These differences are conflict-laden because value judgements often cannot be justified rationally.

There are societies where it is considered shameful for women to ride a bicycle. It just is – nobody can explain logically why. Regardless of this, anybody wanting to provide bicycles for them would fail, even if the women themselves realized that they could take their farm produce to market on their bikes more simply than on their heads.

Differing value systems can make for conflict between church workers, such that partners cannot agree on what is considered in precise theological terms a sin, and what is not. For a Christian with a past in animism, it may well be a lesser sin to commit adultery than to offer sacrifices to one's own ancestral spirits to whom one traditionally turned in need. Christians from a European-Western cultural background are likely to see the issue differently, which leads to conflict in church committees and community organizations having to deal with relevant cases.

In this all-embracing sense the term culture even includes some of the most inhuman atrocities a human is capable of, despite the fact that most of us would not in fact describe such things as pertaining to culture but rather to a lack or a loss of culture. Human aberrations and atrocities even occur in archetypal cultural forms and institutions. An infamous example is the Nazi concentration camp with its uniforms, insignia, forms of address, absurd racial theories and its economic dealings.

The concept of culture as a strategy for coping with life even ultimately includes blatant breaches of law and order like embezzlement and bank robbery. A corrupt cashier takes pains to ensure that the sums he misappropriates appear to be legitimate outgoings. A bank robber walks into the bank he is targeting dressed to suggest he is a normal customer. As a precaution he parks his get-away vehicle not against the traffic-flow or on a no-parking spot but in accordance with regulations, again so as to succeed in contravening other regulations. Exaggerating somewhat, this means that it is only possible to infringe some cultural rules (success-fully) when adhering strictly to others.

This comprehensive understanding of culture, embracing even remote considerations, operates wherever people keep thinking and behaving. Precisely because it is so comprehensive, any definition of the term culture needs to be as general as I have suggested just now. Such a broadly based understanding of culture is thus very different from the usual one which focuses on cultural phenomena such as literature, art and music.

4.6   Culture as a Conceptual Structure

The broader definition does not see culture primarily as the sum total of all behaviour and observed phenomena considered typical of a culture, but rather as something intrinsically *thought-centred* and *conceptual*, some-thing hidden in people's heads as they live in the relevant culture and use its rules (i.e. strategies) to shape their existence. This implies that culture (i.e. the strategy or system of rules) is something other than the activity it-self. The activity is a manifestation of the strategy and only it can be ob-served directly. The visible, discernible elements of a culture make up at best a kind of surface, a tip of the iceberg as it were. Such cultural phe-nomena that are accessible to investigation – being visible, audible and tangible – present themselves as secondary, as something deriving from the conceptual base of a culture; as something resting on its invisible intellec-tual structures; as something which has emerged from them and been gen-erated by them. This is equally true for a stone axe as for an initiation ceremony; however distinct they seem in appearance, they both emerge from the fertile bedrock of rules, mental structures and strategies. In their discernible form they are mere subordinate cultural phenomena whose ac-tual origins are inaccessible to the eye, hidden in the indigenous mind.

This is rarely obvious to tourists visiting foreign cultures. Most tour-ists are on the lookout for the (minimal) visible evidence; this is bound to remain a mystery, because they fail to realize that such things are mere extrusions on the surface of the relevant culture.

What is observable has permanent validity as part of the culture which gives rise to it. The rules governing people's behaviour work by ensuring that the visible surface things have the characteristics of their deep culture. The rules giving rise to Chinese painting, or Arabic script or a simple cooking fire in Africa do so quite typically; we can thus identify them as uniquely Chinese, Arab, or African. The rules by which hunter-gatherers (hunters and collectors) fashion their weapons evolve by necessity and culture; they determine whether the artefact is a blowpipe or a boomerang. (At this juncture I should observe again that rules like this govern human actions in the same manner as the rules of grammar for a speaker: Chinese rules produce Chinese sounds, and so on.)

The close link between culture as a strategy and culture as the manifestations of that strategy is complemented and made more complex by yet another dimension, which we need to acknowledge if we wish to understand peoples of foreign cultures. This dimension is embedded in the way in which *concepts* are related to one another; to be more exact: how the end products of cultures – whether we mean behaviour or material things – are *integrated within a conceptual framework* (see chap. 12 and 19).

To understand what this might entail we need to be aware of what we mean by the term "concept". For practical purposes the most useful definition is that a concept is a thing, a feature, an act of behaviour or a process in *its perceived form*.

This definition views the concept not as the thing, the feature, the behaviour or the process itself, but the cultural aspect hidden in the collective mind of the people. Even concepts are thus to be understood as elements of strategies for shaping life.

The diversity of actual cultures resides essentially in the boundless permutations open to the elements of reality as they combine conceptually. One example may serve to make this clear. If you ask a German child what a house is, the child presumably paints one that looks like the one he lives in, with two diagonal roof profiles. If you then ask about other things that he might call "a house", he will perhaps paint a flat-roofed block, or even perhaps a snail shell... From this we conclude that this particular child is placing the specific concept of a snail shell within the more general concept of house. This is what I mean by concept being integrated within a conceptual framework.

Assigning a snail shell to the concept of house indicates that the thinker is able to think logically. Yet the link is not forced, nor is it the only link that could be made. In other cultures one can find surprisingly different conceptual links.

If we ask a South Sea Islander what a house is he will probably immediately show us the structure he lives in, made of wood, intertwined branches and palm leaves. This does indeed look rather different than a

European building. Yet the differences are not fundamental. If we ask him about other things he understands by the word house he may show us his hat or his cap. At this point the differences become considerable. Conceptually in his culture the idea of housing embraces not just a dwelling but also head coverings, including umbrellas or large Taro plant leaves used as such; but not snail shells! A conceptual store like this demonstrates quite neatly that there is potential for combining things differently whatever their characteristics. For things have more than one characteristic and can relate to others and combine with them.

What must be recognized is that, for two members of two different cultures, a hat (for example) can look physically identical *on* their heads but relate conceptually to quite different things *in* their heads. If one considers that in every single culture there are thousands of concepts all capable of inter-relating in numerous different ways, one gets an idea of what a person needs to assimilate before claiming to know a culture well or even just manage in it.

Numerous difficulties arise from any attempt to access a culture's underlying conceptual structures, since these are not normally embedded in a person's consciousness. Applying them is for the most part a subconscious act; which is just as well, because otherwise our behavioural process would be slowed too abruptly if we kept wishing to apply our culture's regulations as a conscious act. A conscious application of grammatical rules would, for example, deprive our speech of its fluency. Yet precisely because what constitutes our culture is not embedded in us consciously but preconsciously and subconsciously, we find it generally difficult – and in many cases impossible – to identify these elements as cultural or as moulded by culture, let alone to give clear information about them. Culture is a kind of **background phenomenon**; it is something taken for granted which does not strike the community member as being culture.

If the inhabitants of a Swabian village were asked what they understood by the cultural features of the place they lived in, they might be able to mention their men's choir, their association for traditional costumes, or their crafts museum, if they existed. They would probably not think of other things. Questions about whether their farm implements, horticultural methods, country lore and weather lore had much to do with culture would probably meet with incomprehension.

If the same inhabitants were visitors to a different foreign culture, such typical features of life would no longer blend into the background but be conspicuous phenomena, striking the visitors as different from the everyday things of their own world.

In a situation like this we try to understand what is unfamiliar to us. People of a foreign culture appear peculiar, illogical, comic or even offensive, and they are described as such in reports by naïve tourists returning from far-away places. A development aid worker, a doctor, teacher or church worker tries to understand what is unfamiliar to him by first asking questions. From this moment onwards the indigenous people find him similarly peculiar, illogical, comic or even offensive. At the very least they are bemused because he is enquiring about things that are so obvious that any child would consider self-explanatory.

For anybody working as a teacher in a foreign culture, being aware of how these things cohere and can make sense is one of the most vital rudimentary things to know. And because most development aid workers and church workers overseas are there in a teaching role (however informally), they really should engage with these issues seriously or at least be made aware of them as they prepare for service. Yet even today this happens on a very sketchy basis, if it happens at all.

Such lack of awareness is all too evident in the use and particularly the preparation of teaching materials if nobody understands that conceptual storing of learning topics takes on quite different shapes in the minds of indigenous pupils and students than with Europeans; or – worse still – if it is just assumed, out of ignorance of the coherency in the way Europeans conceptualize things, that the relationships are equivalent to those of the foreign culture. This kind of naïve thinking is more frequent than one would suppose.

Western doctors sent to the Third World rarely know anything useful about the medical terminology used by their patients, nor about their understanding of body and soul and what it is to be a person. This leads to countless misunderstandings, as we shall see later (cf. chap. 15).

To sum up, Bible translators have no choice but to acquaint themselves fully with the thought world of the culture they are working in if they wish to ensure the text they are proposing will be understood. The following "translation" of Psalm 23 into a tribal language of South-East Asia shows what can result if the translator doesn't reckon with a different conceptual storing. (The "back-translation" gives some flavour of what the recipient may "understand" on reading the psalm):

> The Great Chieftain is my cattle breeder.
> I have no need of property.
> He leads me to a grassy clearing,
> And he leads me to the river.
> He prompts my soul to always stay close beside me.

When I walk through a gloomy hollow
I am not afraid,
For You are with me.
You use a stick and a club
To make me comfortable.
You set up a wooden table for me to eat at.
My enemies are watching all the while.
You pour oil on my head.
My cup is almost overflowing.
Goodness and mercy will walk
In single file behind me all my life long,
And I will dwell in the house
Of the Great Chieftain for ever.

4.7   Culture and Competence

Because each culture actually uses only a proportion of the conceptual permutations that are logically and technically possible, each one creates a unique, independent and self-contained strategy for existence. This strategy functions only within the particular geographical area over which it has developed a practical mastery, and it can only function in partnership with other people if they too accept the strategy as sensible and can apply it to managing their existence. If they do, the knowledge and capabilities promoted by a culture lead to its users being able to agree about their needs and intentions without undue difficulty and managing to achieve them purposefully. The day-to-day procedures evident at crossroads go to prove this. In other words, a person understanding a culture for the purpose of shaping his life practically within it is empowered *to work effectively* and *economically*. Behind this phenomenon hides a feature of cultures which has far-reaching impact. This one also can be deduced from the example of our crossroads.

Because each of the three drivers knows the highway-code he can *anticipate* how the others will behave. (This prior knowledge is not, of course, foolproof. If this were so there would be no accidents). Similarly one can anticipate people's behaviour in general terms, providing one knows the culture they use to shape their lives. In Germany, any guest invited to a Sunday afternoon birthday party can be fairly sure that they will not be offered beer but coffee, and that the coffee will be sipped from china cups and not drunk through a straw from plastic cups, even though this might be technically possible. The guests also know that they will not be offered roast pork and potato salad but cakes. And so on. Our familiarity with our own culture gives us the knowledge to help us anticipate in general terms what will happen at a birthday party and how the hosts will behave. They also know, broadly speaking, how we will behave as guests. They can reckon with our arriving at the hosts' with a bunch of flowers and not a sack of potatoes. (There are cultures where bringing a sack of potatoes would be expected, and where a bunch of flowers would be considered an insult.)

The *predictability of other people's behaviour* on the basis of our familiarity with a culture is vitally important, for various reasons. A guest receiving an invitation can already cue their behaviour in advance. Guests and hosts alike can adjust their behaviour and the event can pass off without troublesome inhibitions, hold-ups and hitches. Even more important is the following:

Informed familiarity with a culture brings the advantage of predicting its members' behaviour and gives all involved a feeling of *security*, even of supremacy in dealings with others. We are particularly conscious of this in situations demanding our action where we are completely or partially ignorant of the guidelines we ought to be following and the likely response from our counterparts. An invitation to take tea with the Sheikh in his Bedouin tent can cause us to break out in a real sweat. How does one sit down? Does one take off one's shoes, and one's socks? And how does one drink the tea? Should one, must one, sip it? What does one do if one doesn't fancy a second cup, and yet doesn't want to be discourteous?

Uncertainty, which comes over anyone not knowing the appropriate cultural strategies that he ought to have learnt, essentially strikes those who have not long been living and working in a foreign culture. Nothing in a person's behaviour, absolutely nothing, is exactly as one would expect – which is tolerable for a few weeks, perhaps ... But then one begins to grit one's teeth; the feeling grows that one's patience is wearing thin ... One's aggression rises, and there are consequences ... Indigenous colleagues cannot explain one's behaviour and feel alienated. The real trouble occurs when one's patience snaps. At that moment one is just a short step away from *culture shock*. By culture shock is meant a state where one begins to hate absolutely everything in the foreign culture and rejects it, cutting oneself off and becoming incapable of carrying out the allotted assignment.

It is rare for such extremes of uncertainty to be experienced by new arrivals to a foreign culture. They mostly experience what is called *culture stress*. But even this needs to be reduced for a person to work effectively and economically. The only way to achieve this reduction, and the shortest way, is to familiarize oneself as fast and as fully as possible with the rules shaping the lives of the people one is dealing with. It entails learning the language the locals communicate in. (I am aware that this is easier said than done. In work situations where several languages are spoken one cannot perhaps do otherwise than learn the *lingua franca;* nevertheless ...) The quicker we learn the culture and language of our work context the quicker we develop our emotional roots within it and reduce our stress. (The reverse of this requirement should not be overlooked either: one can grow such deep roots in a foreign culture that they can only be pulled up with great difficulty when the time comes to return to one's own home culture.)

4.8   Culture and Understanding among Nations

From the above it is clear that people chiefly perceive their affiliation to different cultures as a *separation*, which engenders in themselves a dual lack of understanding and trust. This is the cause of the ***hostility towards foreigners*** which clearly grows the closer the cultures are set alongside each other. In my view, the separateness which features as a priority by each different culture system is so significant that I cannot see a brilliant future for the much-vaunted ***multi-cultural society***. It just won't work; because it demands from those involved a measure of tolerance which they cannot summon in the long run. For it to work, the costs on the relevant cultures would have to far exceed their means, for example through requiring distinct school systems, teaching materials, departments of education and culture – to name just a few.

The phenomenon of separateness, which is all too clear when people of differing cultures live alongside one another, is also a practical impediment for the development aid worker and church worker. When he is involved in his European sphere of cultural influence he seldom has the opportunity to experience such issues. He only experiences his own culture as an obstacle much too late, namely once he encounters his future second culture. He can only succeed in overcoming the hindrance by taking account of unfamiliar survival strategies then and there, engaging with them, and learning to implement them. The time it takes until a satisfactory outcome is achieved can vary greatly, depending on the temperament of the worker concerned. However long, it requires a considerable personal effort.

Further reading on this chapter's topics can be found in the following:

Baur, Isolde: Die Geschichte des Wortes Kultur und seiner Zusammensetzungen. Diss. München 1951.

Ederer, R.: Zur Begriffsbestimmung von "Kultur" und "Zivilisation". Mitteilungen der Anthropologischen Gesellschaft in Wien (Horn) 115.1985:1-34.

Gerndt, Helge: Kultur als Forschungfeld. Über volkskundliches Denken und Arbeiten. Münich 1981. (Her topic is not cultural studies but the folklore of European peoples: superstition, folk religion, folk justice, art and customs, etc.)

Hansen, Klaus P.: Kultur und Kulturwissenschaft. Eine Einführung. Tübingen, Basel 1995 (recent publication of Veröffentlichung der Reihe UTB [Uni-Taschenbücher] 1984. The author is a Professor of American Studies. His work deals with Western culture and the concept of culture. His writing is fluent and accessible to the general reader).

Kroeber, Alfred L.; Kluckhohn, Clyde: Culture: A critical review of concepts and definitions. Papers of the Peabody Museum of American Archaeology and Ethnology vol. 47. Harvard 1952.

Paul, Sigrid (ed.): Kultur – Begriff und Wort in China und Japan. Berlin 1984.

Renner, Egon: Ethnologie und Kultur: Der Kulturbegriff als entwicklungsprägender Faktor der ethnologischen Forschung. Zeitschrift für Ethnologie 108.1983:177-234.

Rudolph, Wolfgang: Kultur, Psyche und Weltbild. In: Trimborn 1971:54-71.

Trimborn, Hermann (ed.): Lehrbuch der Völkerkunde. Stuttgart 1971.

Znoj, Heinz Peter: Die Evolution der Kulturfähigkeit. Beiträge zur Kritik des ethnologischen Kulturbegriffs. Bern et al. 1988.

Chapter 5
Culture and Environment

In this chapter I explain what relationships exist between the geographical environment of a people and its culture, how its culture develops as a strategy for using this space and at the same time shapes the environmental conditions, how it impacts upon this environment and changes it, and how the changed environment for its part influences the inhabitants and changes them by turn in a continuous pendulum-like process.

Cultures as strategies for achieving mastery over living conditions are largely conditioned by the existing **natural environment**. They are very well adapted for this environment. This is not surprising. Ensuring one's survival by producing food can only be successful if the farming methods and means of transport are appropriate for the climatic conditions and suited to what is feasible as regards growing crops, hunting, fishing or rearing animals. Consequently, cultures in Oceania (Pacific islands) have not developed travel by dog sleigh but by outrigger canoe. In the sub-polar environment of the Inuit people (formerly called Eskimos) dog sleigh travel, however, is a very suitable strategy for solving transport issues.

The influences of an ethnic group's natural environment upon its culture are ramified. In warmer climates people manage with little clothing. A large proportion of their bodies are uncovered, and their skin is thus more visible than in regions with a cooler climate. In Oceania, therefore, this has encouraged the art of **tattooing**; in some ethnic groups, patterns and ornamentation cover more or less the whole body and serve as status symbols, and to ward off evil spirits, etc.

However, tattoos are only sensible if applied to relatively light skin. Where people have dark skin tattoos either don't feature, or else they exist in a special adaptation as scarification tattooing, where the skin is pierced and the wounds deliberately infected so that the resulting scars form a specific pattern – even on very dark skin they are easily seen.

Even the language of a culture is influenced through the natural environment and adapted for it. The vocabulary of a group living in the Arctic Circle contains far more words for types of snow (old snow, recently fallen snow, powdery snow etc.) than professional skiers in Europe tend to use; the inhabitants of the Chuuk islands in Micronesia have more than twenty-five different words for bananas, and almost twenty verbs for the various ways of carrying things; and Bedouins (nomadic graziers of the

Middle East) have a host of terms for sand, mostly short words to enable precise information to be shared with others: for sand where no water is to be found, sand which would threaten to swallow their animals, etc. (Some researchers take issue with this statement, for example, Martin 1986 and Senft 2003:259 concerning the language of the Inuit.)

Of course, a culture's natural environment also has an impact on the forms of religious worship in a community. In the parched areas of Africa there are rain makers, specialists in a particular kind of magic whose practices are said to ensure the regularity of the annual rainy season. In areas where wild animals are the staple diet for the population, respect is paid to a "Lord of the Animals" who sees to it that sufficient numbers are available for people to eat.

These examples serve to show that specific environments demand and encourage specific strategies: *a culture is formed by its environment.* Once strategies have been established they have an immediate impact back on the environment and give rise to further changes; strategies and cultural forms arise afresh. The soil and atmospheric conditions like those at Kaiserstuhl in the Upper Rhine valley have enabled wine production. The strategies gave the slopes of this area their characteristic structure. The individual wine-growing areas were so managed that the soil could be worked by draft animals and by hand. With the progress of technology (culture again!) the wine-growers had an even more effective strategy for dealing with life: machinery relieved the toil associated with draft animals and manual labour, and led to faster and easier production methods. Yet before this could happen the vineyards had to be organized to suit the machinery. The slopes around the Kaiserstuhl became great terraces. (Critics of this change felt compelled to band together in defence of traditional methods and warned of the consequences of mechanisation). A further example of the two-way influence of culture and environment are the rice terraces of South East Asia.

Over recent years transport systems have brought considerable change to the shape of the landscape. For modern high-speed rail systems the need has been for long stretches free of bends and inclines. Accordingly, the land has been contoured and transformed: deep cuttings have needed to be dug, mountains moved and soil smoothed, tunnels excavated, etc.

The branch of knowledge describing the continuous mutual influence of culture and environment is called *anthropogeography*. Its founder is reckoned to be Friedrich Ratzel (1844-1904). A more modern term for this way of looking at the landscape is *cultural ecology*. "It investigates the mutual dependence between cultures and their natural environment. It is guided by the question of how far human forms of culture are marked by the type of interaction with the natural environment, and how far these cultural forms are themselves impacting on their natural environment" (Bargatzky 1986:13[1]. A similar definition can be found in the short, informative introduction to this discipline by Casimir (2003:342, 344).

One of the most general principles underlying the dependency of a culture on its environment is the following: unfavourable areas only allow small human groups to arise, with their corresponding, simply-structured cultures; their individual members do not develop further specialisms. One example of an unfavourable area like this is the arid Kalahari desert in South Africa. The Khoisan bushmen form small groups. The men are for the most part hunters, and the women are gatherers.

There are 8 distinguishable types of environment where people can live and which in turn produce similar cultures. (Taken together they form the inhabited regions of the world, which we have termed *ecumene*, an ethnological word having nothing in common with the theological word except its etymology!) These types of environment are, briefly, as follows:

1. *Tropical forests*. These lie in a circular band between the 20 degrees of latitude north and south of the Equator. Among the areas are the Amazon basin in South America, the Congo basin in Africa, South East Asia and the island of New Guinea. In these regions there is high rainfall. There are tropical rain forests whose existence is greatly endangered by deforestation. The areas vary in the density of population. The Amazon basin is almost empty of people. Java in South East Asia is, by contrast, one of the most densely populated countries of the world. Those living here need to have strategies for cultivating the soil, in the way that is typical for *planter cultures*.

2. *Grasslands*. These are of three types depending on the water content: *steppes* are grasslands which are always covered with grass but which have little water, as for example in Central Asia. *Prairies* have more water and the grass is taller than in steppes; they are a feature, for example, of the Midwest of the United States. *Savannahs* are tropical grasslands. Since they can sustain many varieties of animals they are home to *hunters-gatherers* and *nomadic herdsmen.*

---

[1] German original: "... untersucht die wechselseitige Abhängigkeit zwischen Kulturen und ihrer natürlichen Umwelt. Sie lässt sich dabei von der Frage leiten, wie weit menschliche Kulturformen durch die Art der Auseinandersetzung mit der natürlichen Umwelt geprägt werden, und wie weit diese Kulturformen wiederum ihre natürliche Umwelt prägen."

3. *Arid regions*. There are 5 great deserts on the earth forming two bands around the northern and southern hemisphere, one at latitudes 20°-30°N and one at 20°-30°S. The conditions there are hostile, so these regions sustain only a modest existence; complex cultures cannot be sustained. For people to manage in such arid regions there has to be at least a source of water, however meagre. Areas with no water at all are uninhabitable, empty of people.

4. *Mediterranean areas of brushwood*. Despite their name, these occur not only around the Mediterranean, but also in North America (between northern California and Oregon), in Africa (around Cape Town) and Australia (between Perth and Adelaide), in two bands at latitudes between 30°-40°N and 30°-40°S. They are characterized by mild, rainy winters and hot, dry summers.

5. *Mixed forests of the temperate zone* have a very favourable climate. Here are the highest population densities, and cultures having the most advanced *industrialisation*. However, in earlier periods of civilisation they were almost unpopulated. Only with the development of technology for clearing forests and the invention of arable farming (seed crops) did the mixed forests of the temperate zone become significant. We are referring to Europe, parts of Canada, the Eastern United States, Korea, Northern Japan and vast areas of China.

6. *Subarctic forests*. These occur only in the northern hemisphere (south of the Arctic Circle), because in the southern hemisphere at the same latitudes there is no landmass. The forest lies north of the mixed forests of the temperate zone and the grasslands. The vegetation mostly consists of pine forests. Lakes and swamps contain vast water resources. The climate is characterized by very cold long winters and short rather cool summers. Subarctic forest areas can be found in Scandinavia, Siberia, Alaska and Canada. Even to *hunters-gatherers* they only offer a limited opportunity for eking out an existence, particularly because of the harsh winter conditions.

7. *Polar regions* consist of permanent snow and tundra. In the short Polar summer there is vegetation (even flowers in bloom), but trees cannot grow. So in these regions there is a shortage of firewood, and little timber for construction. There is any amount of food in the form of seals, reindeer, birds and fish, but hardly any edible vegetation, which is why the so-called *circumpolar ethnic groups* (Inuit, and peoples of Siberia) are hunters-gatherers and herdsmen feeding mostly on animal protein. In Polar regions humans can only survive the harsh environment with great difficulty, which is why in these icy coastlands of North America and of North Eurasia the population is so sparse.

8. *Mountainous regions* are a particularly interesting phenomenon as regards features that sustain humans and their livelihood. In terms of geophysics there are only three great mountain ranges on earth which are inhabited at high altitude. A glimpse at a globe shows a range from Western Asia via the Caucasus and the Alps to the Pyrenees, and extending on to the Atlas mountains in North Africa. A second range runs from Tibet (in the Himalayas) via Western China and Eastern Siberia over to Alaska and then down the west coast of North and South America (the Rocky Mountains and the Andes), all the way down to Tierra del Fuego. This is the most impressive of the ranges. The third range begins in north-east India and runs – in places under the sea – to the islands of South-East Asia and Melanesia (New Guinea) and down to New Zealand. (The mountains of East Africa are only inhabited at their lower altitudes).

Mountainous regions are ethnologically of unusual interest because they offer humans favourable or unfavourable habitats depending on their distance from the Equator. The same applies to their altitude. Mountainous regions can include all seven of the above types of environment and their corresponding cultures, in strata: the rain-forest zone lies in the lower levels of tropical mountains, then the grasslands and the other environments up to the zone dominated by polar conditions. On the highest mountain of Africa, Kilimanjaro, there is permanent snow.

The following is also noteworthy: in the mountains of the temperate zone (e.g. in the Alps) natural environments are periodically altered. Depending on the season, grazing cattle is either possible or not. In summer the cattle are herded to the upper pastures and, whenever polar weather conditions set it, are brought down in winter.

Mountain regions are generally inhospitable border regions for cultures; to some extent this is also true for other areas where living conditions are tough. However, distance over sea is not such a barrier for a culture: in the island regions of Melanesia the same cultures exist either side of channels and straits even though they may be 50 or so kilometres across. The Huon Peninsula in north-east Papua New Guinea shows a close cultural affinity with the western end of New Britain island, whereas further inland there are clear cultural divisions east-west and north-south.

If one judges the descriptions of natural environments from the vantage point of whether and in what form they tended to encourage or discourage developments, one realizes that the rise of more complex cultures relates directly to how easily the natural environments sustain farming. If one takes this into account then there are 4 types of habitat: 1) areas with no possibility for farming (tundra, some deserts, savannahs, many mountain areas), 2) areas with restricted opportunities (tropical forests of South America with their poor soils), 3) areas with even greater potential for farming (Andes), and 4) areas with unlimited opportunities.

These last two types gave rise to mankind's early advanced civilisations.

More on the topic of this chapter can be found in:

Bargatzky, Thomas: Einführung in die Kulturökologie. Umwelt, Kultur und Gesellschaft. Berlin 1986.

Beer, Bettina; Fischer, Hans (Hg.): Ethnologie. Einführung und Überblick. Berlin 2003(a).

Casimir, Michael J.: Kulturökologie. In: Beer/Fischer 2003(a):341-360.

Martin, Laura: Eskimo words for snow. A case study in the genesis and decay of an anthropological example. American Anthropologist 88.1986:418-423.

Chapter 6
Economic Systems

This chapter explains what opportunities human groupings have in various climate zones round the world to ensure their survival, i.e. what forms and processes can be used in food production. The chapter also sets out how the four fundamental systems that emerge during the development of human cultures are linked with other areas of human effort required to thrive, i.e. essentially, which religions and typical inheritance traditions are practised under the various systems.

6.0   Introduction

In the previous chapter we saw that a society's culture – in its essential features – is formed by the setting of its natural environment, and that it equips itself with strategies adapted for this environment. Only in this manner can the people shape their existence within their allotted natural setting and master the problems arising.

One of the most rudimentary problems that needs to be overcome is *satisfying the basic need for food*, i.e. *securing a livelihood*. For this reason cultures have a particular *economic system* as their own partial strategy for solving this set of survival issues.

Economic systems are so important and significant for pre-literate societies that their cultures can be classified according to their methods of food production. That economic systems achieve such status is proven by the fact that coexisting religions exhibit a close prominent symbiosis. It looks almost as though certain economic systems are not made to dovetail with certain forms of religions.

In ethnology we broadly distinguish 4 economic systems:

1. *Hunter-gatherers*,
2. *Planters*,
3. *Arable farmers*,
4. *Livestock breeders*, also called *nomads* or *nomadic herdsmen*.

Over and above these are the more complex cultures, mostly urban, which – though pre-literate – nevertheless reveal structures typical of so-called civilisations (artisans, priestly caste, etc.) In this introduction they can only be mentioned in passing.

The systems mentioned above were and are so rarely (if ever) clear-cut. Each ideal-case description below is meant merely to highlight an underlying principle.

The reader should also bear in mind that in more recent publications the *technical names* for specific economic systems *may differ* from those used in what follows. Rössler (2003) calls hunter-gathering simply "food searching" (by contrast with food production). For him the difference between planting for a root crop and sowing for cereals crops is expressed in the words "extensive" and "intensive" growing, or as "Feldbau" and "Ackerbau". For the non-ethnologist working in unfamiliar areas the traditional terms are handier and easier to remember – which is why I retain them in this study.

6.1   Hunter-Gatherers

They are known as such by English-speaking researchers because they do not actually produce their food but take it from their habitat, hunting and gathering what nature presents. This system is *acquisitive*, by contrast with the others termed *productive*.

The task of obtaining food is very clearly allocated in hunter-gatherer societies: the men hunt and the women gather.

A straightforward biological basis underlies this gender-specific tasking. In these societies women are either pregnant during their potential working years, or they have an infant whom they need to take with them all the time. Under these conditions it is impossible to outrun over any distance an antelope wounded in the hunt, or to hoist a seal from among the ice floes; not to mention the fact that hunting can get one into situations too dangerous for young children.

The principle of gender-specific work sharing is common in ethnic groups seeking to make a living from the sea. In Oceania men go deep-sea fishing and turtle hunting, women collect mussels and crabs from the sheltered waters of the reefs and sandbanks, or catch smaller fish with cast nets.

Usually it is the women who gather plant food: fruit, mushrooms, and edible roots.

Hunter-gatherers acquire their food with a variety of *tools and equipment*. The men use hunting equipment such as bows and arrows, blowpipes, harpoons, boomerangs, traps, boats, snow shoes, etc., and the women have baskets for their provisions, and gourds for fetching water, etc. Apart from their clothing, their possessions are almost nil, and their needs are very modest. Yet, to an extent unmatched in any other economic system, they do require a vast *territory*.

With some exceptions, hunter-gatherers *do not live a settled life*; they roam across their territory. If the surrounds of their encampment have been harvested and their prey is dwindling the groups move off, but return from time to time to their bases. In this way they avoid over-hunting, over-fishing and over-gathering.

The life of a hunter-gatherer group requires *extensive land use*. In reality this system needs more territory than any other. One rule of thumb says that the area required for the economic systems, ranging from hunter-gathering and livestock-breeding, through to arable farming, planting and industrial processing diminishes by a factor of 7 for each system. In other words, an individual working in an industrial society would manage on 1 unit of area, but would need as a planter 7 units and as an arable farmer 49 units, and so on.

This huge need for land is an important reason for the decline of hunter-gatherers in recent times. With increases in population densities, for example by immigrants acquiring land (as has happened in North and South America), problems arise which either condemn many hunter-gatherers to death by starvation, during which time of course violent struggles ensue with those seizing land, or the problems compel them to give up their traditional ways of life and become sedentary. This process can be seen at the moment throughout the world.

Because communities of hunter-gatherers must be on the move they remain in *small groups* of 50-100 people. In areas with harsh habitats (Kalahari desert, polar regions) the groups can be even smaller.

In some circumstances hunter-gatherers may reduce their group size to remain mobile. As a consequence, migration to a new hunting and gathering ground may mean that surplus small children who cannot be carried are killed at birth.

In which case conflicts can arise when value-systems and laws originally drafted for European-Western cultures are then enforced in states where hunter-gatherer groups still eke out a living. The right to life, which is considered a basic human right, can seem to hunter-gatherers a threat to their survival if – by adhering to this right – they find the size of their group and the manner of pursuing their livelihood are no longer in equilibrium. The continued life of the group would be in danger, and so would that of each member, since the individual living as a hunter-gatherer can only survive when sustained within the group.

One example of the special significance of the group for each member is the difficulty or impossibility of hunting alone using (stone-age) hunter-gatherer methods. Because weapons do not have a great range, it is only possible to kill larger game if the animal is driven within range by a second hunter (or several others) towards the man with the weapon.

Regarding channels of authority and command, hunter-gatherer groups do not have a complex structure. This generally follows the *prin-*

ciple of seniority: at the top of the hierarchy the last word goes to one man among the elders (excluding any senile members), because he has the greatest experience of life. He holds his position also by virtue of his intelligence and his character, such as his courage in the chase and in combat against attackers.

In hunter-gatherer cultures the ideal of the good and successful (male) hunter is accorded higher prestige than the prowess of the (female) gatherer, although generally her participation in ensuring the group's survival is greater and longer-lasting than the man's. Nevertheless, the dominant status of what are considered male activities is mirrored in the fact that kinship allegiances in hunter-gatherer groups are generally determined through the male line; their *kinship system* is *patrilineal*.

The priority given to the man is reflected also in the hunter-gatherer *religions*. Their basic structure – as in almost all pre-literate cultures – is *animistic* (cf. chap. 14).

The element common to most hunter-gatherer religions is a *superhuman being* of whom it is said that he created all things or perfected the world that was – by some means – already present. In particular this superhuman created the animals and is in every conceivable way responsible for the hunters' prey, and also often for assuring the hunters' food supply generally. This being is a type of personified supreme power called in ethnology *Lord of the Animals*. In rare cases the power is *female*. Alongside these there may be other creator beings.

A part of the *ritual* in these cultures is dedicated to this superhuman being. If the hunters don't manage to kill any animals it must be because the Lord of the Animals is denying them; he must need to be pacified or just reminded that the animals are to be killed. The rituals involve a set pattern of behaviour which in the particular culture means contacting the supernatural (the ethereal, beyond the reach of humankind): mostly entailing a sacrifice as a kind of gift.

Sometimes reconciliation does not follow at the first hint of alienation between the people and the Lord of the Animals. Animals are often thought of as his "children". If hunters intend hunting then they may have to appease him in advance, because it is tantamount to killing one of his creatures.

In cultures like these *hunting magic* plays a significant role. It comprises a whole variety of symbolic acts where the method of hunting and its produce are enacted. The procession of hunters and the killing of the prey are arranged as a kind of dance, with animal models or drawings adding to the scenario, in the hope that the real hunting expedition will match the simulation.

These enactments are a sensible explanation for the *petroglyphs* and *cave paintings* of hunting scenes from the *Palaeolithic Period* (Old Stone Age, c. 600,000-8,000 B.C.) familiar to us from Western France (Lascaux) and Eastern Spain (Altamira). (In more recent times cave paintings were discovered which required a rethinking of this explanation. Perhaps the paintings formed the context for initiation rites.)

Hunter-gatherer cultures and their religions preserve a *mythology* (by mythology here I mean the sum total of all the *myths* surrounding a particular ethnic group, i.e. their own tales of their own religion and world view; cf. chap. 13); in these accounts males and their activities predominate.

A further feature of hunter-gatherer cultures, and a particularly striking one, is the *absence of ancestor worship*. Hunter-gatherers do not retain a long-term link with their dear departed. Because the community is not sedentary, family members' graves cannot serve as memorials or places of cult worship. Quite to the contrary: sites where somebody has died or been buried are feared and avoided. The actual reason for this behaviour is the belief among the hunter-gatherers that a person's soul after death becomes a demon that wishes to snatch those remaining, to bring them violently into its own fateful sphere, and to cause numerous diseases.

Typical of hunter-gatherer groups is the institution of the *shaman*, the intermediary between this world of men and the spirit-world of supernatural beings. Simply stated, shamans are religious specialists who are consulted in situations of need, such as when somebody is ill. They are accredited with the power to send their soul (or one of their souls) on a journey into the world beyond so as to find out from all-knowing supernatural beings (their so-called *auxiliary spirits*) the cause and possible treatment of an illness. During this *journey of the soul* the shaman's body lies in a *trance*, unconscious and motionless, until his soul returns to him.

Hunting and foraging was clearly the first economic activity in the history of human cultures. People pursued this way of life for thousands of years, perhaps for hundreds of thousands; it was the only economic system available to all humankind during the Palaeolithic Period (until about 10,000 years ago).

The life of a forager required humans to adapt to nature as closely as possible. Even now it remains the way of life that imposes the least strain and change upon nature.

Yet this is not to imply that humans and nature had purposely lived in harmony within this system. Life was full of struggles – sometimes harsh ones – against nature and her domineering, intractable ways that battered humans in pre-literate societies, and particularly hunters and gatherers. It is sufficient to take to heart what mortality rates were like in these conditions. There is plenty of evidence suggesting that it was a feat to survive the first five years. Scarcely anybody lived beyond 35-40 years old.

In other contexts, living in harmony was possible only with reservations, for example in the matter of careful use of natural resources. Palaeolithic finds in Western France indicated the following: wild horses were hunted by driving them over precipices where they fell to their death. Archaeological investigations of the area of impact brought to light piles of skeletons whose state of preservation showed that only a few remains had had flesh removed from them; it is likely that these morsels were considered delicacies by the hunters of Stone-Age France. If this conclusion is correct it is a striking example of wastefulness. Similar things could be said of the way ethnic groups of North America treated their prey; Indians there feasted upon buffalo, but sometimes only ate the tongues: on festive occasions so many cattle were slaughtered that the tongues alone were enough, and the rest was left to rot. At no epoch were men so noble as to refrain from inflicting harm on their environment.

The fact that nature was never exhausted – nor yet is even today with contemporary hunters and their quarry – was not so much (then as now) because of lofty moral ideals among hunters (which no doubt existed, then as now); it was because their small and sparse human population allowed them (then and sometimes even now) to treat natural resources in this way without great ecological harm.

Hunter-gatherers exist these days as scattered groups, in so-called *reservations*. The current trend is clear. In a few decades hunter-gatherers will cease to exist, not just because the land, of course, is no longer available but also because they no longer wish to live like this. In the meantime they are in close contact everywhere with cultures affected by technology and civilisation, and they seek to use these benefits to reduce the struggle for existence. They acquire modern hunting rifles, motorised fishing boats etc. to hasten the advances for their own cultures.

Rössler refers (2003:106) in this connection also to "food searchers", as he occasionally terms them; everywhere these days they are "supposedly behind the times and discriminated against." They are seen as an impoverished proletariat in many countries, as are for example the Aborigines in Australia, and are pushed to the margins of society.

We have seen that in their economic system hunter-gatherers do not nurture and grow things, but acquire them. As a rule they are not sedentary, that is, they do not keep animals and plants close by their dwellings to tend them. They set out to hunt when the need arises: the men head off seeking animals and the women go gathering plants, searching for places where edible plants, berries and fungi can grow.

As mankind's cultures developed, the other economic systems might have arisen as specialisations, namely planting, agriculture and livestock breeding (among nomads). This development was certainly not inevitable, because there are examples from the history of cultures where planters became hunters and gatherers, if circumstances forced them to emigrate or move (for example, like the Maoris of New Zealand's South Island).

An extensive overview of particular hunter-gatherer cultures is given by Seitz (1977, French edition 1993) and in the two volumes of Ingold/Riches/Woodburn (1991).

6.2   Planters

At first glance it seems strange to make a distinction between planters and arable farmers. But it is plain to see why such differentiation is meaningful.

Planters grow *root vegetables*, i.e. *taro plants*, *yams*, *manioc*, *sweet potatoes*. These need a tropical climate with plenty of rain or artificial irrigation. Because planters only thrive in the continuous damp of the tropics even *bananas* to some extent belong ethnologically among the root vegetables, and in some areas so does *breadfruit* (i.e. in Oceania).

The produce that planters harvest cannot be stored, or only in a limited way. Root vegetables spoil easily and have to be used soon after being pulled up; only what is needed at the time is uprooted. With taro that is possible all the year round, because in the humidity of the tropics there are no precise seasonal changes where a period without vegetation is followed by one with vegetation. The plants that are required for daily use are kept where they grow; and the plantation becomes a *living storage area*. Because each person plants the same root crops and usually not for selling at market but for his home use, the name for this livelihood is the *subsistence economy*. Bargatzky therefore uses the term *subsistence economy of demand*.

Planters do not lay out great fields like arable farmers do; their plot is the size of a kitchen garden. Suitable plots are the soft ground near water courses which can be irrigated using man-made dams or conduits and channels, particularly suited for plots of taro. Yams or manioc are tubers which require drier ground; they are planted on soil obtained after *slash and burn land-clearance*.

For this purpose an area of forest is cleared, and after the fallen timber has had time to dry out it is set on fire. The ash fertilises the soil. This is man's work. Thereafter, the women start planting. With a digging stick or a simple pickaxe they make holes for the cuttings. Planters do not generally sow seed but propagate their food plants by rooting runners.

Regular fertilising with animal or human excrement is not merely unusual; planters actually consider that increasing the yield in this way is one of the most repulsive of all European agricultural practices: how could anybody wish to eat food grown on a manure heap? If the soil needs enriching the women do it by digging in dry leaves or green plant foliage.

There is a solid reason for women doing the work of planting out. Presumably they were the ones who as the gatherers in a tropical environment hit upon the idea of avoiding a long walk to the plants, by marking out a plot for cultivating them nearer home. Perhaps a further discovery set them thinking; when their group travelled across territory and came back to a previous settlement of theirs, the pile of food waste they had left behind was surprisingly overgrown with one of the root vegetables – all they then needed to do was harvest it without having to go out and spend time foraging.

Laying out plots had consequences. It forced the women who had hit upon the idea and their menfolk to become *sedentary*, although the men could keep their hunting way of life; indeed they needed to keep it, if their families were to have enough animal protein. Becoming dependent on a plot for the provision of basic food meant that possessing land was vital, land that might need to be defended. Holding land was now no longer a collective business, but became a private matter, with particular groups staking their claims, building homes and then settling down.

The discovery of planting meant there was a local supply of food. The number of people who could be fed grew; families and other social groupings increased in size. From this arose the need for political leadership; chiefdoms were organized. From then on it also became necessary for children and other family members to justify and legitimize their claims to landholding. They needed to prove their membership of a particular family or group and prove their entitlement as owners and heirs of a specific parcel of land. Thereafter they had what is known in ethnology as the *land title*. The planters nurtured a distinctive family orientation, characterized partly by an intricate *kinship system* with a carefully nuanced terminology for their relationships – something hitherto unnecessary in the hunter-gatherer clans. In addition, they adopted the planters' principle of *matrilineal succession*.

In most planter cultures family ancestry is traced through the *mother's line*. In ethnological parlance, planters are *matrilineal* in their organisation. Presumably the reason is simple. The birth of a child is difficult to conceal, being evident from the mother's unmistakable pregnancy; and those attending the birth are mostly other women and younger girls. In addition, the ancient Romans had a saying *"mater semper certa est"* (the mother is always certain). This does not apply to the father! Rarely is anybody present at a baby's conception, apart from the two parents. As a result it is usually much less clear who the father is. (In court, evidence of paternity is much more commonly sought than for maternity). One can demonstrate family kinship – and thus lodge a claim to a plot of land and its produce – much more straightforwardly by reference to the mother's line than to the father's (cf. chap. 8).

A caveat is appropriate here: matrilineal inheritance is not the rule in all sedentary societies, only among planters (cf. Müller 1997).

From these few details it can be appreciated that there are considerable cultural differences between hunter-gatherers and planters. The discovery of planting – and the adoption of a sedentary life-style which inevitably resulted – brought in reality such fundamental changes that this is seen as the start of a new era in the history of culture, and is named accordingly; the Palaeolithic age comes to an end and the *Neolithic Age* (8000-1800 B.C) begins. The ensuing arable farming is the hallmark of the Neolithic revolution. Presumably it was evident earlier in the tropics than beyond the tropics.

Being sedentary also had a far-reaching impact in the area of *religion*. As we have seen, planters are much more family-focussed than hunter-gatherers. Their families consist not merely of all their living members but also of those who have died; they too are considered *ancestral spirits* still close by, and – since they are mostly even older than the senior living family members – they are as such even more worthy of respect. They are offered due deference, and are given presents in the form of *offerings*, mostly food offerings. And because they continue to belong to their family after death they are buried on their actual land near their dwelling or even in the house itself. So a family is not just a closed unit in economic terms but also in a religious sense. A hunter-gatherer family is both "the firm" and "the community".

As good spirit beings (good as regards the particular family group or ethnic group) the ancestors possibly have access to a so-called *Supreme Being* whose dwelling is the sky and who is considered *creator* of the world. He is seen as an old man, sometimes very old, who does not look after his creation any more. For that reason people do not honour him especially, at least not nearly as much as their own ancestral spirits who are much more closely involved in human affairs than the supreme being in the sky, far removed from the sphere of mortals.

In planters' mythology the snake is often a type of "Lord of the Plants", sometimes also understood as a water spirit or water god. In ethnic groups in South-East Asia (e.g. the Batak group of Sumatra) there are images of a huge snake-like creature that lives underground and can trigger earth tremours when it moves around.

In addition, planters' mythology speaks of superhuman beings, male and female, of whom it is said that they lived after the creation of the world in a type of pre-historical *mythical age* with humans, until the humans committed a particularly corrupt act by killing one of the superhumans. This act represents something like the Fall, a catastrophe heralding the end of prehistory (only as regards this particular ethnic group) and changing the world into its current state.

Quite possibly this act of evil so roused the anger of the Supreme Being that it moved the sky (which up to then had been near the earth and accessible to humans) far up and away, or else knocked over the ladder which led there. From then on humans had no further access to the sky and the Supreme Being. At the same time there were reports saying that blessings had come out of this evil. After humans had smashed the dead superhuman being to pieces and buried the bits, their first offshoots were root vegetables: from the head came the taro, from the arms came the yams, etc.

These spirit beings are, I repeat, creatures of mythology and of much lesser significance for the daily life of the ethnic group than their own ancestral spirits, who can be contacted directly in crisis situations via a *medium*. This occurs in a very typically different way than for a shaman among the hunter-gatherers who sends his soul on a "journey to the beyond" to his auxiliary spirits in search of important information. With a medium, contact with the being beyond is from the other direction. The ancestral spirits come on a "journey to the here and now". They are "summoned" by the living or else they possess through their own volition the person concerned, who announces in a kind of *trance* (or perhaps not!) the will of the ancestral spirits.

Features typifying the planters' culture are repeated with slight differences, being basically bolder and more nuanced, in the *arable farming* system.

6.3   Arable Farmers

Unlike planters, farmers grow *seed crops* (cereals): maize, wheat, barley, oats, millet and rice. Cereal crops have a dimension which is particularly influential in the history of civilisation.

A famer's cereal crop can be *stored* a long while, for selling at market and, even more importantly, as *reserves* when a season produces little or no produce. As a result of discovering cereal crops the human habitat expanded greatly to the north and south (a nice demonstration of the fact that cultures are strategies for overcoming the harshness of existence!) Whereas planters were restricted to the tropics, arable farmers could survive in areas of prevailing wintry or drought conditions. The only requirement was good soil and sufficient rain at the appropriate time.

The fact that cereals can be stored has further consequences. Because it can be kept for a long time, a bumper harvest need not go to waste. It can be sold at market, or at least exchanged against other goods, or can be used to tide a farmer over whenever his crops fail. Ultimately the *ability to produce surplus crops* allowed humans to feed those who did not produce food themselves: artisans, builders, teachers, priests and soldiers. Even from the earliest farming communities the result was that huge building projects could be achieved (such as the pyramids of Egypt, and the temples at Karnak and Luxor) and great empires be founded (such as the Babylonian), because sufficient food could be produced to maintain a powerful standing army.

The climatic conditions and weather for arable farming were particularly good in the valleys of large rivers, where the annual rain meant the fields were inundated and made fertile by the mud. It was no accident that the early great empires, Egypt and Babylon, were founded on the banks of the Nile, Tigris and Euphrates.

The grain stores so significant for an agricultural economy at first merely had the role as a holding area for the harvest, and were thus sited close to dwellings, since arable farmers are, of course, *settlers* just like planters.

An excess of available food normally causes an increase in the population. In such circumstances a family could reach a respectable size by the third generation. The members built their houses around the food store, and farmsteads came into being. So that the food could be handed round equitably to all and consumed sparingly, a manager of sorts needed to be nominated and made responsible. This steward had to defend the food store against thieves and he probably needed helpers who were armed as well. If the store of foodstuffs was meant for the population of a more sizeable area the steward could not oversee the distribution all by himself, but had to trust a group of officials. He might thereby gain considerable authority. This explains the high status that Joseph enjoyed as steward of the harvests of Egypt (Genesis 41). It also explains why many stewards at the courts of early Germanic rulers, e.g. the so-called heads of households of the Merovingian Frankish kings, were able on the basis of their economic and political position to seize power and become rulers themselves.

The production of surpluses requires the laying out, not of garden-sized plots, but of *extensive fields*. These were worked not with hoes or mattocks, but with heavier equipment: ploughs pulled by oxen. That meant the work was hard men's work. The garden plot had been the woman's domain, but now the field under the plough became the domain of the man and his sons.

This explains why the woman in arable farming in many respects took up a subordinate position, by contrast with her role in planter cultures. Arable farmers reckon their family line through the father (*patrilineal* inheritance). This is particularly exemplified in European-Western cultures by the woman assuming her husband's name on getting married. A woman's use of both surnames, or her choice in the matter, is a more recent phenomenon!)

Farmers are very family-focussed, just like planters. This has a similar impact on their religion, just like planters. Those who have died continue to belong to the family, are given due honour and are consulted for advice or in times of need. In the famer's religion the male element is more significant than for planters. The Supreme Being, identified with the sky and rain, is a male concept. By contrast, the earth is a female concept: its fertility depends on this Supreme Being. In the mythology of farmers this dependency is often illustrated as the sexual union of sky and earth.

It is also interesting that in the farmers' mythology the *snake* is generally viewed in a positive light. Because it lives close to the earth it belongs to the realm of those who have died and is privy to what is known by ancestors; and ancestors – like almost all beings of the world beyond – have access to knowledge of all kinds. On earth the snake is reckoned a wise creature, especially in things medicinal, because it knows the effects of grasses and herbs which are its habitat. This links traditionally with the rod of Asclepius and the serpent twined around it, known to Greeks as a symbol of medicine and healing.

6.4   Livestock Breeders

We saw previously that the origin of farming cultures (planters and arable farmers) can be explained as emerging from the activities of women in hunter-gathering communities. Women made the job of gathering easier by choosing no longer to walk to the plantation but to bring it nearer their dwellings.

One can imagine that the men likewise decided to simplify their life by bringing the animals they had previously hunted closer and taming them. Yet it was not as easy as that. It seems that livestock breeding resulted from arable farming.

Because livestock breeders are not sedentary but roam with their animals from pasture to pasture they are *nomads*. This term is sometimes wrongly applied also to hunter-gatherers, seeing that they live life on the move; yet in ethnology hunter-gatherers are not considered nomads, because they do not breed animals.

Livestock breeders keep the following *large animals*: cows, donkeys, camels, reindeer (close to the Arctic Circle) and yak (in the high mountains of Asia). Sheep and goats also belong among their herds.

The diet of livestock breeders consists largely of *milk* and milk products, and the *blood* of their animals. They get this blood with the aid of a special bow and arrow which is shot from a short distance into the jugular vein of the living animal. The stream of blood from the perforated vein is caught in a basin; only then is the wound attended to.

Surprising as it may seem, livestock breeders rarely slaughter an animal, and eat little meat. When they do slaughter an animal it is a male – and the kill is for sacrificial purposes.

Livestock breeders cannot manage exclusively on the products of their herds, because their bodies require additional vitamins and trace elements from herbs and vegetables for their health. They manage by laying out plots which can be accessed at least sporadically, or else they barter their requirement for plant foodstuffs from growers. (I note in passing that Isaac, though essentially a stock breeder, also had plantations: Genesis 26, 12.)

Working with large animals demands energy. Stock breeders need to exhibit courage and aggression because thieves and predators are on the prowl for their animals. This is why working with animals is for men, including the milking. In nomadic cultures the man has the leading role; which is why the inheritance system is generally *patrilineal*. Women have a subordinate role, even in matters of religion; they are not particularly prominent in society, nor do they have any function in communal rituals. This was also the case back in the Old Testament Israelite community and is still the rule today in Arabic-Islamic cultures: women were expected to be symbolically invisible in public by virtue of their special attire.

The relationship of the livestock breeder to his herds involves elements denoting friendship or even kinship: man and beast in brotherly empathy.

Tending animals is a high calling, whose prestige means that the *bride price* (also called *bride wealth*) paid by a young male nomad to the family of his future wife is reckoned in cattle. In planter societies the bride wealth has a hidden equivalent: throughout his marriage the man is expected to work to assist his wife's family.

Livestock breeders have a markedly different culture from hunter-gatherers and farmers. Because their wealth consists of many individual animals, they have adopted a complex system of numbering; not without reason is the modern decimal system a product of Arab lands. Because the breeders have to be mobile, their material culture has fewer sizeable objects needing to be loaded on to pack animals and transported.

Their *creativity* is, however, very well developed: they cherish a culture of dances, songs and stories in numerous manifestations, styles and genres. (In many ethnic groups the young men compose sophisticated prize songs to their young women, praising their features – e.g. their eyes – by comparing them with those of their favourite cow!)

Even in the matter of religion there are signal differences between the nomadic life and other life systems. Livestock breeders also relate to a Supreme Being which is generally male and all-powerful; they too have a number of spirit beings who are subordinate to this Supreme Being, yet these beings are less significant for them than are the ancestral spirits for arable farmers. The livestock breeders' Supreme Being exhibits some characteristics of a *singular god* (*monotheism*). Typical examples of God as singular and supreme are found in Islam, and consistently throughout the history of Israel in the Old Testament.

The Supreme Being in stockbreeders' cultures is often identified with the sky and the many and varied weather phenomena. One of his most important functions is to send rain. Without rainfall there would be no grass and thus no conditions for life. Correspondingly, rain magic is important – practised by specialists who are held in great awe.

The *snake*, a symbol invested with positive feelings in arable farming cultures, is by contrast an object of danger and evil in stockbreeding cultures, as exemplified in the thinking of the Israelites of the Old Testament (Genesis 3; Numbers 21).

A good introduction to the theme of nomads and their life is Rösing 2003. Her study relates specifically to Asia (the Changpa nomads of Tibet) and issues relating to shamanism.

6.5   Consumerism and Reciprocity

By consumerism is meant people's *use of goods* (Rössler 2003:111). Closely linked with this idea are three more.

Distribution is the way in which products of a culture that are not for exclusive use get from the producer to the consumer.

In societies driven by one of the above economic systems, *bartering* is prominent. To describe its many and varied aspects would go beyond the bounds of this introduction; Rössler (2003: 114-117) gives a succinct survey. In this connection special importance is accorded to the notion of *reciprocity*.

By reciprocity is meant a state of obligation which people are in when they accept a gift or a service. If an islander from Chuuk (Micronesia) accepts a bowlful of breadfruit he becomes "kinissow", which means that from that moment onwards – from the point of view of the giver – he is indebted, until such time as he offers something in return. At which point his state of obligation is annulled or passed back to the original giver.

This kind of reciprocity is not merely integral to the islanders' economy but also to their religious practice. By making an offering, the supplicants expect a "higher being" – such as an ancestral spirit – to be placed just like their fellow islanders in a state of indebtedness. If the ancestral spirit does not similarly fulfil his obligation and does not accede to the request made of him, then rumours start, just as they would in the material world if somebody did not take seriously his obligation to reciprocate.

More detailed introductions to this chapter's topic:

Introductory studies in this area are limited in number, and some are outdated. The following are recommended for their readability: Vivelo 1981, Jensen 1983, Plattner 1989 and Rössler 1999.

A lucid, *succinct* portrayal of the whole topic of the ethnology of economic systems is Rössler 2003. He gives a manageable bibliography with additional relevant publications.

More on the topic of this chapter can be found in the following studies:

Bargatzky, Thomas: Ethnologie. Eine Einführung in die Wissenschaft von den urproduktiven Gesellschaften. Hamburg 1997.

Beer, Bettina; Fischer, Hans (Hg.): Ethnologie. Einführung und Überblick. Berlin 2003. (This is Fischer's 5th ed. of 1983 in a new version.)

Fischer, Hans (Hg.): Ethnologie. Eine Einführung. Berlin 1983.

Ingold, Tim; Riches, David; Woodburn, James (eds.): Hunters and gatherers. New York Oxford 1991.

Jensen, Jürgen: Wirtschaftsethnologie. In: Fischer 1983:91-119.

Kleihauer, Maike: Kulturelle Regression bei Jäger- und Sammlerkulturen. Diss. Freiburg 1989.

Kohl, Karl-Heinz: Ethnologie – die Wissenschaft vom kulturell Fremden. Eine Einführung. München 1993:77-91.

Lee, Richard B.; DeVore, Irvin (eds.): Man the hunter. New York 1968.

Müller, Klaus E.: Der gesprungene Ring: wie man die Seele gewinnt und verliert. Frankfurt am Main 1997.

Plattner, Stuart (ed.): Economic anthropology. Stanford, CA 1989.

Rösing, Ina: Trance, Besessenheit und Amnesie. Bei den Schamanen der Changpa-Nomaden im ladakhischen Changthang. Gnas 2003.

Rössler, Martin: Wirtschaftsethnologie. Eine Einführung. Berlin 1999.

Rössler, Martin: Wirtschaftsethnologie. In: Beer/Fischer 2003:101-124.

Sahlins, Marshall D.: Stone age economics. Chicago, New York 1972.

Seitz, Stefan: Die zentralafrikanischen Wildbeuterkulturen. Wiesbaden 1977. (French title: Pygmées d'Afrique. Paris 1993.)

Vivelo, Frank R.: Handbuch der Kulturanthropologie. Eine Einführung. Stuttgart 1981: chapters 4-8.

Weniger, Gerd Christian: Wildbeuter und ihre Umwelt. Ein Beitrag zum Magdalénien Südwestdeutschlands aus ökologischer und ethno-archäologischer Sicht. Tübingen 1982.

Chapter 7
Technology and Ergology

This chapter explains what both terms mean in ethnology, what components of the so-called material culture can be classified under them, what meaning can be ascribed to them within an overall culture, and why it is not just engineers and artisans intending to operate in foreign cultures who should be informed about technology and ergology.

The previous chapter indicated that the various forms of economic activity are to be seen as cultural strategies for an ethnic group's physical survival. These strategies have emerged from the particular environmental conditions; in order to produce food, certain *tools and equipment* need to be made to suit their purpose. This is why tools and equipment must be considered integral parts of the economies they serve and should not really be studied in a chapter of their own. Yet because in other cultural areas there is a need for artefacts to facilitate interests and activities, artefacts which technologically share many common features with the tools and equipment supporting the economic activities, it is sensible and helpful for their use and manufacture to be treated in a separate chapter.

Among these things we do not just mean tools. In human cultures there are clothes, jewellery, musical instruments, ancestral figurines, and a whole lot more. This is called *material culture*. The specialisms within ethnology which study this are technology and ergology. In museums of ethnology their artefacts are predominant.

Technology comprises the study of the manufacture of objects from raw materials; ergology is the study of a culture's physical artefacts.

A reminder: an ethnic group's material culture is its most accessible aspect for a foreigner, the one which strikes him immediately and which often stays with him: it embodies what he expects from a culture and what he becomes familiar with. Yet the material element is only a small component of that whole culture, a secondary aspect in people's minds, and based on thought structures. These structures exist – hidden but yet retrievable – as strategies for the manufacture and use of such components.

For church workers overseas, dealing with technology and ergology is of rather secondary importance. But it should be understood that a person's cogent opinion on particular topics of his own narrower field can only emerge if these disciplines are first investigated more thoroughly. It is particularly necessary for a person involved in a literacy programme and its related reading material, notably so for a Bible translator. Precise knowledge about the weapon that David used when he killed Goliath (1 Samuel 17) is a requirement, so that the worker can pass on insights to the mother-tongue language advisor. He or she may not be so well in- formed, but the acquired knowledge facilitates a suitable translation which can be understood by the reader later without lengthy explanations. Joseph's trade (Luther calls Jesus' father a carpenter in Matthew 13:55) can cause problems in translating if one is unaware of the variety of tools associated with it over the span of two thousand years between then and now: Joseph the professional builder must have been at least as familiar with masonry as with woodwork, to judge from archaeological finds.

It is self-evident that development aid workers trying to introduce new processes and equipment in agriculture or manual trades should study very carefully indeed what changes they are seeking to bring about.

Broadly speaking the material elements of a culture fall into one of 7 categories:

1. *traditional costume*: including dress, notably clothes, but also hair- style, body decoration (warpaint!) and various adornments (ankle rings, lip pegs – ornamentation worn in the pierced lower lip, or a boar's tooth inserted between the nasal passages), tattoos and other alterations to the body (such as the Hindu-Balinese ceremony of tooth-filing , and the for- mer practice of foot-binding among Chinese women).

Wearing plenty of clothes is necessary in regions further to the north or south, and in mountainous country; tattoos are less common, given that they need to be visible rather than hidden by garments. That is the reason why they are particularly common in tropical climes where the body can be more exposed.

The patterns formed by tattooing the skin have a range of functions. They serve to distinguish particular people from all the others. That is why tattoos are often reserved for chieftains or for the privileged few, and thus function like rank insignia on a uniform. This illustrates a close con- ceptual link between tattoos and clothing, whose styling or patterns ex- hibit social rank or regional provenance – as in days gone by with the costumes worn by European ethnic groups, but which nowadays have a limited function.

It is important for understanding tattoos and body decoration to appre- ciate their link with the supernatural. Certain ornaments are held to be ef- fective in warding off evil spirits, illnesses, curses, spells and other disas- ters. Altering one's face with make-up renders one unrecognizable to evil spirits, or terrifying to an enemy, or attractive to the opposite sex.

In many circumstances clothes are visible status symbols. It is not just kings who can be picked out in a crowd, but army generals as well. They often wear a tall head-dress (a crown or a plumed helmet) to enhance their above-average stature.

A priest's clothing signifies that he has a status above the common people, especially in view of his religious activities. In Exodus 28 there is a description of the splendid garment worn by Aaron for his priestly duties in the tabernacle.

The close link between clothing and status is also apparent in a deaconess's habit. It dates from a time when a woman holding office seldom appeared in public. If she ever did, then only if she was married. Her status was evident from her head-covering, a bonnet which indicated she was married and which conveyed the legitimacy of official approval.

As a matter of principle deaconesses do not marry, but are involved in public ministry. The founding fathers of the work in social care and the leaders of such ministries needed to consider how they might bestow upon deaconesses a legitimacy of office which ensured accreditation in an otherwise male-oriented society.

That we should be considering bonnets should not surprise us if we remember that the actual reason for their existence – the crucial need to give unmarried women status – has since ceased. This is due to the change within our culture and links the demise of the deaconess's garments with that of regional costumes. (The wider aspects of this topic would go beyond the scope of this study).

2. *Food*: Worth mentioning is the huge range of equipment required to produce food, such as tools for digging, and agricultural implements for sowing and threshing. Fishing also has its own range of technology, as do dairy farming and hunting for animal protein, to name but a few of the many technologies.

3. *Shelter*: included here are the various kinds of constructions that serve as living space and protect people against wind and weather: caves and houses; igloos (built of ice-blocks by ethnic groups in Arctic regions) and windbreaks (erected by the Khoisan people of the Southern African bush).

So-called sacred buildings, like temples and churches, cause some difficulty – because they can only be termed shelters with some reservation. They are most usually considered under the heading of a group's religion.

4. *Transport*: vehicles such as carts (thanks to the invention of the wheel), boats, sledges, skis, snow shoes, animals used for pulling and riding (the invention of the saddle) and many more.

5. *Weapons* are particularly imposing and frightening examples of the driving forces hidden in the human mind and heart; they have given rise

to many components of material culture: weapons to hunt with, to defend oneself against enemy attack, but also to conquer territory. The range broadens over history: from the throwing stick or stone, to the rockets or nuclear missiles of the modern world.

Ethnologists distinguish between *aggressive* weapons (bow and arrow, sword and spear), *defensive* weapons (shield) and *hunting* weapons. These last are interesting for being attack weapons and differing only in the particular circumstances of their use.

Hunting weapons can also be bracketed with other required implements of the material culture: with nets, traps, weirs, fishing hooks and lines. One artefact straddles the offensive and the hunting categories: the boomerang used by Australian aboriginals.

Objects such as helmets and armour raise a difficulty for categorizing weapon technology; they can be seen as defensive weapons but also as clothing, indeed as costume. Whenever animals like horses or elephants wear protection against injury it is not sensible to treat it as their costume; it is more appropriate to treat it as their defensive equipment.

6. *Music and entertainment*: this heading comprises a whole number of instruments, from the simple rhythm instruments and the various types of drum (skin drum, slit drum), Jew's harp (which is plucked) through to the various wind and string instruments. The need to be entertained has led to a rich store of strategies and artefacts: *games* (board games, card games, string games, team games), dice, chess pieces, balls and so on.

Under entertainment we have sport, dancing and singing, even though actual equipment is not strictly necessary. Many ethnographers classify them under the heading of *traditional culture and folk pastimes*. *Sports equipment* also belongs to the category of entertainment. Sometimes it may have components which can belong elsewhere: javelins used as offensive weapons, skis as a means of transport, etc.

7. *Actual technology*: technology and ergology have problems categorizing implements for manufacturing clothing, for example, like the weaver's loom. Should they be treated in conjunction with costume, or do they belong with all the other tools and equipment under a heading, for example under agricultural? People hold differing opinions about this. To avoid this problem many researchers deal with the material aspects of a cultural area by relating them to their fundamental context: the loom to costume, the plough to food, etc.

Where appropriate, the implements of a particular culture can be brought under one heading and linked to an existing process (metal casting techniques, resist colour dyeing techniques like ikat or batik), in a chapter whose topic is *actual technology*.

This is particularly the case for objects used in worship (figurines of ancestors, fetishes, rosary beads), objects and paraphernalia used in ritual and magic (stones, dowsing rods) and also for medical instruments used to remove foreign bodies from the eye or skin, appliances for changing the shape of parts of the body (for foot-binding among Chinese women, for binding the skull to produce an elongated head, etc.)

The following account shows that technology and ergology should not just engage the artisan and the engineer but rather all those who are involved with a foreign culture. It is not just people and ideas but also elements of the material culture which occasionally achieve considerable importance and prominence in an ethnic group's general culture: if their significance is diminished by their being replaced with similar but somewhat different things – or if they lose their original position through cultural change – then the consequences can be very far-reaching.

The Yir Yoront people of Australia did not consider the stone axe as just a tool but also as a symbol of authority. When they were introduced to the steel axe during the period of colonisation they adopted it immediately, because the new tool had enormous advantages over the old version. It was easier to work with, it did not get blunt so quickly, and it was more easily obtainable – given that the Yir Yoront had been getting the stone axes from a different ethnic group living a great distance away. Because the axes were for that reason rather expensive, only the more important men in any family group – those in authority – owned a stone axe. If younger members wished to use one, they had to ask. This explains why the stone axe could become a symbol of authority, an authority invested in the Yir Yoront people's mythology and religion, and could thereby derive legitimacy. Cattle breeders dwelling locally employed the younger members of the Yir Yoront as herdsmen and paid for their work with steel axes. It was not long before many members, even women and children, had the new tool and no longer had to ask the elders as authority figures for permission to borrow theirs. Thus began the decline of the Yir Yoront. Nowadays they do not exist as an independent ethnic group. Lauriston Sharp has documented the tragic process in graphic terms (1953, 1970). I call it tragic because nobody forced the Yir Yoront to use steel axes. They themselves wanted them, for understandable reasons. By what authority and with what arguments could they have been dissuaded otherwise?

However, Sharp's arguments can, on the basis of more recent researches, only be validated to a certain degree; they need to be interpreted with some criticism. His predictions concerning the future demise of the Yir Yoront seem rather exaggerated in the light of subsequent research (Taylor 1988). Two things may be noted in this respect.

Firstly, it is extremely difficult to predict even with reservations what direction a cultural change will finally take once it is underway. Secondly, the history of this Australian ethnic group, in whose course of existence the switching of one single element of its material culture for a similar element turned out to be a threat to the survival of its whole culture, is an extreme case. Such occurances are actually very rare. In general, cultures are stable entities which can only alter slowly; they are not easily brought to a point of collapse. Furthermore, changes entailing people coming into contact with others of different cultures are not necessarily negative. Yet in our own attempts to make changes in foreign cultures we do well to act thoughtfully and with care.

Detailed introductions to this chapter's topic:

Feest/Janata 1999 give a fluent and richly illustrated survey, a classic in the field of technology and ergology. Volume 2 contains a manageable bibliography for the individual aspects of this discipline. Feest 2003 gives a brief survey.

The following contain more on the topic of this chapter:

Beer, Bettina; Fischer, Hans (Hg.): Ethnologie. Einführung und Überblick. Berlin 2003.

Harding, Thomas G.; Wallace, Ben J. (eds.): Cultures of the Pacific. Selected Readings. New York (Macmillan) 1970.

Feest, Christian F.: Materielle Kultur. In: Beer/Fischer 2003(a):239-254.

Feest, Christian F.: Janata, Alfred: Technologie und Ergologie in der Völkerkunde. Berlin 1999 (4th. ed.).

Sharp, Lauriston: Steel axes for stone-age Australians. Human Organization 11.1953:17-22. Also in: Harding/Wallace 1970:385-396 (A particularly worthwhile ethnography).

Swain, Tony; Rose, Deborah (eds.): Aboriginal Australians and Christian missions. Bedford Park 1988.

Taylor, John: Goods and Gods. A follow-up study of "Steel axes for stone-age Australians". In: Swain/Rose 1988:438-451.

Chapter 8
Family Relationships

This chapter explains why people consider their family relationships are the most important alliances for survival, what significance their roles have, and what expectations are invested in them. The chapter also explains what a relationship diagram is, what symbols are used, and how to create one's own diagram. The chapter ends with an overview of the meaning of the family and of possible marriage patterns in foreign cultures.

8.0   Introduction

The highest goal of all economic systems is, as we have seen, securing a livelihood; in the narrower sense, producing enough food. In ethnic situations this can only occur within *groups*. The group has a common interest in their members being cared for sufficiently and surviving. This interest is particularly evident in a *family*, where members on the basis of their shared emotional bonds and relationships have a practical fellow-feeling which lends stability to the group. Because they operate for a common cause they create the manufacturing base upon which all its members thrive, the business in which all family members have a stake. The alliance that family members form allows children especially (who have yet to be incorporated into the production process) and old people (who are no longer productive) to survive in a world where there is no institutional care of the elderly.

In these groups not all individuals are alike. They differ in many respects. There are men and women, of various generations and with particular life experiences, etc. A further factor is that they don't all have the same abilities. This results in the members of a family group being given very different tasks. They have a *social role* and *role expectations* accruing from other members. These expectations constitute the duties to be fulfilled by the individual members behaving as a family.

8.1   Basic Concepts

In order to get one's bearings in the network of relational role expectations and functions, and then work within them, a person requires a further set of rules (a strategy) and a relevant set of linguistic terms which help describe the nature of the relationships: the so-called *kinship terminology*.

Ethnologists use standardized symbols to characterize and generally represent the nexus of relationships. A *triangle* represents a *male* relative, a *circle* represents a *female* relative. If they are *married* this is represented by the symbols being *linked with an underlining bracket*. As a rule we are dealing with a *monogamous* marriage of one man and one woman. The bracket symbol can be used for a *polygamous* (more accurately a *polygynous*) marriage where a man has several wives. (The various forms of marriage are dealt with later in this chapter). In ethnology the relationship between two people getting married is called an *alliance*.

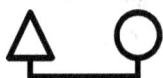

monogamous marriage   polygamous (polygynous) marriage

In a brother-sister relationship the brackets are placed over the symbols, and the relationship is a *collateral* one:

two siblings   more than two siblings

A vertical line linking the two types of bracketed alliance means that the alliance beneath *descends* from the one above. This kinship is called *filiation*:

kinship diagram of a nuclear family

Using these symbols a family can be represented graphically in a *kinship diagram* as a *group of descendants*. In the above diagram we illustrated the simplest form, the *nuclear family*. This is a husband and a wife considered by their culture a married couple with two children, i.e. a diagram showing two generations. The number of children is not relevant for the definition of a nuclear family. There needs to be at least one to merit the term nuclear family. (This diagram depicts a nuclear family even for a polygynous marriage where the man has several wives).

Diagrams like this are an easy way of portraying kinship structures involving several generations.

Starting from the nuclear family, more extensive relational clusters can be defined. These make up *kinship systems*. Broadly speaking, several nuclear families constitute the *extended family*, several such families form the family *lineage* (spanning 3-5 generations), several lineages form the *clan* (in many cultures even those deceased and still remembered by the living are considered to belong to the clan), and all clans taken together make the *ethnic group* or (above a certain size) a *people*. The term *tribe* tends to be used in folklore and is not the usual term in ethnology. (Lineage is pronounced as such when used in German; in French the word is lignage).

In all cultures people are interested in the question of who their ancestors were. Forebears and *founders of clans* are often celebrities. For example in the historic official version, the Japanese imperial family descended from the sun goddess Amaterasu. In many cultures, especially where forebears are not specifically honoured, there are nevertheless accounts of *animals* (bears, eagles, fish, etc.) being considered as *mythical ancestral parents*. In ethnology such creatures are called *totems* (the word is from a North American Indian language). But we are not just dealing with animals; *things* (such as plants, stones, meteorites, etc.) and even *natural phenomena* (lightning, thunder, wind etc.) can also be seen as totems.

Totems are familiar to us from the large North American *totem poles*.

An animal which is considered by its clan as a totem must not be hunted and certainly never eaten. It is *taboo* (cf. chap. 13).

An animal in the above sense is a taboo totem and cannot be hunted and eaten; nor can it become extinct in the lifetime of the particular kinship group. This observation confers on totem animals a kind of conservation order, but for different reasons than in European-Western cultures. There is a whole variety of reasons behind this *taboo against eating totems*; and one should not suppose that the reasons are to do with specific attitudes towards natural and environmental conservation. The most pertinent explanation is the ban on members killing and eating their relatives.

In connection with totemism there is generally a misapprehension among Europeans with their Christian heritage. They classify totemism as essentially a religious phenomenon (animistic or occult). Of course, totemism undoubtedly has religious features, for the killing of a totemic animal brings about the punishment of the perpetrator by a higher power – namely by a Lord of the Animals if such a creature exists in the religion. Yet the ethnological and kinship dimensions of totemism are at least as important as the religious.

Kinship diagrams help to present, analyse and interpret relationships within their structures and systems. In order for us to understand them and to draw inferences from them we need to know the opportunities and the limitations of such diagrams. A practical example will guide us through as follows: Alan and Barbara are married; their children are called Charles, Edward and Diana. Edward is married to Fiona; their children are Graham and Hanna. This is their kinship diagram:

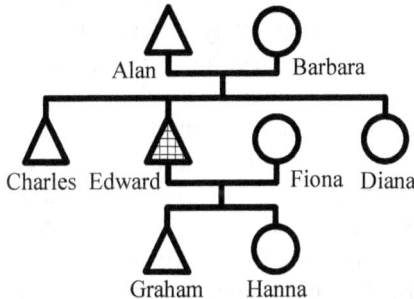

There would be other ways of ordering the names, for instance by reversing them. Usually one is guided by book production technicalities or by the most suitable graphical solution.

One glance is sufficient to glean a few fundamentals from a kinship diagram like this. Firstly, we note the number of generations, the oldest being on the top line. Usually however this is just the *oldest represented in the diagram*. There are other generations further back, because Alan and Barbara themselves had parents and grandparents. Moreover, since Graham and Hanna will presumably one day be parents and grandparents, this kinship diagram is merely an extract from a family tree that is really much more ramified.

In this context Fiona is noteworthy: when she married Edward she was added to this diagram, but it tells us nothing about her parents and grandparents. Because she would not exist without them, this point of contact illustrates where her own kinship diagram meets Edward's. If one wanted to show both diagrams together one would need more space; and then the whole becomes difficult to decipher. That is why Charles's spouse and Diana's may sometimes be left off, if indeed they are married.

In fact, in this diagram two nuclear families emerge: one consisting of Alan, Barbara, Charles, Edward and Diana, the other of Edward, Fiona, Graham and Hanna. In this context Edward is noteworthy. He occurs in each nuclear family but with different functions. In the first family he is "son", in the second "father" and "husband". The three functions are of course only those which are immediately obvious from our (restricted) network of relationships. Were one to include all possible relatives, omitted here, then Edward would have further functions; for example if Charles had a wife and children then Edward would feature as "brother-in-law" and "uncle".

The various functions of each person within a family are of particular interest to the ethnologist of kinship systems. Linked to the functions are the **roles** a relative plays vis-à-vis other relatives. These roles trigger certain expectations which other family members have of the individual. For Edward this means that he plays a completely different role as a son to his father than he does as a father to his own children and again as a husband to Fiona.

In these relationships it is once again clear that a strategy is being applied to enable one to navigate this complex network of roles and expectations; and that the strategy is available if one seeks the words to describe these roles, namely the **words used for relatives**. As a whole they constitute the **kinship terminology**. This terminology has to be well understood, because it is the key to that kinship behaviour an ethnic group would consider normal. This is important because family interaction determines the work habits of a family group and regulates the claims to possessions and to essentials for life.

Thus it is not actually the individuals' names that are needed but the kinship descriptions, i.e. the words for father, mother, brother, sister etc. used by the members of a family for identification.

If one wishes to infer these kinship descriptions from a diagram like the one we have seen, then we need to settle one difficulty at the outset, namely the fact that each member has many roles. The process of simplifying involves identifying a particular person in the diagram, from whose perspective each of the others can only have a single function: from Alan's perspective Barbara is uniquely his wife, Edward his son and Hanna his granddaughter

The person so identified to allow the kinship terms to describe the other members is called in the jargon **ego** (Latin *ego* = I). If we for simplicity's sake change Edward to *Ego* in our diagram, then it looks like this:

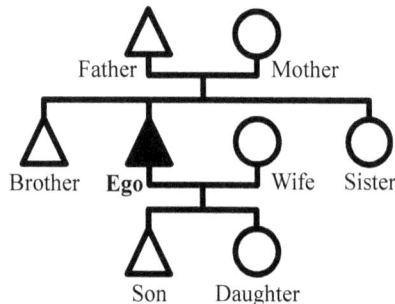

So that the diagram remains as uncluttered as possible the following abbreviations are used:

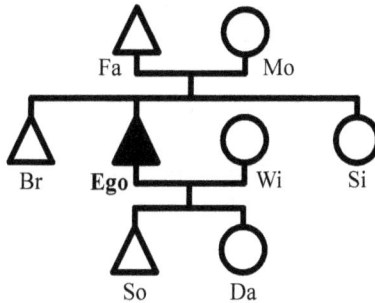

The list of abbreviations for the most common kinship terms is:

Fa	father	*Mo*	mother
So	son	*Da*	daughter
Br	brother	*Si*	sister
Hu	husband	*Wi*	wife

For the kinship terms which proceed from *ego* where the question might be what name *ego* should use for Alan or Hanna a further consideration arises: the distinction between the ***denotative*** term and ***appellative*** term. *Ego* introduces Alan to a visitor as "my father" (denotative), but when calling for him Alan uses "daddy" or "dad" (appellative).

Throughout the world, people's kinship ties extend way beyond the two generations of their nuclear family. In reality a person has dealings as a rule with far more relatives than just with parents, brothers and sisters, their own children and grandchildren. Here is a diagram of a typical extended family:

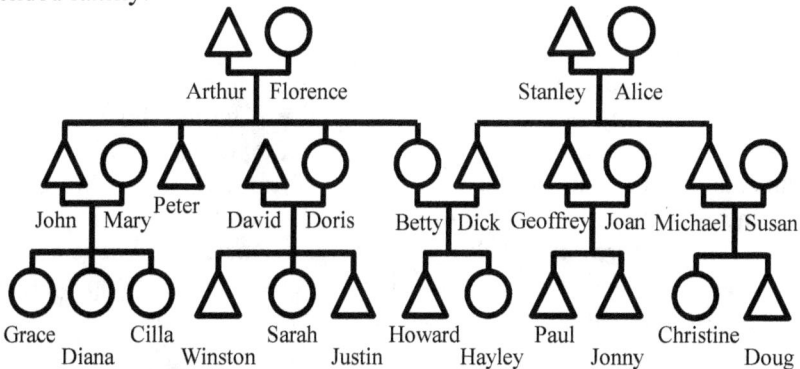

This English middle-class family comprises three generations. The individual names are typical for their generation and reflect a tendency for social mixing and cult of fashion. The grandparents have names which were fashionable before the First World War, with some influence from empire heroes and heroines, explorers and royalty: Arthur and Florence, Stanley and Alice. The next generation, perhaps disillusioned by the economic hardship of the 1930s and encouraged by wartime social mixing seems to have avoided choosing heroic and foreign-sounding names in favour of short English names: John and Mary, Peter, David and Doris, Betty and Dick, Geoffrey and Joan, Michael and Susan. The following generation of the 1960s drew names from countries beyond Europe, perhaps influenced by pop music, cinema and television: Grace, Diana, Cilla; Winston, Sarah, Justin; Howard and Hayley; Paul and Jonny; Christine and Doug.

Individual names, as we have seen, do not say anything about the actual relationship. Instead we have first to substitute kinship terms to identify the structures. This overview is achievable if we first determine an *ego*. In this way our wider kinship diagram is as follows:

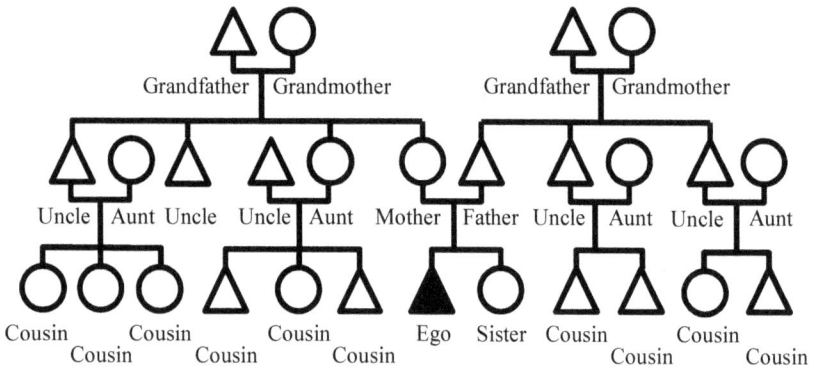

Our new version contains additional terms: grandfather, grandmother, uncle, aunt, male cousin, female cousin. These terms, though precise enough for our context here, are vague in some respects; it is not immediately clear whether the term "uncle" refers to a father's brother or a mother's brother. For us this distinction may not be all that important, but in some cultures it can take on great significance. To achieve a basis for comparison and accuracy ethnologists researching kinship systems use specific compound abbreviations. The result is as follows:

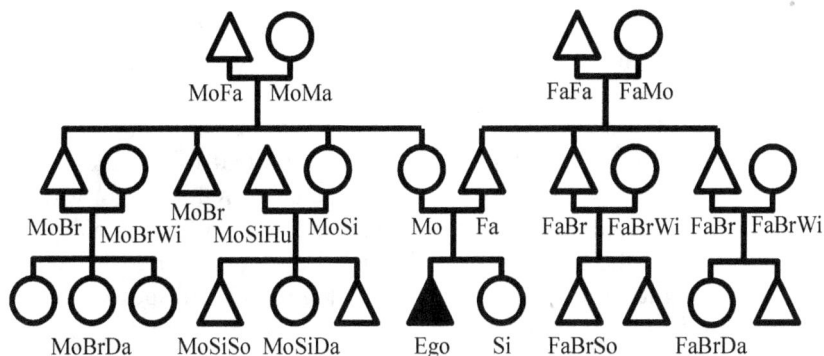

These combinations make for greater precision. *Ego*'s various uncles
are thereby identified as **FaBr** (father's brother) or as **MoBr** (mother's
brother), a distinction which has no special significance in European-
Western cultures, but which in Oceanic cultures and many more is of
considerable significance.

It is more difficult with the term "cousin"; the need for additional
identification ("male/female cousin", and the kinship) results in:
FaBrDa, FaSiDa, MoBrDa, and **MoSiDa**. (Not all of these are shown in
the above diagram.)

Although these four cousins of *ego* are all identifiable in various ways,
ego only uses a single term for them. In other kinship systems this can go
even further. For anybody using these terms there are big surprises in
store, as the following diagram shows:

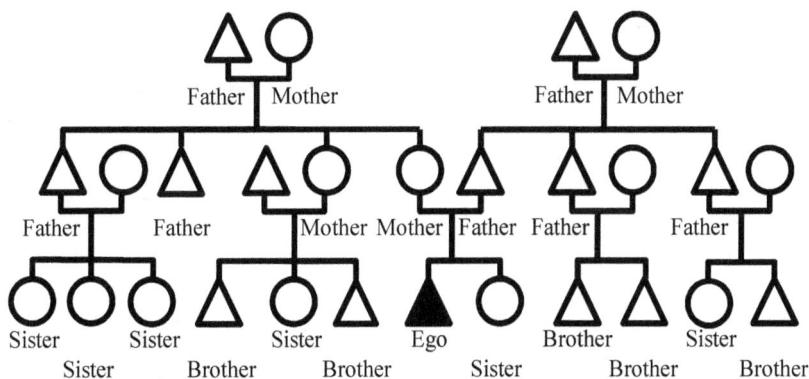

There are systems which only have one single term for brothers and
male cousins, and another single term for sisters and female cousins.
There are even systems where fathers, uncles, grandfathers and great-
grandfathers (and mothers, aunts, grandmothers and great-grandmothers)

are given one all-inclusive yet gender-specific term. Indeed, wife and sister-in-law can be termed alike (and husband and brother-in-law). I shall return to this special case in greater detail in 8.3.

Behind this there may be a logic which raises the question relating to Matthew 12:46, of whether Jesus was the *only* child of his mother or whether he had brothers or sisters. This can be answered in various ways. According to Catholic teaching Jesus was and remained Mary's only son. If this verse uses the term "brothers" in the way that an English kinship system does, then Mary did have several children. If, however, the kinship term "brother" in the culture of Mary's day did include "cousin", then the question as to whether Mary had further children might – with some justification – be answered in the negative. Yet one would still have to be certain that the "brothers" referred to were all just "cousins". Of course, the case is of rather theoretical interest.

In practical contexts one can fall into a trap. A young church worker in Spain was getting to know an African living there who gradually introduced his family to him. It surprised him that every few days the African would mention a new "brother" or "sister". When the number approached 50 the Spanish colleague became sceptical and accused him of lying. The African did not understand the reproach because to him it was groundless: he made no distinction between brother/sister/cousin. The fault was the Spaniard's; he had not reckoned with his friend thinking in the categories of an African kinship system, where the numerous male and female cousins were all introduced as "my brothers" and "my sisters".

8.2   Kinship Types

Kinship systems can be organized on the basis of particular characteristics under four main types, for example: Hawaii, Irokese, Eskimo and Sudan. These are not greatly significant for the hands-on worker. Further information is given in Helbling 2003:129-130.

8.3   Marriage

In societies around the world there are distinctions in the definition of who is considered married. In some societies a husband and wife are considered a married couple from the time they first ate a meal together. It is still widespread to reckon that a marriage comes into being by the agreement of the family groups from which each comes.

Such an understanding of who within a family group is considered a husband and wife can be very different from the understanding of a European-Westerner; thus:

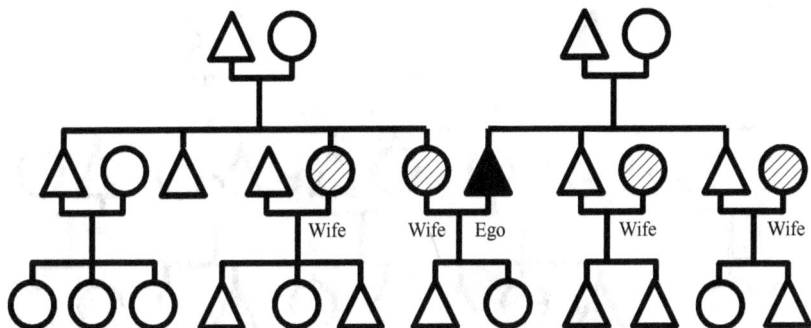

Concerning this, let us look at the diagram above. I mentioned briefly at the end of 8.1 that in many ethnic groups no distinction existed in terminology between a wife and a sister-in-law. Sometimes this has ongoing consequences.

A husband from a culture like this is unable to introduce his wife's sisters other than with the term "wife". Of course for this husband his wife's sisters are "somewhat different" than "his wives", but not in quite the same way as a European sister-in-law is "somewhat different". If the man's (actual) wife has given birth to a child she may sometimes be sexually taboo for him for several years. Her sisters however may be sexually available to him meanwhile, providing they are not in the same situation and providing their own "husband" is in agreement. In a system like this we can discern a kind of *secret polygyny*. (In open polygynous systems a man can legally be married to several wives).

That people share the same kinship term but have different roles does not mean at all that their differences might be insignificant. This point also applies very clearly to "(male) cousins" and "(female) cousins" who may be referred to as "brothers" and "sisters". In many pre-literate ethnic groups there are cousins who are not merely considered possible future wives but who ideally ought to be *given in marriage first*. They are generally FaSiDa cousins and MoBrDa cousins. These are *cross-cousins*, as distinct from *parallel cousins* (FaBrDa and MoSiDa).

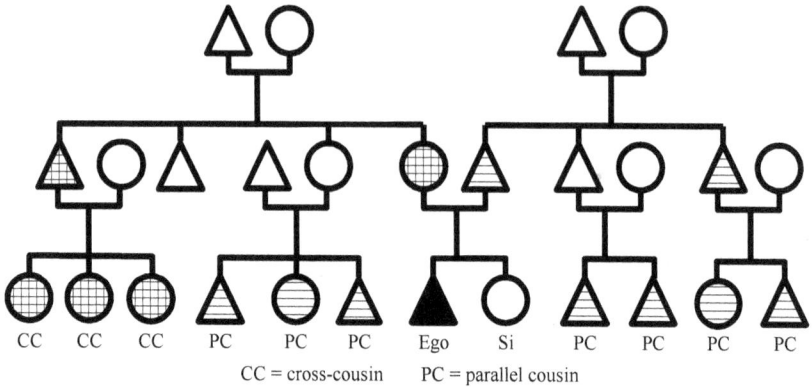

CC = cross-cousin   PC = parallel cousin

The "cross" and "parallel" feature relates to the first two parts of the abbreviation. *Ego's* MoBrDa is "cross-related" to *ego*: *ego's* mother and the father of his (female) cousin are **siblings, but of the opposite sex.** The same is true for a FaSiDa: in a case like this (not shown in the diagram) *ego's* father and the mother of the (female) cousin are siblings of the opposite sex. In other cases above (FaBrDa and MoSiDa) either *ego's* father and the father of his (female) cousin or *ego's* mother and the mother of his (female) cousin are siblings and thus **siblings of the parallel sex.**

Not all combinations are mentioned, in that male cross-cousins do not occur.

Male and female parallel cousins, unlike cross-cousins, are not considered favoured marriage partners, let alone possible marriage partners. They fall under that category of relatives to which the so-called **incest taboo** applies, although male and female parallel cousins are biologically and genetically only slightly different from male and female cross-cousins.

Incest is sexual intercourse between close relatives. In many cultures, even pre-literate ones, there is much more involved than direct sexual contact. Just showing particular parts of the body in the presence of close relatives, or just talking about them, can be considered incestuous and is behaviour to be avoided.

For young children this is not relevant to the same degree, but becomes more relevant as they approach puberty. In many societies a boy must not then sleep in the same house if one of his sisters has reached her first menstrual period; he is then accommodated with relatives where circumstances permit, or in a so-called "men's house" at least overnight.

What is meant exactly by "close relative" is nowhere stipulated, as the example of parallel cousins has shown. There are ethnic groups where on the father's side the female parallel cousin is given in marriage if the bride wealth is cancelled. This occurs, for example in the Berbers of Kabylia (North Africa), especially in poorer families (Helbling 2003:146).

The ban on incest is almost complete, worldwide, for members of the nuclear family. The rare exceptions occur particularly in strictly hierarchical societies having something like an *aristocracy*. In the upper classes incestuous marriages are not unknown, as the history of civilisations shows. The reasons are mostly a concern to maintain possessions and power within one family. The Egyptian pharaoh Tutankhamun married his sister, and Cleopatra was the product of an incestuous marriage.

It is interesting that the various forms of incest taboos occur across the world, and that their rules are strictly adhered to; which has raised the questions of why and how this taboo comes about.

Nobody can say definitely how this taboo originated. It has been assumed that at an early phase of civilisation man recognized that in-breeding led to a *degeneration of the genetic make-up*. This explanation is not likely, because reliable knowledge of this is only possible if one can investigate over several generations and build up a bank of statistics. But the time which a human individual needs for his development is too long: the next generation is only 20 to 30 years away, and in some societies even closer. Furthermore, statistics are not available at all in pre-literate societies. In the early stages of human history infant mortality was very high, so that genetic deterioration only had a small chance of being traced. Indeed, in-breeding does not necessarily lead to degeneration; it can strengthen the genetic make-up. This is a bonus for animal and plant propagation. Cleopatra is traditionally considered an exceptional personality, even though she was the child of an incestuous marriage. What is more, it would be impossible to explain Adam's immediate family in Genesis without assuming that the taboo against incest was not yet active.

Another explanation for the origins and worldwide spread of the taboo against incest stems from the observation that children who grow up together lose the ability to have a sexual relationship. Evidence from Taiwan showed that it was normal in many families there to adopt a girl for the son to marry when both were of an age. These marriages were significantly less stable than those made in the traditional Chinese way where the marriage partners only saw each other for the first time on the wedding day. Spiro (1958) came across the same phenomenon in a kibbutz in Israel. Children who grow up together in the kibbutz community do not marry one another although they are not related; they seek their life partner outside.

The deep psychology or psychoanalysis of Freud's theory states that in the nuclear family there are strong tendencies for sexual bonds between the mother and her sons on the one hand, and between the father and his daughters on the other. These tendencies (called after the Greek sagas the Oedipus complex and the Electra complex) supposedly had such explosive vitality on the basis of their potential to bond people together and arouse jealousy that they were bound to endanger the cohesion of the nuclear family. Since children's development cannot proceed without the stability of a nuclear family it was necessary to suppress these tendencies by invoking incest. This argument is one reason why the taboo exists in the strict form we know.

It stems from this that each individual has to seek his sexual partner outside his or her own family group. The ban on incest leads to the requirement for *exogamy*, also worldwide, although with a range of variants.

Exogamy is a *marriage behaviour*. It is stipulated by the group of relatives stating that no individual can marry within the family circle. This exogamous group is generally the clan, whose members hold that they all stem from a common ancestor. Clans are thus exogamous entities.

The opposite of exogamy is *endogamy*. Endogamous entities cannot, of course, be so neatly defined. Many of them are problematic. They include the issue of race. Racial differences are not significant for the cognitive and behavioural aspects of a person. Yet a white woman's family members tend to signal the displeasure felt by the group if she wishes to marry a black African, because there is still a widespread view that marriage should be confined to one's own race. There are no objective grounds for this.

In reality the grounds are more likely to be the different strategies for organizing life, particularly the values and expectations concerning roles; the relatives may even require of partners from differing cultures a higher degree of tolerance and may heap stress on the marriage and destabilize it and endanger its existence. It is not so much the actual racial differences which are significant, but rather the differences in cultures which give races the appearance of being endogamous entities.

Moreover, it is thus not surprising that religions form endogamous entities with boundaries that many societies are required to observe strictly. The members of a kinship group, or of another social unit holding to a particular religion, do not like it at all if one of its number chooses a life partner from within a quite different religious network. In this sense both Evangelical and Catholic groups are endogamous.

8.4   Matrilineal and Patrilineal Systems

A kinship system does not just allow someone to identify those people who are closest to him and to select what is relevant for their roles and his own; it also allows him to point out his *ancestry*. This is of vital importance, because a person can only ensure his nurture if he is able to name other people; of them he can make corresponding demands, because they have brought him into this world and have the means to produce food, for example by their ownership of farmland. As a rule he is able *to inherit* this land, if he is reassured by his birth status that he is entitled to it.

As well as mixed forms, there are two basic types of working out one's heritage, e.g. via *matrilineal* and *patrilineal* lines of descent (through the mother and father respectively).

The differences are usually a result of particular forms of economic systems which characterise them (cf. chap. 6). Hunter and gatherer societies are very largely patrilineal, and so are arable farmers and livestock farmers. The reason for this is the dominant position of the man in the acquisition of food. By contrast, planter societies are organised to be matrilineal. The reasons for this are the importance given to owning land for ensuring one's survival and the greater confidence one can show when proving one's inheritance via the female line and when staking one's claim to food and care.

The matrilineal reckoning is so embedded that children are often not considered to be related to their father. The father's function is mostly to provide them with food and protection; his function is not to educate them nor to correct their behaviour, nor to be responsible for their actions nor a source of advice about important decisions, such as giving approval when they wish to marry. In a matrilineal kinship system this function is carried out by another male, who is "really" related to the particular children; this is the uncle on the mother's side, the *mother's brother* (sometimes called *avunculus*). He is the one who is effectively the children's father. It is not uncommon in such family systems for the father and the uncle to share the same kinship term.

This aspect of matrilineal systems does not primarily mean that in equivalent kinship groups the women, the mothers, necessarily have the say. This has been misunderstood over time, and people have spoken of a *matriarchy* ("rule by mothers"; Bachofen 1861). As a legal institution matriarchy was never presumably enforced in absolute terms. (Göttner-Abendroth, 1989, holds the opposite view.)

In recent times studies in ethnology have increasingly pointed to the fact that in matrilineal systems men feel less comfortable than women, notably in their subconscious. In certain test procedures (Rohrschach, Thematic Apperception Test) the uncertainties are revealed as castration anxieties. They also seem to suffer under the burden of a double binding obligation. Originally they belong to the family into which they were born. They must care for the family and they are especially responsible for the children of their sisters. When they themselves get married they leave their family of origin and have to work for the family into which they have married. They are however still responsible to their own birth family (their own relatives) as previously. This double loyalty becomes particularly dramatic and oppressive for men in matrilineal societies if trouble breaks out between the two family groups (Thomas 1984).

The fact that women in matrilineal societies seem to suffer less from such symptoms may well be understandable: as a teacher it is a commonplace that during puberty girls become markedly more emotionally stable, more "reasonable" and grown up than boys, who are still at the age of twenty behaving like lost causes and trying to compensate for lack of self-awareness by resorting to demonstrative drinking bouts.

This behaviour that causes so much upset clearly stems from the fact that girls in matrilineal kinship systems experience more care and attention from adults than boys do. As compensation for the deficit in emotional balance which the boys suffer from as they grow into adulthood, relatives sometimes arrange for them to marry; this will require them to become fathers and care for somebody in this way; they will gain a status and a purpose in life, and become "sensible". It is not surprising if a bond like this is of short duration. Marriages made under these circumstances only usually succeed at the second attempt.

The position of the husband and father in matrilineal social structures has a further consequence. The ***Oedipus complex***, previously mentioned with regard to the incest taboo, manifests itself quite differently here from the way it does in European-Western contexts. First analysed by Sigmund Freud, founder of psychoanalysis, the phenomenon of a close, sexually charged soul-relationship between a man and his mother resulting in – among others – a secret jealousy towards his father is not possible in matrilineal kinship relationships; not in the way Freud conceived them, since the "father's" role in the Freudian sense is partly transferred to the mother's brother.

In such circumstances, thought needs to be given as to how the aspects of the Biblical idea of "God as father" appearing even as a disciplinarian figure can be understood in such a conceptual framework, or transposed into it. In matrilineal cultures, an understanding of Mary as the "mother of God" presumably has greater prospects of taking root and growing.

Applying patrilineal kinship is, moreover, not simply the counterpart of applying matrilineal kinship; for the simple reason that in both systems it is the women who bear the children.

Just how important the distinction is between patrilineal and matrilineal inheritance follows from a further look at the example of a complex kinship diagram illustrated previously. In a patrilineal system the family of *ego's* father has, by the third generation, numerous heirs; the family of *ego*'s mother has fewer.

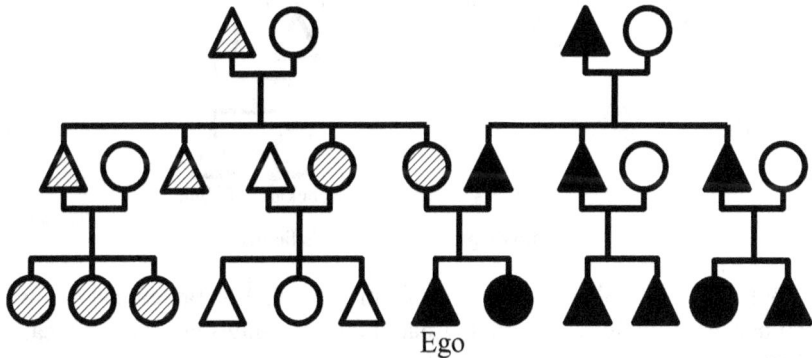

Ego

Application of patrilineal descent

If one proceeds by matrilineal descent the opposite occurs, and the consequences for *ego's* father's family are serious: it ceases to exist in his generation.

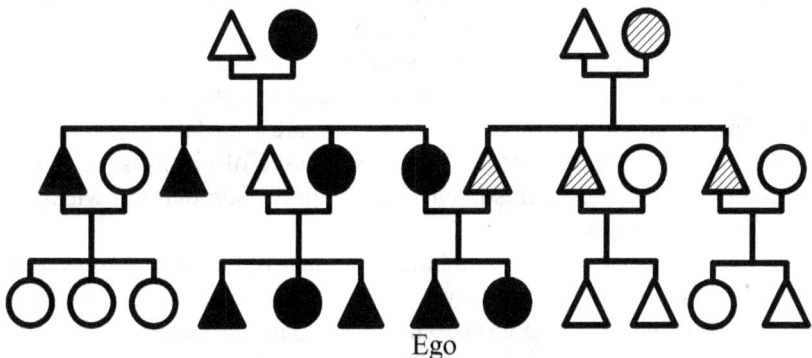

Ego

Application of matrilineal descent

The same fate would have befallen the famous family (known to us from the Old Testament) which established the people of Israel if the inheritance had not been patrilineal. Jacob had 12 sons, but only 1 daughter (Genesis 30:21). If matrilineal inheritance had been in force the "blessing" of multiple descendants for the Israelite patriarch would not have been nearly so considerable.

In this context the kinship diagram of the family of Isaac (Abraham's son) is particularly revealing (Genesis 24:15, 24, 29):

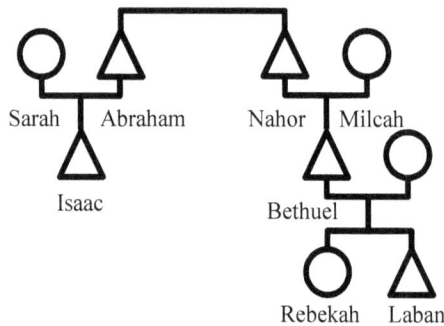

Kinship diagram of Abraham's family

We note the following: 1. Abraham (Rebekah's father-in-law) was also her great uncle. 2. Bethuel (Isaac's father-in-law) was also his parallel cousin. 3. Rebekah (Isaac's wife) was also her husband's first cousin twice removed, and parallel, providing the tradition is patrilineal. 4. If Rebekah adopted the matrilineal inheritance she was not related to Isaac and could thus marry him with even greater justification because no incest taboo stood against her marriage. 5. Isaac did belong to an earlier generation, but since his parents were very old when he was born, he was undoubtedly not much older than his wife.

Admittedly, from a theological standpoint all this is of little significance. Bible translators however need to be thoroughly versed in it, because in the target culture into which they are translating such details delicate matters can arise around the whole issue of kinships; such matters should not remain unresolved. They require thorough knowledge to produce valid answers.

In South Pacific languages care must be taken when interpreting kinship terms for brothers and sisters; among other considerations, the sex of the speaker using the particular terms. This is not so in European languages.

Pidgin, the common language of the peoples of New Guinea and the adjacent islands, is a form of English with a grammar akin to that of Melanesian languages. There the word forms are "barata" and "sisa/susa", which can be identified as the terms "brother" and "sister". In Neo-Melanesian (the alternative name for the pidgin of New Guinea) "barata" only means brother if it is used by a man. If, on the other hand, a woman uses "barata" she means her sister. The same is correspondingly true for "sisa/susa" and its meaning. Therefore in Neo-Melanesian "barata" does not actually mean "brother", but "sibling of the same sex as the person speaking".

Let us assume that a female church worker is speaking about Jesus becoming a person, and that she expresses this by saying that he became "our brother", and uses the word "barata". Her Melanesian listeners' response is bound to be one of incomprehension, since "barata" spoken by a woman means "sister".

Without exception, in their lifetime everybody is a member of at least one family, growing up as a son or daughter; this is called the family of origin (Helbling 2003:127), where they experience *enculturation* (cf. chap. 9), i.e. learn vital life strategies. One of the most important functions of this family is to launch the individual into the world in the best possible way and accompany him or her successfully through life. This is why the term for the child's support network is the *family of orientation*. Membership of this family is through birth.

In European-Western cultures the nuclear family acts as the family of orientation. In other cultures, especially in group-oriented ones, it is the wider family. Each family structure is significant as a protected place like no other, where the individual can learn his culture comprehensively. (For this to happen, the family must, of course, be together!)

Most people only spend a certain period of their lives in their family of orientation. Whenever a person marries and has children a new nuclear family is created. This is ingeniously called the *family of procreation*. (For the children this is their family of orientation!) It fulfils a special social task beyond procreation: that of conferring *status*. This is especially true for women. In many societies outside Europe unmarried women have little or no status. Married women with no children are scarcely better placed, suffering from the same lack of status. This explains the cloud of utter gloom which Hanna, Samuel's mother, lived under for many years; it also explains why she burst out into a song of praise after the birth of her son (1 Samuel 1 and 2).

Even unmarried women in development work and church work overseas can find that their lack of status in this regard creates a problem; their role may be almost indefinable for colleagues in the same field of activity (cf. on this topic chap. 19).

8.5 Forms of Marriage

A person's family of procreation has *marriage* at its core, constituted in four different shapes: 1) a *monogamous* marriage consisting of one husband and his wife; 2) a *polygynous* marriage with one man and several women, 3) a *polyandrous* marriage with one wife and several men, and 4) a *group marriage* with several men and women.

The marriage forms represented by (2) and (3) above are bracketed together as *polygamous* marriages. *Monogamy* and *polygyny* are the most frequent forms of marriage. In societies where polygyny exists most marriages are nevertheless monogamous, because firstly under normal circumstances in all societies the number of men and women is roughly equal, and because secondly a man wishing to have several wives needs to be quite prosperous: polygynous marriages generally have many children and need a correspondingly broad economic basis for food production.

Exceptions to the rule of a balance of numbers of men and women occur in the aftermath of wars where numbers of men have been decimated. In many parts of Asia in the very near future the problem will occur that many men will be unable to find marriage partners because too few women have been born. The reason for this lies in the perception of values prevalent mostly in patrilineal societies: boys are "sons and heirs" and are valued as such; girls by contrast require a dowry, which can work out as too expensive. Further, modern medicine with the aid of ultrasound allows the sex of an embryo to be known at an early stage; and where these cultural and medical circumstances apply, pregnancies are being terminated – when a girl is expected – in large numbers, i.e. in India, for example.

In polygynous marriages one of the women mostly has a higher status than the others, stemming from the order of the marriages or from the ages of the wives.

It is usual in many societies that the husband makes a gift to his wife's family on their marriage, the so-called *bride wealth*. This is a feature among cattle breeders and consists of a number of cattle. This bride wealth is not actually a purchase price. It is not like human trafficking, and for that reason the term bride wealth instead of bride price is less discriminatory.

The bride wealth is sometimes applied further for the same purpose, namely when a brother of the young wife also wishes to marry. The cattle which her family received as a gift for her are then simply given on.

The bride wealth can be interpreted as an act of compensation from the group receiving the woman to the group offering her, an act that acknowledges the loss to the family of her labour when a girl leaves to get married.

The bride wealth sometimes exists as a hidden category, namely when the new husband is obliged (for the duration of the marriage) to assist with the work of his wife's family. This is common in societies organized matrilineally. There is also the case where the future husband has to contribute by working for his intended wife's family for a period before she is given in marriage. This is termed **bride service**. This can be quite aggravating when his future father-in-law exploits the custom. One example bordering on extortion is familiar from Genesis 29: Laban requires from his nephew Jacob 7 years of labour prior to his marrying Rachel, and then proceeds to exact a second similar requirement – with a most unconvincing argument – after Jacob's honourable fulfilment of the first.

Interpreting the bride wealth as a purchase price has led Europeans to attempt by various means to bring it into disrepute and to abolish it. Objections have been raised against this by the people allegedly "bartered" themselves, because traditionally they measured their worth by the number of cattle required in compensation. Without the bride wealth they would have lost their recognizable worth. The brides were bound to interpret its abolition as a simple act of abasement and discrimination.

In addition there are two rather special unions: **levirate marriage** and **sororate marriage**. Levirate marriage is when a husband dies and his wife is obliged to marry one of his brothers, in order to ensure her and her children's livelihood.

This form of levirate is different from the "genuine" levirate marriage (cf. Deuteronomy 25:5 ff.) where the widow is not required to actually *marry* her husband's brother, but to bear his children, who then are considered the children of the deceased. This (Old Testament) form of levirate is still the custom today among the African Nuer and Zulu.

Sororate marriage is to some extent the converse of levirate marriage. It is based on the requirement that after the death of his wife a husband should marry one of her sisters.

A married couple chooses a place to live according to various factors. In European-Western societies this is generally a **neolocal** residence, i.e. a new place, not usually very close to parents or relatives.

If they live among relatives on the father's side of the family this is **patrilocal residence**. Correspondingly, **matrilocal residence** means living among relatives on the mother's side of the family.

Patrilocal residence is an advantage in hunter-gatherer cultures: it allows the best use of a hunting territory, because men familiar with their surroundings are kept together by this form of living. Matrilocal residence is an advantage to planter cultures: as a rule those women who own and those who are in line to inherit remain living close to one another.

In addition, there are a whole lot of complicated permutations for living, for example, living with the husband's matrilineal male relatives: in plain terms, living with uncle, the mother's brother. This is termed **avun-**

culocality. *Bilocality* means choosing to live in two places as the advantages dictate.

More detailed introductions to this chapter's topic

Lucid and more detailed introductions to kinship ethnology and social ethnology are provided by Helmig 1993 and Helbling 2003. Helbling gives a survey of other criteria for the formation of groups other than kinship, for example *age-based groups* and *associations* (2003:146-148). Both publications contain manageable bibliographies for special topics within the discipline. Fischer 1996 writes very well and is indispensable for serious study of the topic.

More on the topic of this chapter can be found in the following studies:

Bachofen, Johann Jakob: Das Mutterrecht. Stuttgart 1861.

Beer, Bettina; Fischer, Hans (Hg.): Ethnologie. Einführung und Überblick. Berlin 2003.

Fischer, Hans: Lehrbuch der genealogischen Methode. Berlin 1996.

Fox, Robin: Kinship and marriage: an anthropological perspective. (1st ed. Harmondsworth 1967), 2nd ed. as: Cambridge studies in social anthropology, vol. 50. Cambridge University Press, 1984.

Göttner-Abendroth, Heide: Das Matriarchat. Stuttgart et al. ²1989.

Helbling, Jürg: Sozialethnologie. In: Beer/Fischer 2003:125-156.

Helmig, Thomas: Verwandtschaft. In: Schweizer/Schweizer/Kokot 1993: 145-174.

Müller, Ernst Wilhelm: Der Begriff 'Verwandtschaft' in der modernen Ethnosoziologie. Berlin 1981. (The author gives a critical survey of ethnological studies on kinship which in his view have been particularly influential in defining the concept.)

Schweizer, Thomas; Schweizer, Margarete; Kokot, Waltraud (Hrsg.): Handbuch der Ethnologie. Berlin 1993.

Schmitz, Carl A.: Grundformen der Verwandtschaft. Basel 1964.

Spiro, Melford E.: Children of the Kibbutz. Cambridge Mass. 1958.

Thomas, John: The Namonuito solution to the "matrilineal puzzle". American Ethnologist 7.1984:172-177.

Chapter 9
Culture and Psyche

This chapter explains what enculturation is, the way cultural rules are taken over into the personality and psyche of a person and become integral to him; and how this process works and what results from it. There follows a description of what is meant by ethnocentrism and its opposite, namely the idealizing of what is foreign; how norms and values arise and how they influence human behaviour; and how all this emerges from the process of enculturation and can be explained by it.

9.0 Introduction

In chapter four we defined the concept of culture underlying all the themes of this introductory handbook: culture is a strategy for overcoming existence. This strategy consists of rules which help to satisfy needs. The strategic rules influence a person's behaviour as he makes headway in a particular culture, rather as grammatical rules govern a person's speech behaviour: culture steers all human activity in a special familiar way.

The rules which need to be followed in culturally adjusted behaviour are *not innate* to the people concerned; they need to be *learnt*. (Innate processes which do not need to be learnt are termed *instincts*). The process whereby these rules are learnt is called *enculturation*. It involves adopting and adapting a culture into a person's psyche.

Enculturation is somewhat different from *inculturation*. By inculturation we mean *transferring* a cultural element from one culture into another; here it takes root and acclimatizes and then takes over functions which enable certain life issues to be solved or simply which support life. Some time ago, for example, the sauna was adopted from Finnish culture (and more recently the pizza from Italian culture) into Germany and elsewhere. Another typical example of inculturation is the spread of Christian doctrine into Europe by Paul the missionary and apostle.

9.1 Enculturation as a Process

The enculturation process involves a few quite specific determining factors and exhibits a number of noteworthy features, the most important of which can be set out in what follows.

When a person is born he does not possess a culture, just as he does not have a language. What he does have on the other hand is an aptitude for one: the potential for a culture. Newborn babies, unlike newborn animals, are equipped with a significant *prowess for learning a culture* and with a definite need; they also have a corresponding potential for learning a language. This natural tendency must be great, from the sheer evidence that we can learn a culture (and language) without being conscious of doing so, and at an age where our ability for the logical thinking of later years has not yet been developed.

Because babies are not born with any culture their first expressions of life (hunger, wish for warmth) can be explained biologically, and are similar in all human societies and ethnic groups. This is on the basis that all human races living today belong to the same species (*homo sapiens sapiens*). (The races living today are from a biological/anthropological viewpoint so alike that their differences amount to less than 1%. From this reason alone discrimination against people of other racial backgrounds lacks any basis.)

But immediately after birth a person comes into contact with culture. Everywhere on earth the treatment of new-borns is culturally specific, from day one – for example in the way food is taken. In many societies babies are given the breast when they cry, in other societies this happens only according to a schedule. A mother's feeding routine that the child becomes familiar with is based on her understanding what is most suitable for her child, and these promptings have given rise to rules on which mothers base their feeding behaviour. Both the understanding and the rules that derive from it are particular cultural elements. That is why the resulting behaviour that the infant experiences is held to be culturally formed.

Insights and behaviour like this are not of course seen as culturally determined, but are all the more so for being *held in common* and only *rarely the subject of rational planning*. That is the reason why they are *long-lasting*, which is itself one more reason why cultures only change slowly. This has advantages and drawbacks.

Because in this way cultures possess a notable ability to endure, they guarantee a high level of continuity over generations when it comes to sounding out their opinions and interpreting their realm of experience, and when it comes to formulating their goals that need to be achieved in common, and when they find various ways of achieving these goals.

On the other hand, by their persistent nature cultures delay or obstruct changes which are deemed desirable or necessary, for example in church work or mission work or medical projects etc. within development aid programmes. Cultures even impede changes which have been triggered from within by the members of the culture. This requires patience.

How mothers behave towards their children is significant in various ways. Among the numerous possibilities available in a particular instance the child is generally faced with just one way of behaving. This way of doing things is, over time, presented to the child as a mother's *normal* behaviour. The child orientates itself to this normal behaviour and ends up by expecting it in all those situations where it has known similar behaviour before. This masks a problem.

Normal behaviour is recognizable here as those forms of behaviour exhibited by members of a particular culture in particular situations and expected by their fellow members. Other ways of behaving in the same situation are reckoned to be less normal or even *abnormal* – depending on the degree of variance – although such disparities in behaviour might be considered perfectly normal in another society. One example: At a wedding in Europe or America it is considered polite and thus normal behaviour to eat with a knife and fork. Persons eating with their fingers on such an occasion would come across as noteworthy or even as abnormal (even mad). In an Indonesian or African ethnic group using the fingers to eat is generally quite normal.

This observation explains why psychology – and even more psychiatry – have problems defining or diagnosing normal and abnormal behaviour, because a person's culture plays such a dominant role in his behaviour that it must be taken into account in the diagnosis if one is trying to avoid being very unfair to the patient. A collection of important contributions to this topic can be found in Pfeiffer/Schoene (1980).

In the main it is the culturally determined behaviour of *people in close contact* with the child from its early years onwards which gives rise to particular views and concepts and steers the child along particular paths. The world view thus built up in a child is directly dependent upon the world view of its contacts and reference people in the immediate,and later in the wider, social setting where it grows up.

The child is not just exposed to this world view in its culturally typical form; the child is *handed over* to its mercy. Because it is born without any culture but possesses a disposition for culture – indeed a marked longing to take on a culture (and language) – the child cannot do otherwise than grasp at what it finds in its immediate cultural surroundings. This too has advantages and disadvantages.

One of the greatest advantages of the need for a culture is that children are highly motivated to work actively towards their own enculturation. Their motivation is all the more enduring the more they find incentives for satisfying their need for culture available in their immediate surroundings; when this is the case the process of enculturation is greatly encouraged and accelerated. Children learn their culture (and language) surprisingly quickly and effortlessly, even in spite of its numerous details and complexities. Without difficulty they even learn two or three cultures (and languages) simultaneously, providing they are in early childhood and in the relevant surroundings. If they have been steered in the right way by the appropriate people, the result of a dual or triple enculturation is of great value to those involved: it makes them culturally mobile and flexible, gives them a broad horizon and it hinders or prevents them from forming prejudices.

The process needs steering because children learning the cultural elements do not sort them carefully into the appropriate cultural matrix where the elements belong. Rather, the elements are combined uncritically according to whatever is feasible. Thus children acquire their own individually mixed culture. If they grow up speaking two languages this mostly comes to the fore as follows: if they are using that language where a thought can only be expressed with a longer construction but at the same time if the other language they also speak fluently uses one word for the thought, then they use this rather than the longer construction. So a mix of two languages thus can arise with a strange impact on any outsider. The consequences are numerous. A problem arises at school if children like this return from overseas to Germany and discover that German is the only language of communication. In their essays they use expressions that serve as a short cut only to themselves: they choose one single word from the foreign language instead of a full German sentence wherever the opportunity arises. Yet this is not accepted because it results in unidiomatic phrases. It is thus important that adults with responsibility for children growing up fluent in two or more languages urge them to use either one phrasing or the other (rule: *zwei* languages should *nie gemixt werden!*)

One of the most far-reaching disadvantages of a child's intense need to adopt a culture is that at the time of acquiring a language and culture a child is most open to being manipulated. A person growing up in a criminal environment scarcely has the opportunity of adopting a world view with full strategies for living well in a socially cohesive community. But even in cultures of normally functioning human communities there are elements which should not be there: prejudices of all sorts, and discrimination towards members who appear to be less well adapted. Because – like all other elements – these too can be part of the uncritical enculturation process, children and young people are especially prone here to manipulation. This phenomenon, for example, can be misused by authoritarian regimes for their own purposes; the National Socialists in Germany deliberately exploited this tendency in the so-called Hitler youth.

The speed at which children adapt to a culture from their social setting is also prompted by the fact that they at first have no preconceived notions: they represent a *"tabula rasa"*, a clean slate, and they incline to what is new for them without judgement and bias. When adults want to, or need to, acquaint themselves with a second culture (and language) the process is much tougher.

Under these conditions a person practising an animistic religion finds it scarcely possible to accept Christian notions of an afterlife (heaven and hell) with perspectives that match more or less those of the Bible. Thought structures that have arisen during enculturation in an animistic environment generally lead in adults to concepts of the afterlife whose representation is quite different.

In young children developing normally the enculturation process becomes more intensive in the second half of the first year of life, then during childhood and youth the process becomes more differentiated, ending only when the individual dies. Because the psyche originally contains nothing to inhibit this process, many cultural elements are absorbed quickly and painlessly. It can be justifiably supposed that by the age of 8 around 80% of all those strategies (in their essential form) required for coping with life as an adult have been learnt. This is all the more remarkable in that during enculturation not only has an enormous amount of stuff been mastered, but intellectual efforts have been also made which in other areas are not possible until after puberty: children abstract the rules of their first language(s) and learn them exclusively by hearing and imitating with no conscious awareness; and 5 year-olds are able to form sentences with logically complex structures with no mistakes. Similar achievements in the field of maths are not expected of them for another ten years!

The enculturation process does indeed continue until death. Yet in practical terms the process is completed when no essentially new elements are being absorbed. This stage is reached for different cultures at greatly varying times. For Indian girls of the lowest caste enculturation is complete by the age of 12 or 13; for Japanese men of the social elite the process is not yet complete by the age of 30. In the societies of Western industrial nations the end of enculturation generally coincides with the completion of job training.

9.2   Results of the Enculturation Process

When this process is complete several goals have been achieved; what a person has been learning culturally up to this point has become self-evident, and affirmed emotionally. Those life strategies which he can now access are not just helping him satisfy his own needs across a broad spectrum; they are also providing for his psychological well-being in the company of others whose behaviour he can now anticipate whenever he is called upon to engage with them. At this stage he has succeeded as a person in adjusting to his cultural surroundings.

The culture instilled into his make-up like this cannot ever be drained out of him once a significant part of the enculturation process has run its course. The process is not reversible.

Among other things, this means that it is impossible for a person to change his culture; but he can learn a second culture, even though not nearly as fully as the first – *those* strategies will always be uppermost in determining his actions

For development aid workers, church workers and especially for missionaries this fact will be a constant source of unhappy experiences and disappointments, unless workers keep in mind that after the end of their personal enculturation people continue learning a lot but they are not able to add a fundamentally new cultural identity ("Therefore, if anyone is in Christ, he is a new *creature*..." [2 Corinthians 5:17], not *culture*!

The process of a person's enculturation is, as we have noted, characterized by a choice of behaviour which selects and standardizes just one or a few of the overwhelming wealth of possible human responses. People thus equip themselves with a set of rules valid only in their own culture, but which they – admittedly without generally being aware of it – use in other cultures.

For migrants of German descent from Eastern European countries it is customary to stand up when talking to people in authority. Remaining seated is a sign of lack of respect, according to their cultural norm. Of course, they also behave like this outside their cultural context, for example when they are back in Germany itself. That is why they consider it unthinkable, and scandalous, that in school pupils answer their teachers, or that in church people pray to God, without first standing up.

The tendency to follow the rules of the society where one has one's own cultural roots, and then use them in unfamiliar surroundings to guide one's own behaviour as well as to interpret the behaviour of others, is called *ethnocentrism.* Behind this response is the (subconscious) notion that foreign culture is to be classed not merely as different but as unusual and of lesser value. One's own culture is considered on a different plane: better, more human.

A typical example of ethnocentrism is the name many ethnic groups call themselves. Many just mean "people", nothing more. This is the case as early as the ancient Greeks: apart from themselves there were only "barbarians", a word embracing all other people who didn't speak Greek.

There is a kind of counterpart to ethnocentrism: *idealizing what is foreign.* In its extremes it can entail the utter condemnation of one's own culture.

During the period of the Enlightenment a tendency emerged to idealize the *topos* of the *Noble Savage*, the outsider born of "nature's race"; it was said he had not been spoilt like Westerners by "culture" (Stein 1984a).

On a similar level are the centuries-long European yearnings for a paradise on the Pacific islands (Ritz 1983; Stein 1984b), which have been nurtured right up to the present day by publications of otherwise reliable authors such as Margaret Mead (Freeman 1983). Descriptions of foreign paradise unreality like these are sometimes called "ethnopoetry". (Perhaps this will not be so for much longer, however, because the term recently – admittedly on rare occasions – has been used in studies on forms of poetry in pre-literate societies).

Conversely, following the need for an idealising portrayal of foreign life, a whole series emerged of descriptions of our own culture through the eyes of supposedly foreign observers. It is significant that they were considered authentic by a broad public. In reality their authors are critics of civilisation from among our own ranks. For example, the German-authored fantasy speeches of a fictitious Samoan chieftain Tuiavi'i from Tiavea are constantly being republished in new editions and pirate copies (Scheurmann 1977, Ritz 1983, Cain 1975).

During the course of the enculturation process two further phenomena arise which are very significant for the individual's behaviour in society: *norms* and *values.*

Norms are culturally determined patterns of thinking or sets of rules guiding human behaviour which are viewed in this way by the majority of those belonging to a culture; norms encourage by their observance what members would consider "correct", "decent" or "normal" behaviour. Norms are not necessarily rigid, since they allow deviations or have built-in tolerance for flexible application whenever the situation requires. For example in Western cultures it is the norm to use a knife, fork and spoon when eating; but when tackling poultry one can use one's fingers if need be, to nibble at a chicken bone. The Christian sacrament of communion is celebrated, according to the norm, with bread and wine. In the Second World War soldiers in the trenches took communion with broken biscuits and tea, and drunk from a tin can instead of a silver cup.

One norm with a complicated structure is the kinship system (cf. chap. 8) of many ethnic groups; it lays down guidance on the care of group members and their inheritance of land. In matrilineal kinship systems people are usually only related on the mother's side, and they thus generally turn to these relatives in times of need. If, however, there is greater wealth on the father's side of the family, by virtue of somebody earning a regular salary, then those in need (or considering themselves needy) seek and perhaps find a way of identifying with that family branch, despite the norm implying they are not related.

When looking for the norms guiding a culture it is usual first to identify the *ideal norm*. We mean here a rule or set of rules which are not fully adhered to in real-life society. This is because the norm cannot be applied in its ideal form, because situations it regulates are not identical in every detail, or because the consequences arising from applying an ideal norm would be catastrophic for those involved.

For example, for the pedestrian intending to cross a busy road it would be the ideal norm to wait at red and cross at green. In reality some individuals in a hurry cross the road even when the pedestrian light is still red, providing it is obvious that all the cars have stopped at the crossing. These pedestrians know that their light will shortly turn green. Similarly it would be nonsense to stop crossing once the pedestrian light turned red if one was stranded in the middle of the road.

With many ethnic groups sexual contact with blood relatives is strictly forbidden by the so-called incest taboo. In reply to the question how those who infringe it are punished, the answer is that people are killed by their own relatives. The pronouncement is nothing other than an ideal norm, because in reality such infringements hardly ever result in killings, but in much less dramatic "punishments" (social stigmatisation, etc.) simply because a killing in that society is a catastrophic event for all involved, including for the survivors. If one points out to interviewees that ideal norms and actual behaviour are not now in harmony, they often say that "in days gone by", however, people had been punished by death. Yet this is unlikely to have been the case, for the same reasons as in the present. The ideal norm nevertheless is justified as a culturally-shaped guideline: it helps resolve issues of life by supplying theoretical points of departure.

Like many other cultural elements and rulings, norms are not always easy to justify in terms of reason, any more than table manners are. Why, when drinking soup, do Germans place their left hand by the side plate, rather than in their lap? This is, after all, quite acceptable in other cultures, in the United States, for example. There is no rational justification.

Educational issues can arise from the fact that norms are not fully justifiable. Children being trained in good table manners begin at a particular age, at the latest in puberty, to ask why they are supposed to behave in one way rather than any other way. At this point parents and others may make the decisive mistake of trying to give a wise and rational justification. Smaller children are easily consoled, but young adolescents are not. They quickly realize that much of what adults prize as "good behaviour" cannot easily be justified, and refuse all the more insistently to behave appropriately. If parents back themselves into a corner with spurious phrases such as "that's the way people are meant to behave" the situation turns awkward: the volume increases and the sparks begin to fly. The proper line of argument is close at hand. One just needs to explain that in certain situations other people (once their enculturation process is complete) expect particular behaviour; they have experienced it and internalised it as the norm for this situation. The person displaying this behaviour appears "well-behaved", and is accepted and approved. A person behaving differently is rejected and cannot expect anything from others. With this guideline the parents offer an option where the adolescent can decide much more directly what he should do or what he intends doing. Sticking to the norm means here just choosing from two options the one which turns out to satisfy other people the best. Defiant adolescents are easier to handle this way and the debate rarely gets to the stage of mutual frustration.

Norms are the most tangible evidence of why cultures differ. Let us consider again the way to make a bonfire. Europeans start with paper and matches, Pacific islanders on the other hand use dried plant fibres ignited with a *fire-plough* (this is a piece of softwood with a groove which when rubbed with a hardwood stick will glow and ignite the fibres). Beyond this is technically a whole variety of ways of getting a decent fire going and maintaining it. For example, the pieces of wood for burning can be arranged in layers, or in a pyramid touching at the top. Of course, this depends on the type of material available locally, but not exclusively. Somehow and at some time each culture has settled on one particular method among the many. How and why cannot always be explained logically. Norms have this feature in common with *values*.

In the cultural sense values are patterns of thought which develop what is considered worthwhile and worth striving for. Examples for values from Western cultures are prosperity, youthfulness, self-confidence, being slim and much more. Even situations can be characterized by our notions of values. Children generally expect from their adult teachers to be dealt with not merely in a relaxed atmosphere, but also in a cheerful and lively manner, a form of behaviour that adults are not always able to achieve.

Values are not absolute. They occur only as values in the context of the relevant culture and may appear in another context as negative. Micronesian society considers slim ladies rather unattractive and unable to bear lots of children. The more well-built a lady is, the greater her husband's reputation grows, because this is the only obvious sign that he is wealthy enough to feed her (and their children) properly. On the other hand, in European-Western societies being overweight is always valued negatively.

There are values which can be named by members of a culture without hesitation or lengthy consideration. These are the *explicit* values. They include faithfulness, truthfulness, being slim etc. But values such as being accepted in one's own group are cultivated less deliberately, and could therefore not be described so easily. These are the *implicit* values. The same applies, what's more, for the realm of norms, such that we speak of explicit and implicit norms.

Values create objectives. They therefore seem to issue challenges, and motivate people to action. People who wish to reach a goal to which they attach a particular value even take paths characterized by negative values. Thus it is proper to refuse to allow somebody to go hungry, because as a rule hunger is not something we strive for. But if a person is going without food to become slimmer, he or she draws our admiration.

The fact that notions of value motivate us to action means that their impact is normative at the same time, i.e. they give a characteristic structure to our way of acting. Because it is seen as a virtue to appear "well brought-up" in the eyes of one's fellows, we follow a series of rules at table: we have the usual table manners for our social group. Maintaining our table manners gives characteristic structure to our behaviour. It seems (gently) dictated by the norm.

On a string of islands in the Pacific one can make a name for oneself by the so-called ceremonial exchange of particular items. The prestige attached to this is considered well worth the effort; it encourages men to manipulate other men with great skill, knowledge and tricks, in order to gain the reputation of being a so-called "Big Man" (Stagl 1983).

A short penetrating contribution to the issue of values in the realm of consumption – the consumption of goods – is found in Rössler (2003:113-114).

Values are hierarchical, i.e. they follow an order or priority. Faithfulness has a higher value than being slim. Within the cultural systems to which they belong, values form complicated and substantial sub-systems. Like other cultural elements they also only fit into other cultural systems rather awkwardly. A person working in a foreign culture experiences the incom-

patibility of his own values with those of his partners as something unpleasant. One particularly stark example is the right to life, which in European-
Western cultures features among a number of so-called human rights.
There are ethnic groups for whom the right to life in this sense sometimes constitutes a danger to their existence. Hunter-gatherers can only
eke out a living if they are on the move. That is, they need to roam across
their broad territory and exploit it. This is only possible if the number of
young children being carried is limited. If such groups are unaware of
contraception methods they have no other option but to kill surplus children, which usually happens immediately after birth. If the children were
allowed to live it would endanger the survival of the whole group. For
members of that culture the right to life is, to put it mildly, a problematic
issue. To demand human rights for these children would inevitably meet
with incomprehension. If one wanted to insist on the demand, one would
have to bring about a complete change of their economy, a process that
would entail great risk for them, and be lengthy and costly. Anybody attempting it would probably be accused of being a destroyer of culture.
Given the incompatibility of value systems, the demand to uphold human
rights and the demand to maintain a culture would cancel each other out.

More detailed introductions to this chapter's topic:

In connection with this chapter's topic the work of the psychotherapist
and doctor Christoph Staewen (1991) is especially recommended. He describes lucidly and in great detail, and from his own experience, the enculturation process of children in Black African societies. He compares
this process with the corresponding situation in European-Western cultures and explains the striking differences in the way adults from both
forms of society behave. Knowledge of this study is not only indispensable for those working in Africa; Staewen's wisdom can easily be applied
to numerous societies beyond Africa.

More on the topic of this chapter can be found in the following studies:

Cain, Horst: Persische Briefe auf Samoanisch. Anthropos 70.1975:617-
626.

Beer, Bettina; Fischer, Hans (Hg.): Ethnologie. Einführung und Überblick. Berlin 2003. (This is Fischer's 5th ed. of 1983 in a new version.)

Fischer, Hans (ed.): Ethnologie. Eine Einführung. Berlin 1983.

Freeman, Derek: Liebe ohne Aggression. Margaret Meads Legende von
der Friedfertigkeit der Naturvölker. München 1983.

Pfeiffer, Wolfgang M.; Schoene, Wolfgang (Hg.): Psychopathologie im Kulturvergleich. Stuttgart 1980.

Ritz, Hans: Die Sehnsucht nach der Südsee. Bericht über einen europäischen Mythos. Göttingen 1983.

Rössler, Martin: Wirtschaftsethnologie. In: Beer/Fischer 2003:101-124.

Rudolph, Wolfgang: Kultur, Psyche und Weltbild. In: Trimborn 1971:54-71. (Very fine introduction to this chapter's topic. I have incorporated much of Rudolph's thinking into my own chapter.)

Scheurmann, Erich: Der Papalagi. Die Reden des Südsee-Häuptlings Tuiavi'i aus Tiavea. Zürich 1977.

Staewen, Christoph: Kulturelle und psychologische Bedingungen der Zusammenarbeit mit Afrikanern. Ansatzpunkte für eine komplementäre Partnerschaft. München, Köln, London 1991 (particularly recommended).

Stagl, Justin: Politikethnologie. In: Fischer 1983: 205-229.

Stein, Gerd (Hg.): Die edlen Wilden – Verklärung von Indianern, Negern und Südseeinsulanern auf dem Hintergrund der kolonialen Greuel. Vom 16. bis zum 20. Jahrhundert. Frankfurt am Main 1984(a).

Stein, Gerd (Hg.): Europamüdigkeit und Verwilderungswünsche – Der Reiz, in amerikanischen Urwäldern, auf Südseeinseln oder im Orient ein zivilisationsfernes Leben zu führen. Frankfurt am Main 1984(b).

Trimborn, Hermann (Hg.): Lehrbuch der Völkerkunde. Stuttgart 1971.

Chapter 10
Culture and Superego (Conscience)

This chapter explains how cultures influence and give shape to a person's ability to live with others in a community; to recognise what is "good" and what is "bad"; to test their own actions accordingly; and to decide upon ethical and moral issues. The point of departure embraces the concepts of superego and conscience. My study sets out in detail what function each has, and what typical development these functions show during the enculturation process under various social circumstances, until the point where – depending on the culture – two main types can be recognized: shame-oriented and guilt-oriented superego or conscience. The final part of the chapter is given over to conclusions resulting from both orientations, affecting the individuals involved and the foreigner who is dealing with their new culture.

10.0 Introduction

The topic of this chapter is part of a specialism which in the last century was called the ***psychology of ethnic groups***, then ***ethnopsychology*** and in more recent times ***psychological anthropology*** (Beuchelt 1983). In the United States it is called ***cross-cultural psychology***. Its topics for research are multilayered, difficult and contested. I shall restrict my attention to the sub-topic of the ***superego*** or the ***orientation of conscience***.

10.1 Anthropological Basics

We must first be reminded of what was said in the previous chapter about the circumstances surrounding the enculturation of a human being: namely that at birth a person possesses no culture, but that his central nervous system (his brain) has the potential for enabling him to adopt and absorb a culture (or even several cultures) into his psyche during the course of his development. By the end of this process the person is equipped with a culture serving as a strategy for solving life's problems.

Along with this culture comes linguistic competence. This allows us as we grow up to learn and assimilate a language (or several languages) into our psyche, and to complete this integration so fully that language and reality are no longer considered distinctive: our words and the things, processes and relationships that they describe seem to us broadly the same.

Furthermore, integral to our aptitude for culture is our ability to evaluate our behaviour and that of others as "good" or "bad", according to particular criteria. We shall see later that this ability even by itself is a strategy for giving form to existence and mastering it. We call this *conscience*. The term is of course rather a popular one; in psychology it is the *superego*. For our simpler, more pragmatic purposes the term conscience suffices.

At birth a person merely possesses an *aptitude for conscience* but not at that stage any ethical or moral standards to measure behaviour as "good" or "bad", and certainly not to regulate personal behaviour. These are acquired through learning as he develops. This learning process works in the same way as all the other learning processes of the enculturation phase, namely by dint of experiencing thousands of specific situations in person.

At the end of this learning process a person has a complex and very detailed set of rules that govern the ethical and moral evaluating of his behaviour and that of others. He thus has a strategy whose aim is to help him relate to others: through it he controls his actions and aligns his personal behaviour to its rules. Conscience and the standards governing human behaviour are almost fully dependent on the general culture surrounding and absorbing a person during his development.

It is a widely held misconception that conscience is something given by nature to a person, a kind of organ which develops in a "natural" way, independent of other people and influencing his social and cultural environment, something akin to a "voice of God". Indeed it is this, as well. However, the metaphorical expression "conscience as the voice of God" is rather deceptive. It narrows our perspective on particular issues and leads us to overlook a series of even more important ones. The narrowing can jolt our insight into quite different orientations of conscience. We should therefore only use them once we are clear about how conscience fully presents itself.

Indeed, every normally developed child is born with an ability which as he grows takes shape as conscience. But that is all it is, a disposition of the same kind and shape as those given at birth for absorbing a culture and its language. During the enculturation process these tendencies are typically shaped by the cultural and social environment, such that great differences can occur in the orientation of the conscience of human societies. This is why conscience and its functions can only be properly understood if they are viewed and described in the context of their cultural conditions.

A person's conscience and its potential for effective exercise are largely dependent on the prior circumstances laid down by the culture in which this person grows up. Only somebody who has been encultured in a Christian European-Western context uses Christian criteria and a very specific and foundational orientation to guide his actions. For example, those who are from a Far-Eastern culture, such as the Japanese, will possess an essentially different grounding, as we shall see.

It is thus wrong to attempt to evaluate people's actions in foreign cultures by making assumptions according to Christian European-Western criteria. We may well be making these mistakes already when judging people from our own part of the world who belong to a different social background from ours.

When interpreting the actions and behaviour of people they come across in their work, Evangelical Christians and especially missionaries tend spontaneously and without much thought to invoke what the Bible says. In so doing they fail to consider that actions and behaviour are being stirred in people for whom Biblical standards are irrelevant; these have never been a part of their indigenous enculturation process, and thus have not been integrated into their consciences. A Christian setting out like this with his theological arguments is blocking his own path towards revealing the real orientation of the conscience of those he works with, an impediment lasting a prolonged period, often years. Presumably something similar occurs in pastoral care in our own society.

Real insight and proper understanding of the foreigner is only possible if the development worker first considers the structure and functions of conscience from purely anthropological perspectives, and only then reflects what the Bible has to say on the matter.

10.2 Functions of Conscience

The worker who sets out to achieve a full understanding of what is at stake must always have in mind that conscience is not first and foremost something to do with religion; it is also involved (indeed particularly so) in areas with little direct bearing upon theology. Conscience primarily guides a person's *social behaviour,* by supplying the criteria for "right" and "wrong" actions towards others. These criteria are present in all societies, irrespective of whether there is a "holy book" expressly describing such standards or not. Whenever two Khoi San men (Kalahari desert) arrange to meet at a particular time of day (according to the position of the sun) and at a particular spot (a rock, a tree) to go hunting, the venture can only take place if they keep to the appointment. For this to happen they both need a functioning conscience. It needs to remind them via their sense of responsibility or their "pangs of conscience" that one of them will be waiting in vain if the other is unreliable.

It is obvious that the individual conscience plays a considerable role in this instance. The question whether the person who fails to keep the appointment is heaping guilt upon himself or is even committing a sin, is on the other hand unimportant, or at least secondary, and perhaps even pedantic. In any case, keeping to the arrangement need not entail those involved fearing punishment by a higher power if they do not keep it. So a theological dimension is not discernible here. At the outset a proper comprehensive description of human conscience requires a purely anthropological perspective. Right and wrong actions are first and foremost defined by the traditions of the society where they are considered right and wrong, and where human relationships are regulated without recourse to a non-human authority. Conscience here fulfils important *social functions*; society cannot be maintained as a coherent structure without it. This could be termed *the horizontal dimension of conscience*. Because good and bad actions are also assessed under the heading of guilt/sin, and cannot be judged in the first instance by society itself but only by a higher authority (namely by God, by a deity) it therefore follows that conscience carries out *religious functions*; using these a person can evaluate his behaviour independently of society's norms. This could be called *the vertical function of conscience.*

As a rule, committed (evangelical) Christians overlook this distinction. They easily ignore that even people without any knowledge of the Bible distinguish good from evil and have a conscience. Christians tend to assign people in foreign societies – whose conscience guides them differently – to the category of "lacking in conscience". Besides, in an overtly Christian orientation of conscience the foreground is so overshadowed by the looming vertical perspective of the religious/theological dimension, so dominant that Christians are depriving the social dimension, the horizontal perspective, of any relation to the conscience. The fact that they do not fully perceive both aspects of conscience can quite often cause them to consider every form of inappropriate behaviour ("that people should be ashamed of") as a grave fault or sin. The following example shows quite how serious this tendency can be:

A European blows his nose "politely" by using a handkerchief. It is also possible of course, to press one's thumb against one's nostril and breathe forcefully through the other. This snorting is not considered acceptable in polite society, yet calling it a sin would invite ridicule. Evangelical Christians are inclined to set up this association; several social conventions such as fashion, especially in women (hairstyle and length of skirt), and going to the theatre or cinema are particularly likely to be considered not just unacceptable but sinful.

To avoid the risk of not considering the horizontal aspect and the vertical aspect in the orientation of the conscience as separate issues, or of overlooking one or both, it would be better to use the usual term in psychology, *superego*, instead of conscience. It is a neutral term and allows the person studying the topic a view of the whole. Yet the term has its disadvantages.

For daily communication with people of different superego orientation it is simpler to stick with the expression conscience, provided one bears in mind that one is dealing with a person's ability to evaluate his actions in relation to his fellows as well as in relation to a non-human authority.

Studies on the topic of conscience easily become so abstract that it is hard to imagine them having a bearing upon real circumstances. So I shall depict three simplified examples from life where conscience plays a role in various cultural and social situations.

Case 1) Peter is a young man growing up in a European-Western culture. He is of school age. One day he goes into the school office. There happens to be nobody there. He notices a five-pound note on the secretary's desk and takes it. He checks to see that nobody has seen him, then leaves.

He could have been relaxed about it all, but he isn't. He can't get what he has done out of his mind. He keeps being troubled by the thought that what he has done has made him a thief. After some time of reflection he reveals the truth to bring matters to light.

Case 2) Namalik is a young man growing up in a traditional culture. (Traditional cultures often mean the oral-tradition cultures of Africa, Asia, etc., which have no tradition of literacy, unless perhaps recently). He also goes to school. One day he discovers that the door to the food store is open. He checks to see that he hasn't been spotted, helps himself to a few tins of meat and makes off quickly.

After a few days the head teacher announces that a few tins of meat have gone missing. He doesn't voice any suspicion or name names. Nothing happens. After a while – time enough for a few empty tins to appear not far from the boy's home – the head teacher lets it be known that he is fairly sure who the thief is. The boy doesn't present himself but disappears overnight and is never seen again. He sends somebody else from his family, an uncle, who settles the matter.

Case 3) "Piggy" (real name Thomas) is thirteen years old. He is very overweight, because he is always eating sweets; hence his nickname. In sports lessons his classmates regularly manage 3 metres or more into the long jump pit. Piggy is the only one barely managing the 1.50m mark; he is extremely disappointed and miserable.

There are conclusions to be drawn from the 3 cases. To begin with it is worthwhile comparing the first two cases. It is worth noting that people have very different personalities and may therefore react very differently to the same situation. Useful conclusions are only likely if we presuppose that Peter and Namalik are of a broadly similar personality type.

There are a series of common features and differences in their behaviour. It is clear to both of them that they infringed a *moral law*. They check to see if their theft has been observed or not. This proves that they have a working conscience. They differ in their response to what they have done. Peter's agitation leads him to admit his action. This expunges the reason for his agitation, his *bad conscience*. Namalik, on the other hand, does not seem to have this need to act. He waits a while and seems to be more at ease with his bad conscience than Peter. Namalik's reaction is all the more stark when he is faced with the threat of being revealed as the thief: he avoids the situation by disappearing and brings some closure with the help of a *go-between*, a *spokesman* or *representative*.

There is a religious dimension in both these cases. We are also dealing with conscience in the theological sense, because theft is not just an infringement against society's norms, but also against the norms which are set by any kind of non-human authority. In the case of Piggy, however, a theological dimension is not discernible.

The easiest approach to understanding the hidden orientations behind these examples is to consider first an adult's fully developed conscience and then to investigate how it becomes like this, how from a disposition in a child to develop a functioning conscience there emerges a fully-fledged ethical and moral competency. In concrete terms this involves distinguishing two aspects exhibited by conscience: its manifestation in adulthood, and its nascent form in childhood and adolescence.

In all human societies a grown adult's developed conscience has the following functions:

1) It *examines* actions, whether planned or already committed, to see if they harmonize with the norms of the society, group etc., or not. It is irrelevant whether an action or behaviour has already occurred or is only intended. Both instances are examined. Examining the conscience is particularly significant where actions are intentional, as we shall see.

2.1) It *signals* compliance with these norms through a feeling of having done right or wrong. Actions and behaviour examined by conscience are revealed as good, proper or conforming to the norms. The feeling that results is popularly called "good conscience".

2.2) It signals non-compliance with these norms through the person feeling they are doing wrong, or that they have done wrong. Actions and behaviour examined by conscience are revealed as bad, improper or offending social norms. The resultant feeling is popularly called "bad conscience". This is held to be a *punishment*.

3) It *controls* the person through feelings of bad conscience and (generally) *prevents* offences against social norms by creating an expectation of punishment.

It is important to note that when a person's conscience identifies his action or behaviour as good it frees him to take action. On the other hand, if the conscience signals that the action or behaviour offends social norms, then its function is to punish. If the action is wrong and norms have been ignored the person will be punished by his feeling of having done something bad, inappropriate or improper, i.e. by "bad conscience". If the offence has not yet occurred, but has been planned and recognized as such, then conscience functions as a *barrier*: it impedes bad, inappropriate or improper behaviour by the fact that the person *expects* to be punished by conscience signalling feelings of bad conscience.

Of crucial importance is the very *varied quality* of the experience of a "good" and "bad" conscience. It would be natural to expect that in contrast to punishment by one's own bad conscience, a good conscience is experienced as a reward. This is generally not, however, the case. Among the thousand and one specific situations a decisive and active person engages in every day, he tends to feel the embarrassing ones more keenly; regrettably, he is much less conscious (if ever) of the numerous small incidents of correct behaviour. Only slight importance is accorded to the feeling of good conscience. A person behaving according to the norms does not experience his conscience as a faculty expressly freeing up his path for action, nor does he feel his correct actions present or past as particularly emphasised. In one's daily actions and behaviour the exercise of good conscience feels commonplace and self-evident.

Bad conscience, on the other hand, feels quite different: a person intending to act against the norms of his culture, his society or group will experience conscience as an institution blocking the path to action in a near authoritarian manner. The feeling of not having acted according to custom and practice is experienced as burdensome. In daily dealings one's bad conscience is by nature conspicuous, heavy, dramatic, constraining and impeding.

10.3 Feelings of Guilt and Shame

This increased conceptual burden of bad conscience on people's thinking and feeling is yet another feature absent in good conscience. Bad conscience functions on two distinct fronts. It prevents and punishes infringements against the norm via a *feeling of guilt* and of *shame*. This issue is crucial.

Feelings of guilt are generally triggered in a person's conscience when he responds to violations against norms formulated in terms of *right* and *law* by the person's culture, society or group. It may be a matter of written regulations (byelaws, Highway Code, etc.) or mere verbal agreements (committing to a speaking engagement). Feelings of guilt are however also responses of conscience where a person reacts to infringements against norms that he knows are set by a non-human authority, such as a god. Infringements like these are termed sins, a concept that is not confined to Christian cultures

Feelings of shame on the other hand are generally reactions in a person's conscience when he responds to violations against norms considered generally accepted rules of *decency, propriety* and *civilised behaviour*, everything that "people" should rightly uphold; such things as table manners, dress codes, an acceptable body weight, the ability to achieve a sporting target that other members of the particular group have also achieved.

Piggy's feelings as an inadequate long-jumper can clearly be interpreted as reactions by his conscience, although he is not committing a fault or a sin. He is ashamed because he cannot manage what his classmates manage; he has a sense of disgrace at falling short of the mark, the norm set by "the others" in his group.

Relevant situations can be separated boldly into categories, but not into ones where feelings are exclusively either guilt or shame. In fact there is always a mixture of both, and the boundaries can be very fluid. It is, however, important to recognise that conscience does not just involve guilt (sins) and the feelings associated, but also shame (disgrace) and the feelings associated there. A person's actions and behaviour are guided both by the sense of guilt and of shame in such a way as to enable interaction with other members of the culture, society or group and eventual integration into these groupings. Only when a person is thus equipped in his conscience with a range of abilities, however small, is he ready to integrate. People "lacking in conscience", devoid of guilt and shame, cannot thrive in any society over the long term. There can only ever be human societies and groups because their members possess a conscience whose nature has been developed in a characteristic way to exhibit a particular common orientation.

10.4 The Orientation of Guilt and Shame

It is significant here that conscience displays its dual orientation of guilt and shame only in the realm of bad conscience; here its effects are significant and unforeseen, with consequences that are frequently disregarded or not even recognised.

If the various cultures, societies and groups are examined for their common features and for their distinctiveness the results show *two fun-*

damental manifestations of human conscience. There are cultures, societies and groups whose members are mainly ***predisposed to guilt***, and others whose members are mainly ***predisposed to react in shame***. The point is that there are cultures, societies and groups whose members are punished largely by their conscience with feelings of guilt whenever they transgress norms; and there are other cultures whose members are punished by their conscience largely with feelings of shame, whenever they transgress norms. From both these criteria emerge profound differences in people's behaviour, impacting on the cultures themselves.

Societies made up of individuals tending towards guilt are generally much less tightly-knit and governed by fewer norms. They allow pluralism of opinions and tend to tolerate a range of standards of value and patterns of behaviour. Because *freedom of the individual* is held in high esteem, these societies are rather threatened with breakdown, because individuals are permitted to consider their own opinions and needs, and to view themselves as more important than "the others". In decision-making requiring a common opinion a discussion is generally pursued only until the majority view emerges.

Societies made up of individuals tending towards shame are tightly-knit in structure, and often have a strict hierarchy. They tend to require unity in opinions, and common standards affecting values and patterns of behaviour. Members tend to be forced to subordinate their individual freedoms to the group interest: they are less important than "the others". In decisions which require them to fall in line discussion is usually prolonged until all participants can agree about the solution. (Europeans invented the term palaver to describe this drawn-out business).

The type of culture which is predominantly guilt-oriented is mainly found in the complex, industrially influenced European-Western societies. Note that this is particularly true for the culture of upper classes of society and in urban settings. In lower social classes and in villages a shame orientation is quite pronounced. The spread of the principle of guilt orientation seems to coincide with those areas where Christianity is the dominant religious expression, or at least where its social foundations are determined ("the Christian West"). Nevertheless, the circumstances are not as straightforward as they seem. Beware of generalisations over such things!

The type of culture which is predominantly shame orientated is mainly found in the less complex societies, the pre-literate ethnic groups holding to their oral traditions as hunter-gatherers, planters, arable farmers and nomads (herdsmen); occasionally also in such complex modern industrial societies such as the Japanese or Chinese.

10.5 Enculturation and the Orientation of Conscience

At this point we can now turn to the question of how the ***process of conscience orientation*** actually works; or more precisely how its typical guilt orientation or shame orientation is laid down in childhood and adolescence.

Two requirements must be fulfilled for conscience orientation to occur at all: 1) A child needs (at least) one ***attachment figure***, 2) the child must be pre-disposed to want to build a ***harmonious relationship*** with that person, and then want to maintain it.

Every normally developed child is born with the need for a harmonious relationship with at least one attachment figure. Generally this is its mother, as the first person it comes into physical and emotional contact with. She decisively guides the formation of the child's conscience, and much else besides. During the child's development other attachment figures come into focus, depending on how its capabilities for responding to them grow and diversify.

We saw that the process of enculturation is determined by a child's attachment figures; it absorbs their culture and makes it personal. This is particularly true also for its conscience orientation which is of course integral to the culture the young child is absorbing. Consequently the norms and values that it internalises and which gradually determine the conscience are firstly those of its attachment figure(s). Here is an example to clarify how we should envisage this process unfolding:

In the living room a mother (or father) is talking to a four-year-old child about a rose in a tall thin vase. When the phone rings in the next room the parent explains to the child that she/he needs to answer it and needs to leave the child alone. The child must leave things alone, and particularly not touch the vase until the parent returns; the call won't last long.

There are a host of possible (and impossible!) situations which the child can create before the attachment figure comes back. Let us take the simplest one: The vase is still there. The child was obedient and heeded what the attachment figure said. How does the parent now respond to the child? Here too there is a range of possibilities.

First possibility: the attachment figure is attentive, ascertains that the child has done what it was told, and says that she/he is pleased with the child and its behaviour. By responding in this way the child experiences harmony between itself and the attachment figure; more precisely, the child learns that the harmonious relationship it has established with the parent is fully maintained, indeed confirmed, since the attachment figure is sending signals which convey this. The experience is positive, but not particularly striking, certainly not dramatic, just something it experiences as *normal*.

Second possibility: The attachment figure not only notices that the child has done what was wanted but tries deliberately to encourage behaviour like this with enthusiastic affirmations and effusive hallelujahs. The child experiences this response as a positive one, as confirmation of the cherished harmony. It is unable to perceive mother's exuberance as problematic. Indeed, why is her response excessive?

The attachment figure who praises enthusiastically every "right" act of child behaviour misses the opportunity to modulate praise appropriately in cases of really excellent child behaviour: the praise is devalued by inflation, and the child gets a false impression of the significance and intrinsic value of its action. Over time, children with consciences formed in such circumstances expect more and more attention and recognition from their peers, even for quite ordinary behaviour. Their response is to sulk if this attention is not forthcoming.

Generally, however, the attachment figure does not realise that the child has behaved as it should. Consequently the parent will not dwell on the matter: their response is normal, or at least not excessive. This is an important consideration, as we shall see.

Meanwhile, let us consider a quite different situation confronting the attachment figure after the phone call: The vase is in pieces on the floor, and the rose is in a puddle on the table cloth (or vice versa). How does the attachment figure react now?

Again, even here there are several possibilities, a broad range – from picking up the pieces in silent disregard through to outbursts of anger and physical punishment of the child. As a rule the attachment figure somehow gets "angry", responding in each case more dramatically than if the child had been obedient. This is the crucial difference in the two situations.

The child understands the response of the parent as a sign that the harmony between the two of them has been destroyed, and it experiences this breakdown as harm and trauma. From this moment on a normally balanced and developed child will do something, or everything, to reestablish harmony in the relationship with its parent. It is, however, more important that the child is clear that it has done something "bad", meaning that its attachment figure (the parent) has become "angry". The hurt experienced by the child is received as its "punishment".

From thousands of similar incidents occurring over the period of enculturation in childhood and adolescence an individual extracts what its world – the social surroundings of its attachment figure – perceives as good and bad, proper and improper, honourable and shameful, faulty and correct behaviour, what counts as worthwhile and worthless endeavour. The growing child learns the norms and values of its culture from the responses of its attachments figure(s) to its own actions and behaviour.

These reactions seem positive to the growing child if it experiences harmony with the attachment figure; they seem negative if the child reckons the harmony has been destroyed. The good and the bad, proper and improper, and what counts as worthwhile and worthless are thus essentially value judgements about actions and behaviour; these judgements are distilled from parental responses and are internalised in the child's conscience.

Internalisation processes only occur through such experiences. Without these experiences there can be no orientation towards the norms and values of a society. Thus conscience orientation does not occur naturally; it is guided and imposed by the attachment figure.

From this it is obvious what a responsibility an attachment figure has for the development of a child's conscience. Scarcely anybody understands this or is aware of it.

Internalising the reactions of attachment figures does not just involve being able to distinguish between good and bad, proper and improper, between behaviour that is honourable and shameful, blameworthy and blameless. Once the "angry" attachment figure and the perturbation have been internalised as punishment, then for purposes of inculcating ethically appropriate behaviour he or she is no longer needed, having been built into the child's awareness to function in good and bad conscience as an authority for control or punishment. What has emerged is a superego.

A child perceives and experiences an attachment figure's reactions more vividly when norms are infringed than when norms are followed. The difference explains why a bad conscience later has a more dramatic impact on the mind than a good conscience.

What has been stated thus far about the emergence of a person's conscience still does not explain how a conscience adopts a guilt orientation rather than a shame orientation, or vice versa. The origin of the distinction is surprisingly simple. We know the origin from researches done by Melford E. Spiro (1958 and 1961) into various cultures characterised by particular orientations of conscience. A rule of thumb is as follows: societies where a *small number of attachment figures* are involved in the enculturation and socialising of children give rise to a tendency for guilt orientation; societies where a *large number of attachment figures* are involved give rise to children tending towards shame orientation.

To clarify how conscience orientation works in societies tending to shame here is a further example:

On the islands of Micronesia the length of a church service is not fixed. It lasts just as long as the preacher has something to say, or as the people have a mind to listen. Children start to get restless, and their mothers then have difficulty calming them in church if they are not willing to take the children outside and listen from where they can occupy them.

A European mother would talk to her child directly and appeal to its ability to be patient, would point to her watch and explain that the service will stop when the watch hand gets to a particular time. An islander on the other hand tries to distract her child, a ploy which succeeds only for a short time. Finally the mother resorts to a surprising method: she points to the other church-goers and says: "They can all see now what a naughty child you are!" If a (white) foreigner is in the congregation the mother will choose to point him out and say: "He can see what a naughty child I have". The child's response is typical: it hides its face. From thousands of such experiences a child extracts during its enculturation very precisely what is considered good and bad, proper and improper, honourable and shameful, what counts as worthwhile and worthless. The child does not learn this from the reactions of its direct attachment figures, but by constant reference to a wider circle of folk, to the group, to *the others* whoever they are. As it grows up the child gears its actions and behaviour increasingly to what these others may expect, becoming thereby predominantly shame oriented.

Even a conscience formed like this has internalised the norms and values of its culture, including those pertaining to the organs for control and punishment; yet not in the same way, nor to the same degree. It is clearly less distinctively a superego. Of course, the individual internalises "the others", but they are much more clearly significant in determining its actions and behaviour than is the case with a guilt oriented individual. Only when these significant others are actually present are norm infringements actually controlled and punished.

The punishment expected by shame oriented persons for their non-conforming behaviour is much less a feeling of guilt than of shame; this shame is what a shame oriented individual perceives primarily as bad conscience.

10.6 Shame Orientation as a Group Orientation

There are reasons why ethnic societies in particular are made up of decidedly shame orientated individuals. Their economic form and lifestyle are only possible if members cooperate as an established *group*. An individual cannot live satisfactorily without actively belonging to a group like this, and may not even survive.

Big-game hunting, for example, is too arduous for a lone hunter with simple weapons (bow and arrow, spear), for various reasons. One individual with a weapon cannot hunt down his prey, because the prey senses his presence and maintains its distance, and may be too large. The hunter needs his fellows to drive the animal towards him, so that he can approach close enough to be certain of killing it.

By virtue of the fact that people can be grouped via a shame oriented conscience, then kept together and even moulded for a purpose, it is possible to achieve high productivity at work. It is not unusual for the Japanese, whose culture results in shame oriented individuals, to experience some embarrassment if they take their full entitlement to holiday. They suffer feelings of having let down their colleagues. This is one of the reasons why industry in Japan has tended to thrive. The Japanese subordinate their individual interests not merely to their circle of relatives but also to their work collective.

Can it be inferred from this that shame oriented people might be better at team work than guilt oriented ones? The answer is not easy. In firms in European-Western industrial societies attempts are being made today to increase employee productivity using deliberate ploys to encourage group practices, in order to harness the dynamism operating in all kinds of groups once they are in place.

Group dynamic processes are complicated, and I cannot describe them here fully. One key element they exhibit is that all members of the group become more approachable. Over a period they become imperceptibly part of "the others", opening up and even disclosing things about themselves to the extent of sharing personal thoughts and feelings; a kind of intimacy emerges, creating close emotional bonds between group members. This keeps the group together over a sustained period and concentrates members' performance, because at this point in the group momentum they do not feel they can just withdraw from the goal that the group itself has set or that has been set for the group to achieve. On the other hand, by their cooperation individuals give up certain freedoms to act independently and differently from what the group wants; otherwise they would necessarily lose face and be considered spoilsports or betrayers. I shall return to this point later.

Because members of ethnic groups cannot survive on their own, these societies have developed a very effective strategy for compelling their members to submit to the group and its interests: the shame oriented conscience. The interests of "the others" in the group – and thus the interests of the group as a whole – are more important than an individual's interest; it will be said of a member wanting to withdraw that he wants to be different. The potential dissenter feels this disgrace, fears the blight of a bad conscience and is thus compelled to conform to the wishes of the group.

10.7 Group Orientation and the Individual

In societies which largely give rise to shame oriented individuals it is a person's *prestige* which is key. Prestige is the opposite of disgrace. Prestige only lies in the eye of the "other", the beholder, and from this fact alone it is recognizable as a special feature of group oriented situations. Only the person who conforms to the norm and is ready to submit his individual needs in the broadest sense to his group's needs is a candidate for prestige, however this may occur. In prestige oriented societies the consequences are many and various.

In these circumstances it is highly desirable to win **great prestige,** which lifts the person above the rest of the group. This earns him **status**, and can qualify him for public office. In hunter-gatherer societies a man wins prestige by demonstrating that he is a particularly successful hunter, whom others go to for advice. As such he has a better chance than others of taking over the leadership of the group, not because he may have been designated expressly as a leader, but simply on the basis of the status that "the others" recognise in him; he has earned prestige in a realm reckoned essential for survival. Women can gain prestige by being particularly successful as planters.

There are ethnic societies whose structure is built on shame orientation; the prestige here is recognised in a quasi-institutionalised form. In numerous cultures of Melanesia there is an office-holder called *Big Man*. This term is the English translation of the various terms for this person in Melanesian languages, as well as the term used by ethnologists.

The most important qualities for Big Man are ambition and drive, the ability to manipulate other people and instigate a range of activities. His actual prestige, however, rests on his success in accumulating wealth, in the form of pigs, horticultural produce, and objects of value, together with his generosity in sharing his wealth with others. In addition he needs to fulfil other conditions. He must be courageous when fighting, knowledgeable concerning magic, and articulate. Nevertheless, his prestige derives from his being surrounded by a group of shame oriented followers assisting him and subordinating their own needs to group needs, so as to be able to share this prestige.

Societies like these do indeed foster the emergence of Big Man. Yet at the same time they work against it by demanding (not openly, of course) that this happens discretely, in all *humility*. In other words: what such societies reckon to be unassuming action and behaviour is of great worth, seen as an actual desirable attribute, and typical of conformist members of the relevant group. The person behaving immodestly in the meaning of the above is bound to be ashamed, suffer from bad conscience, and lose face and prestige. This mechanism prevents all group members from embarking on an unseemly race for the position of Big Man. Yet the mechanism also exerts a great pressure on the individuals themselves to moderate and suppress their wish for self-fulfilment. They already have to humble themselves often enough to demonstrate that they are in a position to serve the group's interests.

Pressures like these lead to tensions in a person. In shame oriented societies it is the men who appear to suffer particularly from not being allowed to fulfil themselves, from not being allowed to stand out in the group without feeling a sense of shame and a loss of face. They have acquired inhibitions during their conscience orientation phase and cannot do other, because they would then have to act against their conscience. In such circumstances men have recourse to problematic behaviour to rid themselves – at least temporarily – of their sense of frustration: they turn to drink, to grant themselves freedom to show what they are made of and who they really are.

This is one of the reasons for the *popularity of Rambo films* and of a particular kind of *alcohol misuse* in societies made up of largely shame oriented individuals. By that I mean not so much the alcohol dependency that comes from social deprivation or inadequate perspectives on life, but the need for validation which drives young men in particular to get drunk from time to time in order to get noticed, to pick fights and destroy things of value. Without alcohol their inhibitions at behaving like that would be too great. With alcohol they lose their shame-focussed inhibitions, and the result is bad behaviour: they can act out the role as individuals that they are not supposed to act out by the circumstances of their group orientation. That we are not dealing with alcohol misuse arising from social deprivation or inadequate perspectives on life is shown by the very different accompanying circumstances: the drinking often occurs in groups and then only occasionally. Yet behaviour like this is destructive even without the rampage. The benefit which the group hopes to gain is going down the drain; the satisfaction drawn from such goings-on is not genuine self-fulfilment.

The foreign observer finds it unusual that alcohol misuse like this occurs in social situations which are actually quite settled. Societies whose

very structures encourage similar alcohol misuse are promoting this behaviour by excusing it: The men who behaved destructively were, after
all, just drunk. What else could be expected of them?

To be excused in these terms, or even to boost one's own self-
assurance, it is sometimes enough just to create the impression of being
drunk. Three grammar-school boys from a shame oriented society wished
to make an impact at a school party by planning to appear confident in
front of the girls. They knew that they could only mask their inhibitions
and inferiority feelings by absorbing some Dutch courage. They were
well aware they couldn't afford the required amount of alcohol – their
pocket money was only enough for one can of beer. This they shared, intending just to smell of alcohol and not get really drunk. For the sake of
their self-esteem and apparent self-confidence it sufficed that the girls got
the impression they had been drinking.

There is also, of course, alcohol misuse linked to social deprivation
and poor future prospects, but this occurs only in circumstances that are
themselves problematic, such as the slums of large cities and similar areas. Mandelbaum (1980) gives a survey of this topic.

Yet another example of extreme behaviour arising because of the
shame orientation of a person's conscience might be the phenomenon of
running amok, common in many areas of South East Asia (e.g. Malay-
sia). The runner offloads his aggression – stored in him because he has
had to suppress his individual needs over a long time – by becoming violent and killing people. Even this behaviour is partly excused by the societies where it occurs, with the remark that the person running amok was
incapable of reacting differently, was under enormous pressure to prove
himself, win back his prestige and save face (Karim 1990).

10.8 Group Orientation and Ethics

When a person's conscience shows a shame orientation whose highest
aim is to maintain the group, what comes to the fore is a *characteristic
ethos*. This goal is the backdrop, according to which all actions and behaviour are good if they serve the group, and bad if they threaten its existence. Outside the member's group they are of lesser ethical significance.
Infringements against norms, such as selfishness, meanness, lies, theft,
murder etc. become weightier matters if they are committed against the
member's own group. Against members of an alien group such actions
and behaviour are less bad and are reckoned as lesser "sins".

Sin occurs here in terms of a person's relationship to the group. Sin
tends therefore to be *defined socially* rather than by commands from a

non-human authority such as a god. In many such societies members take it for granted that group members who have died continue to watch as ancestral spirits (and thus as quasi-divine beings) to see that those still alive do not infringe any norms. A person who "sins" in this sense has to reckon that he or another member will be punished with sickness, disaster or death. He will not be threatened with this punishment at all or only moderately if he infringes against non-members; the same sin committed against them is viewed as less serious. The sinner can even assume that his group members will support him and protect him against any vengeance from outside. If they are unwilling to support him, they will run into problems of conscience because they acted against their own group. The sinner can even expect solidarity like this from his own ancestral spirits; they will defend him against attacks by the spirits of the other group.

This mechanism is the reason why in African countries, for example, *tribalism* occurs – the preference for one's own ethnic group or clan (from Lat. *tribus* = tribe) to the disadvantage of the others. A minister bestowing official jobs who thinks he can deny preferment for one of his own ethnic group, or a teacher who gives bad marks to pupils he is related to, at once becomes the subject of criticism and is faced with a moral dilemma: he will be ashamed and will suffer from bad conscience, because his social group aligned him to shame oriented responses; these do not allow for unbiased judgements.

Members of European-Western cultures generally think of behaviour like this as *corruption*. Yet it can only be understood as corrupt behaviour if the person concerned has a guilt oriented conscience. For the shame oriented person, conforming to the group is the only option for morally correct behaviour; if the person were not to favour his group members they would inevitably consider him corrupt.

It is clear from all this that orientations of conscience are essentially determined by the cultures in which they arise and operate. Each culture makes strategies available to those who need them to cope with their lives. Under these circumstances a person's conscience, with its guilt or shame orientation, is an integral coping mechanism, best understood as a cog within the workings of the culture as a whole.

10.9 Group Orientation and Community

We have noted that people with shame oriented consciences tend to be more prepared than those with guilt orientation to subordinate their interests to the group interest. This circumstance is an issue for what Christianity understands as *community*.

People in our Western civilisation with its roots in Christianity who join a church fellowship (or community) must face up to what is probably a new situation regarding conscience: They seem to have experienced a shift towards shame orientation, because they feel they *need* to align their actions and their behaviour from now on towards "the others", the members of their fellowship or community; or they really *wish* to do so. These "others" do indeed form a group, unconsciously setting norms and in some situations quite specifically requiring that norms be adhered to. In some cases they only count as genuine members if they wear (or avoid wearing) particular clothing and favour (or avoid) a particular hairstyle, or drink no alcohol, or watch no television. The need to identify with these norms may not in itself indicate an orientation towards shame. However, as soon as the new member feels apprehensive about not being acknowledged as a member if his actions and behaviour are not in line with the norms of the community or fellowship, at that point shame orientation is involved. There can be a potential problem here.

There are people who develop the need to match their actions and behaviour largely or indeed fully to these "others". The anxiety a person feels in losing face may lead to a state of permanent bondage and remove his power to decide, act and behave autonomously; his predicament gives a massive ascendancy to "the others". There are people who are so badly twisted in their emotions that they require psychiatric treatment. Critical situations like these are more frequent than generally admitted.

10.10 The Potential for Misusing Group Orientation

We return now to the results and effects of the previously mentioned group dynamic processes where an individual is held up to scrutiny, or even to the full glare of public exposure. These can continue as significant factors, finally leading to the person offering himself up completely, and reaching a stage where he is open to total manipulation.

There are areas of life where conscience orientation like this is misused. We know today that extreme political groups and terrorist organisations compel their members to conform; anybody wanting "out" must reckon with being branded a "wrecker", and a "traitor"; this is an accusation that people inclining to shame orientation cannot live with. They are sometimes more ready to commit a crime than to be exposed by this accusation. So – against their own will – they conform to the group will.

Shame orientation runs parallel to the individual's need for the group's recognition, and parallel to the fear of losing it. People with shame oriented consciences generally show a tendency to exaggerate their need for recognition; and so they suffer from the increased pressure to maintain recognition. Many are ready to make great sacrifices for this; they permit themselves to do the most unusual things. Such individuals are particularly open to persuasion to conform.

For example, in youth gangs members volunteer to commit the worst criminal actions and behaviour, just to maintain their reputation and pecking order. The decisive self-exposure which binds a potential member to the group may consist of an "initiation", an act where a condom machine is broken open or a defenceless old lady has her handbag snatched with "the others" watching.

Sometimes even fundamentalist religious organisations have recourse to group pressure and use shame orientation against their members. Persons cancelling their membership must reckon with total loss of face. There are sects where a former group member is no longer acknowledged by those still in membership.

Such mechanisms are also at work when a person gets into the clutches of a so-called *psycho-sect*, and severs all ties with his previous life, often with dire consequences, such as financial ruin and the end of his education or professional career. The ultimate disclosure, which ends in self-sacrifice and manipulation is a detailed public confession of "sins" (or whatever sects call this kind of thing) in front of the whole community (functioning as "the others"). The absolution consists of the person being taken into the bosom of the new community. (Cf. Boston Church of Christ "Soldiers for God", Der Spiegel 1.1994:55-57).

Once he has integrated himself somewhat into a group like this, and felt accepted and found some kind of perceived or genuine recognition, a shame oriented individual has no way out again without massive loss of recognition. Experience shows that separation from the group is a disgrace and a cause of anxiety, an inhibition weighing on the individual and of great significance.

People who have been taken into membership are followed closely by the others. Sometimes their lifestyle is carefully monitored, even to the extent of what they should wear and how they should think. Members of these communities are sometimes called upon to check on each other, all in the name of some vague purpose to do with maintaining group allegiance, or even in the name of an extra-human authority. This can even extend to collective suicide, with a whole series of incidents occurring up to the present. Such "churches" – or rather cults – have all the externals of totalitarian party and state structures familiar to us from dictatorial systems.

Misuse of people's shame orientation is evident whenever Marxist social systems require people to spy on one another and compel those of different persuasions, such as critics and "dissidents", to conform to state ideology. In former East Germany a person who put himself "socially offside" was officially denounced and stripped of any prestige by being declared unworthy to join the local volunteer fire-brigade – a classic case of being ostracized from a group for non-conformity to the collective interest.

This practice is widespread in socialist countries, and is even an educational principle in schools. Pupils who do not conform to the ideology are publicly exposed. Undisciplined behaviour, even minor infringements of house rules, are debated in front of the whole school, the "collective", the significant "others". It has to be said that it is a very effective instrument for binding a person into the group.

Abusive influence on a person's conscience orientation occurs in cases where, for example, a child is brought up using shame-based processes to make him conform to a particular tendency; where not only his direct attachment figures such as his parents but a greater number of "others" are in the know and exert influence on his actions and behaviour. When a misbehaving youngster is constantly faced with the question as to what "people" (a kind of imaginary group) think of him, he will end up justifying his actions and behaviour less and less by reference to himself, but taking his cue increasingly from such "people"; he will allow strangers to govern him and will suffer from feeling captive to them.

In our European-Western cultural circles the children whose conscience tends more towards a shame orientation often come from a Christian home. Just at a decisive phase of their development and enculturation process children of pastors, preachers and missionaries are exposed to role-strain. Sometimes they adjust their actions and behaviour to a community and its values for years on end, because to do otherwise would put at risk the family's relationship to the outside world (via the father's position in society). In addition, maintaining the internal harmony of the family is a strong impulse. This pressure can just as well come from parents as from community members; parents fear being talked about if their children fail to behave according to the expectations set by other members, for example when the children are unwilling to attend regular Sunday fellowship events.

Many youngsters survive without long-term adverse effects but nevertheless are loath to look back and examine their feelings. For others the consequences are more serious. Children who are by nature strong-willed escape the group pressure at the latest during puberty, then revolt and turn their backs on the community. They often turn right away from Christianity. Some are so distorted in their thinking that they become incapable of taking their own decisions; they are unable to behave without fearing that "the others" might somehow disapprove, and punish them with mockery, and consider them as outcasts. This is how shame orientations develop into clinical cases of *ecclesiogenic psychosis*. The instances of this are quite rare, but suffering in silence is much more widespread than we are led to believe.

It is appropriate here to mention children's *adjustment*, or rather the *degree to which they are adjusted*. It is clear that only individuals having a certain level of adaptability to their group's valid norms and values are in a position to live within a group or community. Somebody who does not have sufficient adaptability either cannot become a member, or will remain a marginal figure, or will be an active trouble-maker in the group.

Marginal types find it hard in that they are forever feeling dissatisfied; they have to devote mental and emotional energy to avoid being pushed out of the group or community. By contrast, individuals who have experienced in their conscience an accentuated tendency for shame also suffer, because they can easily fall victim to group blackmail. They are over adjusted and easily succumb to the will of others, for the very reason that they do not have the power to set their own wills in opposition to others.

For this reason it is wrong to leave children stuck in their enculturation phase without any conscience orientation. Their attachment figures may give them no experience of norms and the consequences of infringing these norms, for whatever reasons – such as wanting to avoid curtailing their children's freedoms, and wanting to facilitate their children's own decisions. Such lack of guidance can lead to a child having no conscience orientation whatsoever. It is evidently crucial for a child's conscience orientation to exhibit the minimum necessary potential for conformity. This must lie somewhere between the extremes of guilt orientation and shame orientation. Where exactly this point is between the two extremes will be determined by the culture of the society where the individual has to live. In our European-Western cultures this is evidently closer to guilt orientation; in other cultures closer to shame orientation.

What I have just said applies particularly in pre-literate, largely Third World, cultures, but also applies to many of the more complex cultures, such as the Japanese, and to specific religious groups. Being attached to a group is here either a person's means of survival, or else we are dealing with a form of conscience orientation which has emerged from a person's past and which has not lost – for a variety of reasons – its hold upon that person.

In passing, a shame orientation was probably standard in the proto-cultures of current European-Western societies: the Germanic and Gallic tribes with their clan organisation patterns would seem to allow this observation. (A proto-culture is the source for other emerging cultures).

A common method of "punishment" in the Middle Ages for those norm infringements considered minor rather than criminal was the so-called *pillory,* also called *the pole of shame.* For example, unmarried women who had become pregnant were pilloried; they were put on show in front of "the others" with a dual purpose, both as a punishment (which they experienced as shame, loss of face and honour) and to warn "the others" about acting or behaving similarly, and about the need to conform to the norms.

10.11 Group Orientation and Mistakes

It would be wrong to claim that a shame oriented conscience is of lesser value in comparison with the Western tendency for guilt orientation. Every culture is dependent on the environment in which its members live and, by extension, on a whole lot of historical imponderables. If this environment requires a particular culture as a strategy for overcoming life's obstacles and excludes any other culture, then it can happen that the home culture so formed only allows as its strategy either the one or the other conscience orientation. There are consequences and compromises arising from this, which the individual must take on and accept.

One of the prime consequences is the general heightened fear – common among shame oriented individuals – of *making a mistake,* however slight this appears in the eyes of a rather more guilt oriented European. Mistakes mean loss of face and prestige, especially where "the others" recognise what this loss entails. With increased anxiety there comes increased pressure to hide this mistake.

In societies like these it is considered a gross impertinence to *criticize* somebody in front of others for a mistake. It discredits him and causes loss of face and prestige

A foreign visitor notices that shame oriented people frequently burst into uncontrollable laughter when doing something wrong in front of others or when caught out. This laughter is not easy to explain. Those who are foreign to the culture consider such behaviour arrogant; but this is a misreading of the situation, and it can have near disastrous consequences. As we learn from experience, laughter is almost always a mask behind which hides deep shame with all its forsakenness.

10.12 Group Orientation as a Problem for Teachers

The general mind-set of shame oriented individuals when they make mistakes has enormous impact in teaching situations, whether with schoolchildren or with adults in church and fellowships. The contrasts with equivalent teaching situations in European-Western cultures are very marked. Scarcely any development aid worker or church worker teaching in the Third World is prepared for it. Because of it most people get into real difficulties, at least in the initial stages of their work.

In European-Western research into teaching methods and teacher training there is a principle of group learning introduced by the pedagogue Georg Kerschensteiner (1854-1932). His theory requires that the teacher does not give a lecture but sets out the material to be taught in a detailed chain of questions put to the class. The individual answers given by pupils represent their available knowledge in a kind of mosaic, with additions being learnt as they connect to it, and expand it.

Yet a technique of questioning only produces pupil activity if those being asked are not afraid, and then only if their answer turns out not to be wrong. If a child is afraid of losing face at giving a wrong answer, it will take pains not to run the risk.

For this reason the teacher's question to a class of shame oriented pupils generally results in a pregnant silence. When the teacher calls out a name everybody is hoping that it won't be his own. One can easily imagine what a deadening impact this can have on the lesson. The only visible gain to be had is when muzzling the pupils can be used as a simple way of solving disciplinary problems, by asking questions that everybody is afraid of and responds to in silence.

Another type of reaction to a teacher's question is when – instead of the targeted pupil replying – the pupil next to him has caught the almost inaudible answer and repeated it boldly. This second pupil suffers less from fear of losing face if he says something wrong, given that he is not being directly asked but only repeating what another pupil has said. His reaction is recognized by "the others" as helpful and therefore reduces the tension, even if the friendly classmate repeats a wrong answer, because it can be accepted that he himself has not been the author of the mistake. His loss of face is thus kept within reasonable bounds; it was not, after all, his turn. If what he says is correct nobody can object. Conversely, the honour of the pupil whose turn it was has been somewhat rescued or his disgrace mitigated: if the answer turns out to be wrong, at least he has not given it himself.

It is impressive how patiently fellow pupils accept inaudible answers. Pupils in European-Western cultures would be protesting even after a brief period and announcing that they could not understand a thing. Experience tells me that a class gets restless if incomprehensible answers accumulate. For a shame oriented class it would be inappropriate for a teacher to hint by requesting a repeat answer that the pupil concerned was behaving in an unmannerly way. The point that an inaudible answer is just as meaningless as no answer at all does not alter this fact.

Of course, shame oriented pupils can – in an extreme case – react dramatically, especially if the teacher is not aware of their orientation and provokes by his clumsiness a corresponding act of pupil misbehaviour. The following is a possible scenario: The teacher asks a question and the class falls silent. He then concludes that his question has not been understood, and he rephrases the question, several times, although this is not really needed. Even then nobody replies. The fear that the teacher might not greet an answer with fulsome praise, leaving the pupil inevitably feeling ashamed, is so great that silence persists.

The teacher could in such situations give the answer himself. But this would eventually lead to nobody bothering to think about the question at all. Finally, he could try addressing a particular pupil, expressly requiring an answer and emphasizing at the same time that the answer need not be a complete one.

With frequent repetitions even this method leads to a dead end. If the teacher insists on a silent or soft-voiced pupil giving an answer, he is signalling indirectly but clearly that the particular pupil is behaving inconsiderately. This turns the pupil's anxiety into aggressiveness. He either ends up answering in a loud, clear and cross voice, or he refuses point blank by throwing his book across the classroom and leaves the building in a rage, even permanently. A reaction like this is rather rare, at least with younger shame orientated pupils. With older pupils during puberty the response is triggered more promptly, and is more blatantly hostile. With adults the aggressiveness unleashed by confrontation like this tends to be hidden and controlled by reason, yet it is a considerable aggravating factor in inter-personal relationships.

In shame oriented societies there are, nevertheless, some brave souls who answer boldly because they are sure of their ground, because they wish to shine, or just because they know that they will cause merriment by their wrong answer.

As a rule, however, a learner's personal initiative is greatly curbed by shame orientation. Pedagogy, and particularly the principles and practices of class teaching, is duty-bound to make adjustments for it. Classes should be taught using an orientation towards the group and its concept of shame, not individually centred in guilt orientation. What do I imply by this? Putting it simply, teachers need to bear in mind the following:

Teaching shame oriented individuals, children or adults, has to take into account the group, not the individual. The teacher presents a topic by explaining in broad outline, then proceeds to ask questions on the details which can be framed along the lines of the European-Western model of the principle of group learning. The teacher's technique for asking questions must in any case anticipate the formulation of answers and smooth their path so that these are quite recognizable for the majority of the class; they must seem for the pupils to be "easy" answers. Only in this way is the level of inhibition kept low enough for pupil answers to be prompt. Alternatively, group answers can be anticipated by the teacher issuing the challenge: "Let's all give the answer together."

In a Western-guilt oriented classroom this would lead to chaotic scenes, especially with larger pupil numbers. Experience shows that in classes of shame oriented pupils this risk is much lower, or does not exist at all. Of course, for this style of teaching as well, the class or group should be small.

The shame oriented, group-centred learning style marked by the corresponding influence of pupils' conscience operates by the teacher announcing the topic content, with the words being repeated by the pupil group in chorus, or often just shouted out. This is a widely used learning style in the Third World. The principle of continuous repetition is indeed an important and effective element. However, individual thinking – converting the knowledge content into a matter of personal insight – cannot be achieved by this style.

10.13   Group Orientation and the Representative

Another characteristic feature of cultures with a high proportion of shame oriented individuals is the *spokesman* or *representative*. In the classroom situation in which the teacher's question is answered not by the pupil questioned but by his trusted classmate who has understood his almost inaudible answer, we are dealing with a representative. He is alleviating or preventing the threat of loss of face. The phenomenon of the representative is even more important in situations where somebody has already lost face and prestige by being pronounced guilty of something, for example of theft.

Even shame oriented individuals have the need (as described above in case 2) to repair the damage that they have caused. Indeed, the threshold of shame that they have to cross is a much greater barrier than for individuals with a guilt orientation. This is the likely reason for the role of the spokesman whose interventions help alleviate the vexations pressing upon a shame oriented individual when he is required to admit responsibility for his deed.

In shame oriented societies a person cannot in fact set about rectifying what he has done to another. Anybody doing this would be demonstrating publicly that he was indeed a "shameless individual". This would place the person himself under even greater stress of conscience. He would be forced to act against his conscience if – instead of sending a representative – he himself went to apologize. This much he has learnt in his enculturation phase.

Foreigners from European-Western societies are frequently annoyed about behaviour like this because they are not familiar with the context, and they react accordingly. Church workers try, often unsuccessfully, to encourage shame oriented individuals to settle past injustices by requiring those who have done wrong to speak with those whom they have affected and open up to them, which is an unthinkable ploy and the height of "disgrace" for somebody who has been accused and pronounced guilty. In his eyes the unpleasant episode is made even more unbearable. This can only be avoided by having recourse to a representative.

This representative is active in other circumstances as well, for example as a petitioner or go-between. If a young man wishes to marry, he cannot himself disclose his plan directly to the girl's parents, so for example, he sends his uncle instead. Very often a person wishing to avoid losing face will not even borrow an item or request help with a difficult task without involving a representative.

In this connection it is mostly overlooked that there are distinct parallels here with the New Testament: Jesus as representative/petitioner on man's behalf before God. Shame oriented Christians will appreciate this more easily than others.

10.14 Group Orientation and the Pressure of Suffering

On the whole a shame oriented individual suffers from his conscience orientation far more than a guilt oriented individual. This is obvious from letters where somebody says why he wishes to disappear, why he cannot bear to be seen any more, because he has already heaped disgrace on himself or thinks that this will happen. Superlative expressions ("this is the last letter that I shall ever write"), symbols of death and metaphors of hell ("I am drowning in fire and blood") are symptomatic of this suffering.

Sometimes conscience orientation creates a problem for individuals involved in group dynamic experiments; they open themselves up to "the others" during the process to such an extent that they find out too late how very exposed they feel, something they did not anticipate at the outset. By disclosing so much of themselves they have to a degree surrendered sovereignty over themselves as individuals. The result is a feeling of pain and suffering.

10.15 Group Orientation and Suicide

Suicide is a dramatic expression of the suffering that shame oriented people experience; it is stirred up by constraints and by the requirement to fit into their group. Bouts of depression in people having European-Western lifestyles may be triggered by overwork, or desperate situations, such as may occur when life perspectives seem inadequate or when opportunities are misjudged: feelings like these can be a classic motivation for suicide in a Westerner. Yet in a shame oriented person they arise essentially from the disgrace which he has brought upon his group. This causes him to feel that he himself has engineered his exclusion, even though this perception may be his alone.

A person who has lost prestige can sometimes regain it by removing himself from the group through physical annihilation. Suicides resulting from this motive are common in Japanese society: Japanese pupils failing to reach the class goal, and students who fail their exams, kill themselves to redeem their disgrace or the disgrace brought upon the family.

In the shame oriented societies of the Pacific it can happen that a person hangs himself because he has been criticised by a high-ranking family member. In this case there is yet another motive beyond regaining one's prestige: the person committing suicide wishes to punish his critic for his reprimand by causing him pangs of conscience over the death, in the short term or even for ever. This is sometimes linguistically precisely defined. The islanders of Chuuk in Micronesia have a short word (*mwún*) for the feeling of guilt experienced by a person who has taken the prestige from another person through criticism, and has eventually caused his suicide. This word is used exclusively in this connection.

10.16 Group Orientation as a Prerequisite for Church Workers

It is not possible in an introductory study even to go some way towards analysing shame or group orientation in foreign societies, and the many various consequences arising, all of which a European-Western church worker comes across in group oriented communal structures. However, the following should be taken into account in all situations:

Members of shame oriented societies and groups are quite overwhelmed or at least in a difficult position when they decide to become a Christian and want to make this a reality *as individuals*. The decision will isolate them in an elemental way from their group and cut them off. It will equate to trying to act against one's own conscience. The decision is easier if at least two decide together to commit themselves. Therefore the rule applying in this decisive step is: either together or neither. (It is worth noting the passages in the Old Testament and New beginning "Me and my house wish ..." These indicate a group decision.)

Individual decisions taken by a shame oriented person sometimes require considerably more mental and emotional energy, and renunciation of self, than is the case with a guilt oriented person.

A similar victory over self is involved when a shame oriented person is expected to make a public avowal of sin to his own community or some other audience before he can be baptised. In many evangelical circles in our Western Christian societies people place great emphasis on this kind of "testimony". A shame oriented person finds this so much more difficult because he is giving an account in front of his group, close-knit or extensive. They already know what kind of person he was and is, and he is required to disclose still more of himself. Experience shows that it can happen that individuals try to gain prestige under pressure from the testimony by declaring particularly drastic "sins" which they have committed "in the past". This, too, can be explained by the shame orientation of their conscience.

Sermons given by shame oriented pastors to shame oriented listeners are more likely to mention the *law* to be followed; less common are sermons about the freedom that Christians are called to. The result is that communities in shame oriented cultures can have a rather Old Testament feel about them.

On the face of things it can seem that shame oriented societies are attached to a form of religion whose theology holds *self-redemption* to be a key issue. This would need a more specialist study.

If Western Christians are asked the question whether Bible passages reveal shame oriented themes or guilt oriented ones, the answer comes back pretty directly that the Bible emphasises guilt orientation. Those questioned are quite amazed that this can ever be a matter of debate. However, further research reveals something striking.

In the revised Luther Bible the term guilt and its derivatives (guilty etc.) occur about forty times. The term shame and its synonyms and derivatives (disgrace, disgraceful, to be ashamed, scandal, scandalise etc.) occur on the other hand about seventy times, almost twice as frequently. What is unexpected are the proportions when one just considers the New Testament and the two thematic fields: guilt and its derivatives are mentioned sixteen times, shame etc. on the other hand about thirty times, i.e. also twice as frequently.

The raw figures vary according to the translation: the English edition of the KJV or the RSV. In both these, for example, the prevalence of the word shame is even greater (Noble 1975:26).

Of course, it would be tricky to deduce from statistics like this any theological conclusions. I am not persuaded to do that! Nevertheless the following is thought-provoking: The church communities in Asia Minor and Greece planted by Paul – for which he wrote a large portion of his important theological messages – were not people from the educated and governing classes of his day; they were from the lower classes and from slavery, and belonged to ethnic groups whose territory had been con-quered by Greece and Rome. Both groups, the lower classes and ethnic groups, can be expected to be shame oriented rather than guilt oriented. Is this the case also for the church fellowships of the New Testament? I am unwilling to give a definite answer on this matter. If this is the case, then we would have to look at Paul's theology of conscience from a different perspective, and understand it differently from the way we as guilt ori-ented Europeans do nowadays. In this view, Paul would have set out his theology of conscience from a shame perspective according to the needs and issues of individuals and their related community structures. Scarcely any European theologian or church worker overseas gives any thought to this. An important exception is Stockitt (2012).

Generally speaking it would also be completely wrong to view shame orientation of conscience in an essentially negative way. Groups consisting of shame oriented individuals bond better, and for longer. Viewed in this light, shame orientation can be said to be a community-building principle.

In the secular world shame orientation evidently prevents criminality rather effectively. The social situation in village structures, as distinct from city structures, bears this out.

Furthermore, in missiology there are new approaches towards a differ-entiated theory of conscience. It is called *elenctics* (Müller 1988, 2010) and is strongly aligned to the ethical/moral aspects of conscience, such as guilt, sin and forgiveness, i.e. aligned to its significance for religion. So-cial functions of conscience are rather adrift of its main preoccupation. What is new is that in its theoretical foundations great account is taken of the dimensions of anthropology and ethnology which have impacted on the topic of the superego and conscience orientation.

Two relevant works have recently performed great service in this re-spect. In his broadly conceived study (2003) the missionary doctor Han-nes Wiher working in West Africa has presented the dimensions of the concept of conscience from the standpoint of theology, philosophy, anthropology and missiology; his study is an informative manual for mission practice, making for easier access via its extensive bibliography to the numerous gradations which typify conscience orientation. Ruth Lienhard, a colleague at SIL (Wycliffe Bible translators) deals in her PhD thesis (2002) with the sociological and theological aspects of conscience orientation among the Daba and Bana of Cameroon. She demonstrates that human relationships and personal honour form a close bond of great significance for the harmony in society at large and in the Christian community. Her arranging of the social system into cultures that are "honor oriented" and "justice oriented" is illuminating.

More on the topic of this chapter can be found in the following studies:

Bakhtiar, Mansour: Das Schamgefühl in der persisch-islamischen Kultur. Eine ethnopsychoanalytische Untersuchung. Berlin 1994.

Barloewen, Constantin von; Werhahn-Mees, Kai (Hg.): Japan und der Westen (vol. 1 Philosophie, Geistesgeschichte, Anthropologie). Frankfurt am Main 1986.

Barloewen, Constantin von; Werhahn-Mees, Kai (Hg.): Japan und der Westen (vol. 2 Wirtschafts- und Sozialwissenschaften, Technologie). Frankfurt am Main 1986.

Beuchelt, Eno: Psychologische Anthropologie. In: Fischer 1983:345-361.

Bock, Philip K.: Rethinking psychological anthropology. Continuity and change in the study of human action. New York 1988.

Fischer, Hans (Hg.): Ethnologie. Eine Einführung. Berlin 1983.

Gadamer, Hans Georg: Psychologische Anthropologie. Stuttgart 1973.

Gestrich, Christoph: Christentum und Stellvertretung: religionsphilosophische Untersuchungen zum Heilsverständnis und zur Grundlegung der Theologie. Tübingen 2001.

Hirschmeier, Johannes: Grundlagen des japanischen Arbeitsethos. Die Firma als Schicksalsgemeinschaft. In: Barloewen/Werhahn-Mees 1986:270-285.

Kaplan, Bert (ed.): Studying personality cross-culturally. Evanston 1961.

Karim, Wazir Jahan (ed.): Emotions of culture. A Malay perspective. Singapore et al. 1990.

Kasdorf, Hans; Müller, Klaus (Hg.): Bilanz und Plan: Mission an der Schwelle zum dritten Jahrtausend. Festschrift für George W. Peters zu seinem achtzigsten Geburtstag. (English ed: Reflection and Projection. Missiology at the threshold of 2001). Bad Liebenzell 1988.

Lienhard, Ruth: Restoring relationships. Theological reflections on shame and honor among the Daba and Bana of Cameroon. (Ph.D. dissertation Fuller Theological Seminary) Yaoundé, Cameroon 2002.

Müller, Klaus W.: Elenktik: Gewissen im Kontext. In Kasdorf/Müller 1988:416-454.

Müller, Klaus W.: Das Gewissen in Kultur und Religion. Scham und Schuldorientierung als empirisches Phänomen des Über-Ich/Ich-Ideal. Lehrbuch Elenktik. Nürnberg 2010.

Mandelbaum, D. G.: Kulturelle Bedingungen und Funktionen des Alkoholkonsums. In Pfeiffer/Schoene 1980:116-131.

Noble, Lowell L.: Naked and not ashamed. An anthropological, biblical, and psychological study of shame. Jackson, Michigan 1975.

Pfeiffer, Wolfgang M.; Schoene, Wolfgang (Hg.): Psychopathologie im Kulturvergleich. Stuttgart 1980.

Schwartz, Theodore; White, Jeoffrey M.; Lutz, Catherine A. (eds.): New directions in psychological anthropology. Cambridge 1992.

Spiro, Melford E.: Children of the Kibbutz. Cambridge Mass. 1958.

Spiro, Melford E.: Social systems, personality, and functional analysis. In: Kaplan (ed.) 1961:93-127.

Sun, Longji: Das ummauerte Ich. Die Tiefenstruktur der chinesischen Mentalität. Leipzig (Kiepenheuer) 1994.

Stockitt, Robin: Restoring the shamed. Towards a theology of shame. Eugene, Or. 2012.

Wiher, Hannes: Shame and guilt. A key to cross-cultural ministry. Bonn (Verlag für Kultur und Wissenschaft) 2003.

Williams, Thomas, R. (ed.): Psychological anthropology. The Hague, Paris 1975.

Yamamoto, Shichihei: Ursprünge der japanischen Arbeitsethik. In: Barloewen/ Werhahn-Mees 1986:95-129.

Chapter 11
Forms of Thought

This chapter explains how cultures – and the habitats where they are to be found – shape people's thinking in their logic and their conceptualizing; and why racial differences ought not to be equated with differences in intellectual abilities. The chapter gives significant examples of the considerable differences in the world-view of different cultures, differences in their learning styles, their concepts of quantity and measurement, their orientation in time and space, and their attitude to planning.

On the basis of how complex their own culture is, many Europeans incline to the view that people of foreign cultures are not intellectually on their level. They casually make this comment about members of pre-literate (or only recently literate) ethnic groups, often in the same breath – strangely – as their further claim that the groups are living ideal lives protecting the environment. Europeans who think like this explain the paradox in terms of biology. They deduce that *racial differences* signify differences in mental and moral capacity, in intelligence and character. What is more, this same fundamental attitude characterised the beginnings of academic ethnology. Occasionally this mindset re-emerges, even today.

Whenever mention was made in the past to people in pre-literate societies they were known as *primitives*. This meant that their intellectual and personal make-up was held to be somewhat animal-like. It was, of course, conceded that certain intellectual abilities were more advanced than with so-called *civilised people*, for example their ability to sense things, their faculties of sight, hearing and orientation, as one might observe in intelligent animals. At the same time however, it was agreed that their logic – their ability to imagine and remember and draw deductions – was limited. The natives were held to be naïve and childlike in their feelings, and were, naturally, impulsive and not in a position to free themselves from their immediate material needs to strive for "higher things".

What was not known then was the fact that the way people think, feel and wish is substantially tied to the culture they use to shape their existence. Set against the background of European-Western cultures the so-called primitives were bound to appear intellectually and spiritually challenged, and their behaviour, norms and values were inevitably classed as abnormal.

This is also the case the other way round, as we know these days; development workers and church workers, but particularly tourists of whatever sort, often create quite an impression on the inhabitants of foreign societies – also seeming naïve, childlike, arrogant and lacking in imagination. Their emotional and intellectual make-up comes across as puzzling; the locals question whether they are dealing with right-thinking people at all.

It is wrong to claim that people in pre-literate societies are unable by their biological make-up to think logically or make deductions, or think creatively; it is wrong to suppose they are without insight and incapable of recognising mistakes, or of drawing conclusions, or of unscrambling dead-end thinking and sterile arguments. The fact that they appear like this does not just stem from the false conclusions we draw if we take their behaviour out of its particular cultural framework, and interpret it in the light of some other, alien, framework. We can also come to wrong judgements by not distinguishing between a person's mental/emotional capacity and a person's scope for fulfilling this potential, given the constraints determining his life, in the form of social and cultural structures.

When one has seen how adults in South American Indian ethnic groups seldom stimulate creative thinking – or even creative play – in their children, it is no longer surprising that children's cognitive abilities do not develop in the same way as in Europe.

An ethnic group's environment does not require a routine of stockpiling where this would be contrary to common sense (for example in a planter culture where vegetation grows throughout the year). In this case the people cannot be expected to show any interest in having a savings account when – as part of their country's economic "development" – they find themselves in a few years facing a cash economy they have to come to terms with.

When Europeans are critical of these circumstances they usually emphasise the irrational element that is undoubtedly at work here. Because it jumps out at them, Europeans emphasise the irrational element as a lack of logic and as a sign of an inability to perceive things that are self-evident in "civilised" societies. This criticism overlooks the fact that circumstances are not always as straightforward as they seem from a European-Western perspective.

It has been claimed that so-called primitive thinking is in fact fixed and orderly. The French psychologist and philosopher Lévy-Bruhl (1857-1939) posited in his writings a "law of mystical participation" at work in primitive peoples. He meant by this that they were only interested in the mystical aspect as the true essence of things; they could not distinguish between themselves and objects. For this reason he supposed that their thinking was "prelogical".

Today we know that describing an ethnic group's thinking in these terms is superficial, *eurocentric* and speculative. The corresponding judgements are prejudices because they have been formed before experiencing the true situation; they are groundless misrepresentations.

Indeed on closer inspection one can spot "prelogical" behaviour (whatever that may mean) in modern civilisation as well, without much effort. What, for example, is rational about driving in fog at 100 m.p.h. with 10 yards' visibility, when fatal multiple pile-ups are the consequence? And what is logical about the rampant individualism of societies excessively promoting the rights of the individual and his self-centred ambitions? This reaches the point where the state's ability to conduct communal affairs becomes nil, as we see increasingly in the mass democracies of the West.

Extreme examples are often brought up as proofs for "primitive" thinking: a bow and arrow seems at first glance to be hopelessly inferior to a machine gun. Who among sophisticated people using a machine gun would be in a position to manufacture a bow and arrow, or simply use it to acquire food? In addition, this argument would not take into account an important time aspect: if this kind of hunting is primitive then our own ancestors who used these weapons were also primitive.

In every period and in every conceivable environment people have made their lives possible and secure by developing strategies, techniques and thought structures. Sometimes these have been quite astounding. Consider the skills shown by Polynesian, Micronesian and Melanesian seafarers (Lewis 1975). The same is true in the realm of the abstract: the mythology and metaphysics of the Maoris of New Zealand or the religion of the ancient Egyptians are examples of the rich prowess of such imagination and thinking.

This cannot be appreciated without reference to the purpose it serves, or without considering the environment where all this happens and has an impact. A European's knowledge and technology are quite ill-suited to an expedition for food in the Arctic or the Kalahari desert. Seen like this the circumstances are reversed: the cultures of European-Western civilisation appear primitive in these conditions; by contrast the Inuit people and Pygmies are developed and superior.

Cultural sophistication, therefore, cannot be equated with the presence or absence of mental or moral abilities; nor is it a prerequisite for effective learning of skills and for ingenuity. The fact that we Europeans can learn how a bow and arrow are made and used is also valid without reservation the other way round, even for members of pre-literate cultures.

Cultures and their products arise, as we have seen, through the prevailing environmental conditions. A combustion engine can only be developed where the following environmental factors apply: metal, chemicals, electricity; what is also needed is expertise acquired in various other branches of knowledge which occur only at a later date – often quite fortuitously – and result in a recognizably meaningful link with what is to be processed as a new venture. It would be absurd to assume that living in an environment lacking the relevant conditions (or even just the requirements for them) makes people intellectually less capable. To argue this would be tantamount to stating that Africans are incapable of inventing a car engine just because they have not invented it. I would consider it a significant misrepresentation if somebody pronounced that I was not capable of learning Chinese because I had never in my life learnt it. What people have actually achieved cannot serve as a yardstick to determine what they are capable of as a whole.

Much of the technology that we Europeans possess has actually been invented beforehand by so-called primitive peoples, often thousands of years before. We have just developed it, refined it and put it to special use: the wheel, pet animals, the calendar, the week (invented by the Chinese), the regular communal cleaning day (invented by the Swabians), paper, and much else.

Differences in mental characteristics are not marks of racial differences. These days we know that all living human beings belong to the species *homo sapiens* and that the biological differences distinguishing the races are so minimal that they can be left out of the equation. They amount to under 1%.

The mental aptitudes possessed by people of different races are in actual fact so moulded by the process of enculturation that they can only be compared after much analysis. Differences in mental aptitudes can only be determined reliably if the subjects themselves are equal in terms of their human interests and motivation. This is why a meaningful comparison can only emerge within the same culture and within a limited geographical area. The study by Krebs on intentional and implicit education, 2004, makes a useful contribution to this topic.

One of the most important differences in the ways of thinking between European-Western and pre-literate cultures resides in the *type of learning* which underpins their knowledge and learning strategies. European-Western oriented learning is basically *institutionalised* learning. In ethnic societies the learning is *functional*. In specific terms, we Europeans attend school where learning procedures are systematically organised, where the content is divided into graduated steps, and where practice is preceded or followed by a theoretical stage. Learning through observation and imitation, hence functional learning, is also of course a process which we use; but it is integral to the learning institution and is perceived as complementary.

This is not the case in pre-literate cultures. There, functional learning is by and large the only principle, and there are consequences from this. Learning in this setting is understood as an accumulation and summation of knowledge: facts and processes, feats of memorising and other skills, all of which are relevant to the immediate needs of the world at hand. The European-Western way of institutionalised learning tends much more towards thinking logically and drawing conclusions. This is valued as a skill in its own right.

It has been shown that institutionalised, graduated and schematic learning leads to a person being able to solve a theoretical or a practical problem in familiar situations; and not only there, but also to manage in completely new situations occurring unexpectedly. A person who has learnt how to think in a connected, logical way can more readily identify the principle behind any problem unfamiliar to him thus far; he also knows he needs to find the principle to find an answer. This is more of a challenge for a person who has only learnt these processes through their function or by rote.

In pre-literate societies learning and knowledge are seldom cultivated for their own sake but more for their immediate application. The topic to be learnt is reduced to its essentials, because in that way simpler and more plausible explanations can be found. This is evident in the *worldview* of pre-literate societies. It is similar to the worldview our ancestors held until quite late in the Middle Ages: the earth as a flat disc with the sky overhead as a hemisphere.

Thought forms as strategies for coping with existence are strongly related to an ethnic group's natural world and are geared to what their people need. *Number systems* are often limited to what is strictly necessary. The Asheninca, an Amazonian Indian ethnic group, know no other quantities than "nought", "one", "two" and "many". (Where schooling is available they learn the corresponding Spanish words and, of course, the extended number concept).

The decimal system is not used worldwide. For more straightforward purposes the duodecimal number system, which was previously the norm in the West (dozen, the twelve-hour day, etc.), was much more convenient, because twelve is divisible by more numbers (1,2,3,4,6,12) than ten (1,2,5,10).

The *systems for measurement* are related to the human body: an inch (twelfth part of a foot), a hand width, a span (the stretch from thumb tip to little finger), cubit (elbow to tip of middle finger), and so on. The outrigger boats of the Pacific peoples were built by specialists using their own body measurements. The results are thus hand-made in an individual sense.

Greater *distances* are measured in terms of how long it takes a person to walk, for example a day's journey.

Direction of travel is related to rivers where they occur: upstream, downstream. On Pacific islands places are considered "seawards" or "landwards". The four cardinal points, familiar to Westerners, are not known everywhere; and where they occur the concept is sometimes rather different. South Sea islanders go "up East" and "down West", "into South" and "out North". In Nepal there are ethnic groups which consider their own territory as "above", but the rest of the world as "below". When speaking to European and American visitors returning to their countries a Nepalese will enquire politely when they might be "coming up" again, meaning coming back to Nepal.

The differences between European-Western cultures and pre-literate ones are particularly great with regard to the *concept of time*. Time already presents an interesting structure within our own thinking, by seeming to indicate through our idiom that time, a point of time or a regular fixed appointment, moves towards people, such that we say: "Spring is coming". Time can, however, be conceived as standing still, with people moving towards a period or an event, such that we say: "We are getting nearer to Christmas".

Since history in our thinking plays a bigger role and of course is institutionalised as a taught subject, the idea is established that events follow in a straight line. This sequencing can be called a *linear* interpretation of history. In pre-literate cultures without the knowledge of greater historical perspective (people just are more knowledgeable on what occurred within the last two or three generations) this linear concept of history does not emerge to the same extent. There, one is more conscious that the world in which people live is indeed always altering, but that after a year it is just as it was twelve months before. In addition, certain events such as the Spring festival or Harvest occur at regular intervals to give an annual "round of events", a pattern based on a *cyclical* concept of time.

Furthermore, in pre-literate cultures the smaller time periods are not as nuanced as in the West: There are no hours, minutes or seconds. People reckon time using periods of the day: darkness, dawn, morning with its pleasant temperature, the heat of the noonday, etc. If people are arranging a time to meet they do this with reference to where the sun will be in the sky, often indicating with their arm a particular angle to the horizontal.

By and large people of pre-literate societies are only sensitive to time in a very indirect way. Unlike Europeans, they are much more clearly *sensitive to the requirements of the event*. A meeting or a church service does not begin at a particular time (even if this is stated!), but only when all the participants are there, or when it has stopped raining. Correspondingly, the event is only finished when everything has been said and done, when participants are hungry, or when the sun is about to set.

We **time-conscious** Europeans often have quite a curious impact on event-oriented local workers if we say "It's time to go and eat". A phrase like this causes great jollity, because locals eat when they are hungry, when there is food available, or when they reckon that the work is rather irksome and one could profitably do something else. For event-oriented people it might be considered unreasonable for an inter-city express to arrive two minutes past the full hour or to depart without waiting for passengers who have been delayed.

This thought framework often causes us time-preoccupied Europeans great stress, because we are programmed to suppose that time and rate of work determine the productivity we hope to achieve. It is indisputable that there is no way of by-passing some alteration to the event-oriented framework of thinking if ethnic groups – in which pre-literate cultures still determine the pace of life (or did so until recently) – today want changes or improvements, for example schooling or a functioning traffic system or a workable economy. Without a shift of orientation from event focus to time focus these things simply cannot be achieved.

A culture's orientation towards a time focus or an event focus is in direct relation to a further feature distinguishing very clearly those who belong to European-Western societies from those who belong to pre-literate cultures: the requirement for any enterprise to be **planned**; the more people involved in the project and the more complex the expectations, the more detailed and thorough the planning needs to be.

As a rule, we Europeans plan a venture from beginning to end, including its finance and the time involved, because the sooner the goal is achieved the lower the costs. There may sometimes be several alternatives, in case things go differently from planned.

An important aspect of European-Western ways of planning is evident when during the course of the project itself a significant unforeseen event occurs to thwart its outcome. From that moment on the whole plan is revised including the cost and time calculations. This, of course, is also true of building a house, just as much as for a scientific expedition.

In all this planning, the time dimension is a significant one, since it can easily become the cause for all manner of stress and nervousness, for sleepless nights and heart attacks.

Peoples of pre-literate cultures are quite different in their preoccupations. When they know what they want, they begin with the means at their disposal. If during house-building some material (or the money for it) runs out, the work comes to a standstill until the remainder is available

again. Nobody mentions a time-scale. Between the idea and its imple-
mentation there is a long period of improvising; this also leads to the outcome, but one without a foreseeable schedule. Gladwin (1964) has drawn
attention to an interesting example.

This way of doing things does indeed spare the nerves of those involved, because it happens without agitation. For a mixed team comprising locals and Europeans it is mostly unwelcome as a source of stress and
constant discord, even serious conflicts. These can only be avoided if
both parties are able to summon a greater degree of patience than would
be needed in a one-culture team.

More detailed introductions to this chapter's topic:

Publications on the topic of time: Gell 1992 contains numerous contributions. Wienecke 1992 holds particular interest for missionaries.

More on the topic of this chapter can be found in the following studies:

Barnett, Homer G.: Innovation: the basis of cultural change. New York et
al. 1953.

Egli, Werner; Krebs, Uwe (Hg.): Beiträge zur Ethnologie der Kindheit.
Erziehungswissenschaftliche und kulturvergleichende Aspekte. Münster 2004.

Gell, Alfred: The anthropology of time. Cultural constructions of temporal maps and images. Oxford Providence 1992 (1996).

Gladwin, Thomas: Culture and logical process. In: Goodenough
1964:167-177.

Goodenough, W. Hunt: Explorations in cultural anthropology. Essays in
honor of George P. Murdock. New York et al. 1964.

Hallpike, C. R.: The foundations of primitive thought. Oxford 1979.

Krebs, Uwe: Erzogen ohne Erziehung? Vom Nutzen impliziter Erziehung
und der Bedeutung der Ethnologie für die Erziehungswissenschaft. In:
Egli/Krebs 2004:21-41.

Lewis, David: We, the navigators. The ancient art of landfinding in the
Pacific. Honolulu 1975.

Wienecke, Werner A.: Die Bedeutung der Zeit in Afrika in den traditionellen Religionen und in der missionarischen Verkündigung. Frank-
furt/Main, Berlin, Bern, New York, Paris, Vienna 1992.

Chapter 12
Culture and Language

This chapter explains how languages should be seen as systems within cultures; not just as systems for communicating between speakers, but also – on the basis of their typical grammatical structures – for approaching and representing those things, processes and characteristics that are part of the surrounding cultures. The chapter deals with the issue of what links there are between language, thought and reality, and with the fact that thought and logic are impossible without language. The chapter also explains how linguistic structures influence the form that concepts take, and how the concepts, once formed, impact on the perceptions and actions of the language user.

Of all the component areas that make up a culture there are two by which people define themselves in a manner that gives them pride of place. Of the two, it is the *language* of a culture that is the most significant element for the group members, by which they consider each another "equal" and identify foreigners as "different". (The other significant area is their *religion*, which I shall treat in the next two chapters.) In conversation with Swabian villagers one can occasionally hear references to the fact that people in the next village pronounce certain words differently or refer to an item using a completely different word. Their comments imply that people from the neighbouring village are to be somehow earmarked as "different".

Language is in fact one element which – unlike virtually any other – gives various cultures their characteristic permanent hallmark; this is all the more significant if the languages have been given particular scripts, as in the cultures of South Asia and East Asia.

Languages are far more than elements characterising a culture. They actually form complex structures within which the culture is encapsulated and mapped out. Languages do not just help their speakers understand one another, as a superficial perspective might suggest. Nowadays we know that languages are the fullest automatic and unconscious facets of their particular cultures (Beer 2003:63-64). Yet we know more, namely that they influence and shape human thinking to such an extent that we can justifiably claim that a particular language forces its speakers to perceive and understand the world around them – with its things and events, conditions and features – and pronounce upon them so as to be able to achieve mastery over them. Consequently, as part of the whole strategy for coping with life, language constitutes a tool of great complexity and significance.

Language is not simply a vehicle for thought. Many people consider that thinking and logic are identical in all peoples, and independent of language: they think that it is just the sound of languages and the words that are different and unfamiliar, but that the meanings of the words are the same. This belief is only true in a very limited way. On the basis of numerous studies into languages of very different cultures, we now know with certainty that on the one hand languages are the expression of the most varied forms of thinking, and on the other hand that languages create through their particular structures a great range of forms of thinking in those who learn to speak them (or have to speak them) as their mother tongue. This was the proposition made by scholars in the European Renaissance, but it was Wilhelm von Humboldt (1767-1835) who finally clarified it. For a long time afterwards his ideas were not properly acknowledged, because – for one thing – general linguistics was only able to establish at the beginning of the twentieth century the methods which led people to recognise the pioneering value of Humboldt's initiatives. In particular, two Americans, Edward Sapir (1884-1939) and Benjamin Lee Whorf (1897-1941), both ethnologists and linguists, took up Humboldt's ideas on the link between language and worldview and made them the object of their research. In the *Sapir-Whorf hypothesis* they triggered a world-wide debate among scholars; this was not achieved without acrimony, but it eventually enriched ethnology by a method called "*cognitive anthropology*" (cf. chap. 19).

During their study of the languages of American Indians, Sapir and his student Whorf had established that speakers understood and spoke about certain environmental phenomena in quite a different way from speakers of English or other Indo-European languages. Whorf noticed, for example, that Hopi Indians in the South West of the United States conceived of the terms "lightning" and "wave" not as phenomena but as processes, of short duration; he ascertained that Hopi speakers did not describe them using nouns as in Indo-European languages, but using verbal word forms. Whorf drew his conclusions in line with Humboldt's thinking.

If one compares the means and processes that enable natural phenomena such as "lightning" and "wave" to be represented in the grammatical system of the Hopi people and speakers of Indo-European languages, it is immediately noticeable that in this example the same human perceptions have been *classified* in different ways, in the one system as things and in the other as processes.

If languages are examined using these criteria, and a sufficient number of relevant phenomena are compared according to the principle of clustering examples, it is then obvious that language forms an *organising system* by means of which people label their experiences with connotations in the broadest and most elementary sense; they do so by classifying things, processes, features, circumstances and conditions under concepts, and they build these associations into a conceptual structure.

The system that emerges organises its elements not according to a large number of criteria, but to just a few. This does entail some limitation, but it ensures careful handling of the reduced capacities of human linguistic ability and memory.

Language as a classification system functions not only in the one direction where what was (originally passively) perceived takes on a meaningful connotation. When the things perceived, the processes, features, circumstances and conditions have been conceptually organised – and thus have become parts of a language system – they appear so meaningful to us that when we talk we give them no further active thought. For a European "lightning flashes" and "waves" are now natural phenomena, for a Hopi Indian they are processes, so self-evidently and largely unconsciously that neither would consider querying the matter. Where the need arises for them each to exchange information about perceptions there can be difficulties of mutual comprehension.

Indeed, the words of a language have the ability to confer upon reality perceived through senses a characteristic form in the human brain, or at least an ability to confer certain qualities which they as words would not have without language. By the fact that "lightning" and "wave" in English and related languages like German are termed "substantives" or "nouns" they take on the nature of things. This is known as the *hypostatising effect* of the substantive category. Because this effect is largely anchored in the subconscious its ramifications are hard to grasp; they cause a significant problem by sometimes preventing real links from being recognised over a sustained period, or even preventing any recognition at all. The following is a demonstration of this.

Because substantives in English or German mostly refer to things, the converse applies: speakers perceive the reality-elements (to which they refer using substantives) primarily as things; this is the consequence of hypostatising. We have seen from the Hopi language example of "lightning" and "wave" that this cannot necessarily be seen as the absolute "correct" interpretation of reality.

The same hypostatising effect could be the reason why chemistry and physics in their infancy were convinced for several centuries that "heat" was a substance, because the phenomenon was described using a noun. This may well have delayed the understanding that heat "in reality" (in the sense of physically) constitutes a particular scenario where atoms and molecules move around, and behaves quite differently from a substance. In this example language is describing the "real" circumstances in a distorted way, such that blind alleys in the history of researching into heat were inevitable.

Whorf's studies in this area and his thoughts on the consequences of the various options open to humans in verbalizing their experience of the world led him to formulate the ***principle of linguistic relativity*** as it is known these days:

"We are thus introduced to a new principle of relativity, which holds that all observers are not led by the same physical evidence to the same picture of the universe, unless their linguistic backgrounds are similar, or can in some way be calibrated" (in Carroll, 2000, p. 214).

During the course of my own field research in ethnology I have experienced various striking examples of Whorf's principle of linguistic relativity influencing people's thinking.

The inhabitants of the Chuuk islands say *"kinissow"* when they thank somebody for a present. A European might conclude that it means "thank you". Yet the islanders also say *"kinissow"* when they say sorry. In a specific situation like that the word cannot mean "thank you", and conversely the first situation cannot give rise to the need to say "sorry", because one doesn't excuse oneself when receiving a gift.

In ethnographical reports dating up to the 1950s observations on this phenomenon are not infrequent. They tend to assert that "the natives" are not able to think "logically", that they express themselves unsystematically with no logical grasp of reality. These days we know that our conclusions need to be quite different.

The Chuuk islanders use the same word for two situations which are profoundly different for us Europeans, or which even seem to have nothing in common. Yet because the islanders can use the same word in both situations we must accept that for them these situations have features which are identical or similar and which thus offer parallels. We foreigners first need to make an effort to discover this overlap which is all too obvious for the islanders: namely that on the Chuuk islands a person receiving a gift feels obliged towards the giver, just as though he has done somebody a wrong. This is the overlapping feature in the situations which justifies the use of the word *"kinissow"*.

We should nevertheless be cautious about applying this principle, because it is not always the case that two "different" situations present common features just because they share the same vocabulary. We can "get over" (cross) a river, "get over" (convey) a meaning and "get over" (overcome) a sorrow. In other contexts there are identical words which have arisen by chance during the development of a language and which would, without closer attention, inevitably lead to misinterpretations. (Two examples: a Hamburger is either a native of Hamburg, or a fast food with or without ham. A Beefeater is a guard or tour guide at the Tower of London, who may or may not be a vegetarian, despite the suggestive origin of his name). To find common links between the two would be beside the point.

Behind the fact that processes and things are typically considered separate categories lies a principle valid for all languages. Because nothing here can be predicted, a foreigner finds language learning more difficult if he is not alerted to this phenomenon, because understanding among people is harder if they are speaking a common language but have very different mother-tongue backgrounds. Difficulties in understanding arise often enough even when the speakers know the language very well. On the other hand the learner's inability to predict combinations of concepts often results in joy at such delightful surprises, once he has reached a particular level in the language he is committed to acquiring.

One does not need to search beyond the European languages to experience such delights. In French a dog's paw or a cat's paw is "patte", but the French designation is wider in its application: even to elephants and horses; also to flies and fleas (where English says "leg"). In English the attribution of "paw" is restricted to the soft foot (not "leg") of a clawed animal, such as a dog, a cat and a monkey. At the end of their legs English elephants have feet – and horses have hooves!

The fact that languages (and therefore cultures) group their concepts differently and often unpredictably has further implications for language learning. Only in a few instances are the groups predefined by nature – only seldom are they justifiable rationally. Most have arisen with the particular language systems and the indigenous speaker is unaware of them. In order to speak intelligibly it is not enough to learn vocabulary and use it. In addition to mastering the sounds and grammar and writing, the foreign learner must learn the conceptual grouping if he wishes to convey meaning that his listener can recognise. He has to go about things differently from the way he did at school.

At school he kept a vocabulary book for the supposed "word pairs"; "patte" = "paw". This matching is only correct for a restricted range of reality (dogs, cats and monkeys). In the wider language jungle of all possible situations for "patte" (elephants and horses, flies and fleas, etc.) the boundaries do not match.

The mismatch increases as the degree of family relationship decreases. (French and English are both Indo-European languages, and yet distinctiveness is already apparent!) Thus foreign languages must be taught fundamentally differently from the "word matching" method when it comes to semantics and "acquiring vocabulary". How this can be done is not easy to explain in a few words, but I shall endeavour to do so.

Let us suppose that an English person learning French is trying to understand the meaning of "la patte". He has perhaps heard of the word in the context of a dog's "leg". If he is an inexperienced language learner he might then apply the French word to a table leg, and cause general amusement (which is the usual extent of success with word matching!) The learner would make proper progress if he asked somebody what things and creatures had "pattes". Then, gradually, he would collect the animals, i.e. would circumscribe the concept associated with the word, and would then be able to use it "appropriately", just like a French mother-tongue speaker.

This method is useful not just for vocabulary learning, but for learning the concepts and the wider culture that the language belongs to. Thomas and Elizabeth Brewster (1977) and Ursula Wiesemann (1992) have written fluent and lucid books on how language can be learnt using these criteria. The authors elaborate on how the issue can best be tackled in a non-European situation. Those interested in ethnology would also profit from reading the book by Robbins Burling (1984).

Whorf's principle of linguistic relativity, which is properly acknowledged in the Brewsters' book, is not without its critics. What is interesting is the observation that the linguistics researchers who fail to see a deep and consistent relationship between language, thought and reality are not ethnologists. Among those who support this relationship there are a sizeable number of ethnologists, especially those coming to similar conclusions as Whorf via their own studies into non-Indo-European languages (Gipper 1972:77-78). I, too, became a staunch defender of the Sapir-Whorf hypothesis during my many years of field work in linguistics and ethnology in Micronesia. The following was one key experience.

To tackle the language of the archipelago where I was working I had been compiling a list of words I had recently learned relating to the human body, i.e. the vocabulary of anatomy and physiology. My purpose was to investigate its structure and the general concept of "body" as represented in the islanders' thinking (Käser 1989). While working on the breathing process I came across a word which did not mean much to me, but which proved to be my entry point for understanding a striking and unexpected conceptual relationship. The word was *ngasangas* and it occurred regularly in situations to do with breathing.

One morning I was standing at the jetty in the village where I lived. I was chatting to some locals. Suddenly one of them pointed down to a splendid umbrella jellyfish which swam past us pulsating as it pushed onward. I heard a short phrase which included the word *ngasangas*, which surprised me because jellyfish, in my experience, did not "breathe" like this. I asked a precise question or two and soon had two contexts, i.e. two acceptable, correct sentences in the local language, which then revealed a further surprise. They were in translation "a jellyfish swims" and "a person breathes". In the language of the Chuuk islands the two sentences were *emén nimmaatong aa ngasangas* and *emén aramas aa ngasangas*. My astonishment can be appreciated as soon as the underlined parts are compared: complete matching, quite unlike the Indo-European versions. Up to then I had always felt and understood a person's breathing and the pulsating movements of a jellyfish to be entirely separate. So I was not ready to hear somebody explain the two processes with the same word.

I was suddenly made aware that the reason for the same term was to be found in the rhythmic movement of each process, but I only managed to recognise this by encountering a linguistic structure.

Thinking about it later, I realised that the islanders do not use the word *ngasangas* just for the rhythmic rising and lowering of the chest, but also for the heartbeat; the matter then took on a dramatic dimension. When I asked the people I was with where the breathed-in air went to, each one said without exception that it went to the heart. Nobody, it turned out, made a link with the lungs, which – significantly – they call "sponges".

That was still not the end of it. When I finally asked what kind of illness coughing, asthma and pneumonia were, and when again everybody said without hesitation that they were all heart diseases, I was convinced that I had hit upon unshakeable evidence for Whorf's principle of linguistic relativity.

The fact that the islanders conceived of asthma as a disease of the heart might sometimes have a consequence, as follows. Let us assume that a nurse development worker from Europe is training indigenous nurses. Let us also assume that one day an emergency patient comes in suffering from an acute asthma attack and requires immediate help. The European health worker intends giving an asthma injection, so asks the local worker to get the medicine. She rushes off and gets a heart medicine, which in her own view is a sensible choice. Because neither person in their hurry asks a question or even checks the wording on the dosage, the patient is bound to die. The mistake occurred because of a difference in the mind-maps reflected in the two languages.

The example is hypothetical. But I assume that the enormous problems in development aid with its astronomic waste of money and materials have arisen at least as often through misunderstandings of this kind. It would be worth investigating.

Further surprises were in store for me. I worked through the physiology of the breathing process and how it becomes speech with one of my informants, Namiyo. At first he said, just like all the others I had spoken to, that the breathed air goes into the heart. When I then asked him whether he had ever noticed when slaughtering a pig that the airways did not go into the heart but into the lungs he interrupted me on the spot and said that he had indeed often been surprised at this. He had assumed that pigs were different, and that nevertheless breath generally ends up in the heart.

This observation is significant in many respects. Namiyo had discovered that in reality the breathing passages work differently from the way he and people generally assume to be correct. He was puzzled by this and could also recognize the inherent contradiction and express it. Remarkably, he obviously could not fully accept the situation that he had often observed as reality, because the concepts, the "theory" that he and all others held about it, were at odds with observable reality.

Namiyo cannot have been the first to be struck by the contradiction in the nature of things; there must have been many other islanders before him. So what had led to so many maintaining the theory, even though it was contrary to their perceived reality? The reasons are quite clearly to do with language; the linguistic concept had prevented a theory from being overturned, and continues to do so. The breathing process and the heartbeat have been illustrated by the same word *ngasangas*, and this association has been influential in maintaining the concept that breathing involves the heart and not the lungs.

Of course a linguistic configuring like this does not inevitably lead to misunderstandings, as we have seen. The fact that "block" in English means an impediment, or a group of flats, or a building brick does not mean that people will inevitably confuse their meanings. Even in the language of the Chuuk islands there are many words which on the basis of a single common characteristic may yet mean several "different" things, without giving rise to confusion. Indeed the semantic features of the word *ngasangas* have resulted in false conclusions uncorrected over a considerable period, even though the most tangible experience of reality would deem it otherwise: my informant was puzzled that reality as he saw it did not match up with generally accepted "theory", but was yet very happy to espouse his home-grown "theory".

In studies of the links between language and reality it is always emphasised that the repercussions of linguistic structure on people's perception of reality are considered slight because, primarily, it is reality which has given the structures of human languages their form; this is because reality existed prior to the advent of linguistic structures. But this argument is not valid here with our example; quite the reverse. *Ngasangas* shows how a concept has led to opinions which counter reality, and it also shows how a concept can maintain the thinking. On the basis of thought patterns like these, Micronesians are reluctant to acknowledge that observable phenomena in this realm of human perception indeed constitute the reality.

It must be borne in mind, with some reservation, that this of course has serious consequences only in rather spontaneous speech. Nobody is so at the mercy of the structures of his language that he cannot come to appreciate the actual context, even when this is contracted by linguistic structures. It has been obvious for centuries that the pattern of day following night occurs because of the earth's rotation. Nevertheless we still say that the sun "rises and sets"; nobody is thereby prevented from understanding the full reality. This includes the Micronesians, of course. However, what is relevant for them from the linguistic structure of *ngasangas* is the fact at least that their language is pre-structuring the perception of reality in a way that may lead to wrong assumptions. A Micronesian child acquiring the language of his human environment takes on its thought patterns without being able to consider alternatives. In the example of *ngasangas* a child is exposed to these structures immediately and thus learns a false interpretation of the reality adhering to this word. Language is clearly the primary lens, the filter, by which reality has to be discerned. I am convinced that the same is true, *mutatis mutandis*, for a child growing up in Europe.

From what I have said thus far it follows that what we might term the surface of conceptual structures can be observed in language structures: these language structures help us, as it were, to describe and analyse conceptual structures. But what also emerges is that development aid workers and church workers serving overseas must be challenged not only to use the language of the local people they are working with but also to learn to examine the conceptual structures conveyed by the language. Surprisingly, this is expected of church workers (missionaries) more than of doctors and nurses, although both groups alike must be in a position to understand how people of foreign cultures depict the world in their minds, and how the things in their world find their rightful place. It is not until a person masters a language along these lines that he can make himself understood as a foreigner and thus work effectively.

The many and varied close links between culture and language – this needs saying for the sake of completeness at the end of the chapter – are the business of what English and American scholars call *anthropological linguistics* or *linguistic anthropology* (and Germans call *Ethnolinguistik*). There are two important introductory studies by Duranti 1997 and by Foley 1997. Senft 2003 gives a brief overview of the discipline.

More on the topic of this chapter can be found in the following studies:

Beer, Bettina: Ethnos, Ethnie, Kultur. In: Beer/Fischer 2003(a):53-72.

Beer, Bettina; Fischer, Hans (Hg.): Ethnologie. Einführung und Überblick. Berlin 2003(a).

Brewster, E. Thomas; Brewster, Elizabeth S.: LAMP. Language acquisition made practical. Field methods for language learners. Colorado Springs 51977.

Burling, Robbins: Learning a field language. Ann Arbor, Michigan 1984.

John B. Carroll (ed.): Language, thought, and reality: selected writings of Benjamin Lee Whorf; with an introduction by John B. Carroll; 25. print. Cambridge, Mass.: MIT Press, 2000.

Duranti, Allessandro: Linguistic anthropology. Cambridge 1997.

Foley, William A.: Anthropological linguistics. An Introduction. Oxford 1997.

Gipper, Helmut: Gibt es ein sprachliches Relativitätsprinzip? Untersuchungen zur Sapir-Whorf-Hypothese. Frankfurt am Main 1972.

Käser, Lothar: Die Besiedlung Mikronesiens: eine ethnologisch-linguistische Untersuchung. Berlin 1989.

Senft, Gunter: Ethnolinguistik. In: Beer/Fischer 2003(a):254-270.

Whorf, Benjamin Lee: Sprache, Denken, Wirklichkeit. Beiträge zur Metalinguistik und Sprachphilosophie. Reinbek bei Hamburg 1963 (and later).

Wiesemann, Ursula (ed.): Verstehen und verstanden werden. Praktisches Handbuch zum Fremdsprachenerwerb. Lahr/Schwarzwald 1992. (The author was on the staff of Wycliffe Bible Translators, as head of the language learning department).

Chapter 13
Religion

This chapter explains what it means when people act in a religious way, relating to the "holy" and ascribing a sacred and a profane realm to it in their world, their environment and their time. The chapter explains that religion delivers a system whereby the cosmos can be shaped into a worldview at whose centre stands a picture of man as an autonomous being. As a result, religiously motivated strategies (such as initiating relationships with higher powers; rituals; etc.) can be drawn up to overcome the problems of daily life, and answers can be found to the issue about human existence continuing beyond death.

13.0 Introduction

Religion, the second cultural area in which people identify one another as similar or different, is just as complicated and all-embracing as language. It forms a similar high-level classification system within the individual culture and is one of the most significant auxiliary strategies people employ to shape and master their existence.

In humankind's various forms of religion there are two opposing but also interrelated aspects of reality, embracing space, time, being, things, processes and characteristics: the *holy* or *sacred*, and the *profane*. With the help of the concept of holy – which in all religions typically seems distinct from the profane – the realms of the *supernatural* are known and structured, and made available to human thinking and feeling. Answers are sought to fundamental questions concerning a person's dependency on uncontrollable powers to which he feels a prey, and which he would wish to influence or indeed master. In these particular cultures, the contrasting elements "natural" and "supernatural", so self-evident for a European, are not distinguished.

Religions include strategies for solving a whole lot of life problems, chief of which is the answer to the meaning of death: What is a person to expect when he dies?

Many forms of religion include realms of culture which a European would tend to class as philosophical, scientific, medical, etc.

In pre-literate cultures religion is thus seldom a distinctive, defined issue of life, but is essentially omnipresent and active. In all that they do people try to ensure successful outcomes by offering prayers to their ancestral spirits to gain their blessing; or else they use talismans and amulets to protect an undertaking from harmful influences. Yet people are largely unaware of religion as a *framework for thought*; religion remains a pervasive **background phenomenon.** On this depends not only its great effectiveness, but also its stability in the face of life's vicissitudes: religions are by nature *conservative*, more conservative than other areas of cultural life.

In European-Western cultures on the other hand religion appears as an independent category alongside economics, art, relationships, technology, politics, etc. Its nature as an independent category is evident in the fact that religion becomes visible institutionally, for example in Sunday worship. On the other days of the week scarcely any European behaves in an openly religious way such that his religion would be recognisable. More and more these days religion has become a celebration of festivals at Christmas and Easter when churches are full, or else of an observable *rite of passage,* such as a baptism, a confirmation, a marriage, a funeral or a burial.

The observation that religion in pre-literate cultures is something of a background phenomenon correlates with the fact that hardly any language in a pre-literate culture has a word for the concept of "religion" as a European would understand it. Teachers involved in development aid programmes who have to organise materials for their religious education lessons often struggle for a long time to find a usable term. Words which in the particular languages are used for "religion" sometimes also mean "tradition", "order", "law", "manner of thinking" and even "old-fashioned belief". A religious dimension is, of course, part of all these concepts, but is below the surface.

Even early Indo-European languages did not have a word for it. The Latin word "*religio*" actually means "care" while observing the *omina* (omens or signs) of nature (such as the way an augur viewed the flight of birds), from which the will of higher powers could supposedly be interpreted. The opposite of "*religio*" is "*neglegentia*" (being negligent or careless while watching and heeding the *omina*). Only later did the concept of religion assume the form we are familiar with today. (The derivation of its meaning from the Latin verb "religare" = to fasten, bind to a supernatural authority, is unsatisfactory and has little evidential base.)

One difficulty attaches to religion as an independent concept of European-Western cultures. If we set out to identify in foreign cultures what religion means in our own thinking we often only end up finding part of the whole, because not all areas of our own religion are equally distinctive in foreign manifestations of culture. Therefore we often remain unaware of what other elements also make up religion. The result is that we overlook them because we do not anticipate seeing them. Thus a precondition for successful research in the ethnology of religion is not just a longish experience of living in the society one is studying, but also an above-average knowledge of the language.

Roughly speaking there is a distinction between so-called *high* or *scriptural religions* on the one hand and the *religions of pre-literate societies* on the other. Religions with scriptures usually have one god and are thus *monotheistic* (Islam, Christianity). The religions of pre-literate cultures tend to acknowledge a pantheon of gods, with a so-called *Supreme Being* at their head, which shares some features common to a monotheistic god, but which is distinctive in other respects. But this statement is to be understood as a rough approximation. Concepts of god can vary considerably and must be studied for each culture individually.

It can be stated with some justification that no human grouping exists without some form of religious practice. What we call atheism is a rather rare and individualised phenomenon which only occurs with any consistency in intellectual circles. Those living in pre-literate societies cannot conceive of atheism or godlessness.

Around the world the elements comprising religions vary in their development and expression. In several religions priority is given to belief in miracles. This is generally the case in religions of pre-literate cultures. In the societies of so-called high religions belief in miracles is a mark of the lower classes, or at least of those sections of the population where education and knowledge play a lesser role; or of people who particularly link religion with their emotional life. Examples of these religions range from various charismatic groupings to ecstatic forms of religion and to cults familiar with spirit possession such as *Voodoo*, *Candomblé*, *Macumba*, and *Umbanda* in West Africa and Latin America.

In any population the middle classes are less preoccupied with any belief in miracles than with the *ethical and moral aspects* of their religion. What is uppermost in their minds is what one might call appropriate (decent!) and inappropriate (indecent!) behaviour. Inappropriate behaviour is decried not just for being immoral but for being broadly identified with what the Bible calls sin. In European-Western societies this has consequences for middle-class attitudes to fashion and several forms of entertainment (dancing and stage shows), and consequences for issues surrounding individual work ethic. A person who is hard-working and consistent etc. and can bring morally positive attitudes (virtues) to his work is often considered blessed by God and accepted. This is one of the basic tenets of Calvinism.

The ruling classes, on the other hand, intellectualise their interest in religion and select those aspects which are philosophical in nature. Theological phenomena and the theoretical structure underlying them are the issues debated. There is a tendency for the link between religion and life to get lost.

Religion as a cultural construct can be unusually multi-dimensional, as mentioned before. It can comprise a limitless number of individual phenomena; yet the full range of possibilities is never actually brought to fruition in any particular single religion – hence the enormous differences between the various religions world-wide.

The more general the concepts being compared, the more commonplace are the features they share. Differences are greatest at the most specific level of conceptual thinking. In concrete terms this means that notions of God are revealed to be surprisingly alike, but over something like the issue of sacrifice considerable differences are evident: a comparative study reveals more significant problems of definition and mutual understanding.

One of the areas that various forms of religion frequently share is the belief in the existence and potency of powers over an individual's life, powers that are greater than him. The differences lie in what he believes and holds to be of value, and in the forms of his religious experience and expression.

A more recent introductory survey (Mischung 2003:201) distinguishes three broad areas for religion:

1) notions of existence and the nature of "supernatural" powers,
2) myths,
3) rites.

In his article "Lehrbuch der Völkerkunde" (in Trimborn 1971) Josef Haekel gives a handy breakdown of the issues relating to religion; many of them have been the starting point for areas raised in this chapter. Here is my summary of the most important ones. According to Haekel religion consists of:

1) a person's *notions* about his religion,
2) his *attitudes* towards his ideas,
3) the *actions* that result from 1) and 2).

13.1 Notions

Among the notions an individual has about what his religion comprises is a *worldview*. From this worldview stem explanations for much of what could not be understood without it. A worldview comprises general views about nature and the cosmos; speculations about the nature of things; and attempts to explain rationally the processes pertaining to physics, chemistry and biology. In specific terms this means that in many pre-literate cultures it is accepted that the earth is a flat disc, at the centre of which live human beings, and over which the heavens arch like an up-turned bowl. As proof of this they declare that the distance from the place they are living to the horizon is the same in any direction. This worldview is akin to the one that our forefathers themselves held, right into the Middle Ages and beyond.

Despite its simplicity a worldview like this can highlight interesting features. During my involvement with fieldwork in ethnology and linguistics in Micronesia when I was looking for a word to express "sky" I was faced with a whole range of words. This was at first confusing. An informant told me that the whole space under the hemisphere was "sky" and it began right at the earth's surface.

In some cultures sky is divided into various layers each with its name. (A remnant in English is the phrase "to be in seventh/highest heaven"). This in itself can cause difficulties when translating Christian notions into a similar thought structure and needing to decide which of the many words for sky is appropriate in any particular Bible context.

An Asheninca Indian of the Amazon region once described to me a similar worldview, where the earth is a disc, surrounded by water and with a hemispherical sky. When I asked where on the earth's surface we were standing he said in a confident way "right in the middle". When I asked him to justify his view, he said: "Look, the sky is furthest away from us right overhead!"

Among the Iraya people of the island of Mindoro in the Philippines there is a complex model of the firmament with eight layers, the lowest of which begins at the treetops. Each layer is accorded a specific phenomenon: meteorological ones like cloud formation and rain, birds in flight, heavenly bodies such as sun, moon and stars. Each layer is also the dwelling place of particular spirits.

The layered structure of the hemisphere above the earth quite frequently has its counterpart in the space under the earth. Here dwell spirits having generally hostile and evil intentions towards man; sometimes the spirits of the dead hold sway here, although they usually live as invisible spirits in the world of the living and in the firmament.

Powers whose existence and influence hold sway over us play a dominant role in the realm of human thought. One example of personalising is where spirits, good or bad, are portrayed in human or animal form, are given a name and assigned typical abilities and behaviour. An example of impersonal powers is the force of **mana** ("the unusually effective one") in Pacific island ethnic groups, or the **manitou** ("supernatural power") of North American Indian groups.

Among the ideas to be found in most religions is the central one of a being higher than any other being or thing or process throughout the world: this is the so-called Supreme Being.

In religions having no script the Supreme Being is usually a man, very old and frequently *otiose*[2], i.e. inactive. He mostly lives on the highest level of the firmament, far removed from mankind. If he chooses to intervene in the affairs of the world it is usually through his instructions to spirit beings under the command of the Supreme Being, often the ancestral spirits of men on earth.

The Supreme Being is considered benevolent and wise. However, he can also become angry. Among the most notable features of the Supreme Being is that he has accomplished a heroic feat: (usually) he has created the world – more especially the things of this world accessible to everybody: the sea, water and fire. The act of creation itself is immaterial, like thinking and wishing, or singing and speaking. After creation the Supreme Being lived with humans for a while; then because of their evil he went back into the sky far away. Since then he has had no part in human activities. For this reason people have held him in respect, but have paid him little attention, have not made sacrifices and have hardly even prayed to him. Yet people have indeed been responsive to spirits which are beholden to the Supreme Being.

We need not always suppose that the Supreme Being made the world from nothing. Some religions hold that the world has always been in existence, but that over the course of a *primeval period* it continued to be enhanced and perfected by so-called *primeval beings* or *culture heroes* adding springs and rivers, mountains and seas, until they had imparted the features of the current world.

The names used in relation to the Supreme Being are of interest. He is called the Unknown, the Great Spirit, the Merciful One, the Unique Being, the Embodiment of Self, the Radiant One, the Sublime, etc. (cf. Isaiah 9:5). The emphasis here is on the unfathomable nature of the Supreme Being: compared with humans, he is all-knowing and all-powerful, eternally.

---

[2] The Latin *otiosus* has a broader range of meaning: idle, active as regards knowledge, peaceful, withdrawn, sedate. The Supreme Being is characterised by the meanings "idle" and "withdrawn".

It is not unusual for the Supreme Being to be married, sometimes with several wives; and his offspring are numerous. If he is married he may be portrayed as rain, and his wife as ground made fruitful by the rain. These notions are particularly current in the religion of agriculturalists. Sometimes his offspring are reckoned to be purveyors of culture inventing the technologies and tools of individual cultures: the Supreme Being's daughters bring weaving, singing and dance, and sons bring hunting, fishing and agriculture. Humans have been granted these skills through dreams, or through a love relationship, or else by simply stealing them.

Sometimes in this mythology one of the Supreme Being's offspring is the black sheep of the family, usually a wayward son. He is idle, has designs on women, being well equipped with an overlarge penis and sexual potency. He takes pleasure in staging floods and landslides, volcanic eruptions and other phenomena, and spends his time making all kinds of mischief. He is known to ethnologists as the *trickster*.

The Supreme Being has many features in common with Supreme Gods like Allah or Yahweh, especially in his capacity as creator of the world. Yet an ethnic group's term for its Supreme Being cannot simply be appropriated when it comes to the God of the Bible. A Supreme Being is quite distinct, in significant ways. He is not the God who has sacrificed his son on a cross to rescue mankind. Furthermore, a Supreme Being does not always have the function of a judge before whom people must appear after their death to answer for their actions during their lifetime. If one is wanting to use an indigenous term (one in use by the group's members) then one must be very careful to check what associations people have with it. It is not unusual for many Bible translations to use the (Indo-European) words "God" or "Deus" in a form matching the phonology of the particular language, for example "Koot", "Tios" or similar. Of course, these terms need first to be filled with meaning, a process that may take quite some time; they are, at least, free from the connotations associated with the Supreme Being in the various religions. Nevertheless it should not be expected that introducing a foreign term solves all these related issues.

Among the manifestations of a religion is its mythology. By this is meant either the totality of all the myths that surround a religion, or the (academic) study of myths. *Mythos* in Greek means "saga", "narrative of heroes, spirits or gods." Myths are orally transmitted stories rooted in the worldview of a culture. Their particular function is to give to what cannot be easily explained the form of a story that can be told; narrating these myths gives meaning to the inexplicable and justifies its occurrence. Moreover, myths form a significant portion of an ethnic group's narratives, representing one aspect of its *spoken* ("oral") *literature*. They are, however, determined far more by the religious than by any other area of spoken literature such as songs, riddles, etc. Haekel distinguished the following types:

a) *Cosmogonic myths* tell of the origin of the world or its creation by the Supreme Being or Most High God.

b) *Anthropogonic myths* depict the circumstances surrounding the emergence of human beings, who were either created by the Supreme Being or Most High God, or else were directly the product of creation, from fruits such as coconuts, mushrooms, eggs and many other things.

c) *Primeval myths* deal with events occurring in the period shortly after creation. In Australian cultures this period is known as the *Dreaming*, because it is assumed that the world was then akin to what we experience now only in a dream. During this period the creation as it existed was augmented by powerful, seemingly superhuman ancestors. As they bestrode the earth they created natural features in the landscapes: dominant rocky outcrops (such as Uluru/Ayers Rock), water sources, valleys, caves, etc.

In those times in many cultures the Supreme Being lived on earth with the first humans and their families, mostly until the humans committed a crime. Their punishment was that the Supreme Being withdrew from the human community, or excluded them from fellowship with him. Yet another type of myth deals with the dramatic events linked with this crime.

d) *Transformation myths* tell of drastic events causing a sustained change in the world leading to its present form. The separation from mankind that the Supreme Being set in motion is presented in the myths as the unbridgeable distancing of earth and sky, which originally were so close that humans could reach either realm at any time by means of a ladder or a liana plant. But from that moment on the ladder is tipped over, and the liana is cut back. Thereafter the Supreme Being lives totally separated from mankind.

Transformation myths also include events such as universal floods or conflagrations which result in the earth and creation losing their Paradise status. The catastrophe ushering in the new status amounts to a punishment of humanity for having reached such a degree of corruption that the Supreme Being is forced to intervene.

e) *Myths of the Gods* portray the life, behaviour and destiny of beings who have been fashioned by men but granted superhuman qualities and who quite frequently are seen as offspring of the Supreme Being. Examples of this type of myth are found in the Greek myths (Heracles/Hercules, and Odysseus/Ulysses)

Myths of the Gods often contain accounts of how particular technologies or material elements from their culture were imparted to humans. For example, the Greek demi-god Prometheus stole fire from Olympus and brought it down to earth. By similar means, for example by seed stolen from the sky, humans in other cultures learned how to grow crops. Myths like these are called *aetiological myths* (aetiology = the study of causes).

f) *Nature myths* sometimes have aetiologies like these, for example to explain physical phenomena like lightning (Zeus's weapon), thunder (the hammer-blows of the Germanic god Wotan), the starry firmament (including the man in the moon). Nature myths generally reveal the particular ethnic group's economic life: in the myths relating to hunter-gatherers we have accounts of the origins of wild animals, and the techniques and weapons for hunting them.

g) *Messianic myths* are rather rare. The events they depict lie in the future. They tell of an imminent saviour, of a messiah who is coming to rescue man from his condition that has become unbearable. This condition can be simply economic, such as famine and devastation caused by drought, or political, such as succumbing to a colonial power. Myths like these are the basis for the *movements announcing the hope of salvation* (cargo cults, Chiliasm, Nativism, see chap. 16.)

h) *Eschatological myths* recount future events, such as end-time catastrophes which re-establish the world and creation in its ideal state; here the Supreme Being returns to the world of humans and the dead are resurrected (eschatology = the study of the end of the world and the advent of a divine kingdom). As a category eschatological myths are rather rare.

Fundamental motifs like a universal flood or fratricide are called *mythologems* – the most basic elements of meaning in the myths of countless ethnic groups and cultures.

It is remarkable that there are parallels between the myths of the various cultures and particular accounts in the Old Testament. God brought the world into being by speaking – just one mythologem from the cosmogonic myths. The Fall is an event driving humans from the immediate presence of God – a mythologem from the primeval myths. The universal flood is a consequence of mankind's corruption and an event which altered the world drastically – a mythologem from the transformation myths. The list of parallels can be prolonged effortlessly, but for us here two aspects are of greater significance.

In their teaching, missionaries and other church workers usually seek points of comparison between what the Bible says and the statements of the religions they meet in their work. For them the parallels between the foreign culture's mythology and the biblical accounts above are often welcome opportunities to link indigenous thought patterns and knowledge of religion effectively with the new thinking that workers bring.

This is only possible to a certain extent, but it is more feasible in the isolated case than with general notions of a Supreme Being.

Another issue – a difficult one – is the historical reality of events depicted in mythological accounts. We must, of course, suppose that they have a historical nucleus of some kind or other. But we must also suppose that they have undergone changes through their long oral history before being written down, and that during this period certain details have assumed particular prominence. Undoubtedly, one particular reason for this is that these accounts are meant to make it easier to imagine what is hard to imagine, or indeed unimaginable.

I dare say that the mythological accounts in the Old Testament were given a function similar to that of the parables Jesus used in the New Testament, namely to lend a memorable perspective to the teaching: the events of these parables also occurred outside historical time.

Of course, it would be rather one-sided to classify the relevant Old Testament accounts as pure myths akin to those found in cultures around the world. Jesus himself referred continuously to the Old Testament to support his sayings, and – if I am not mistaken – he quotes everything there as factual. The believer takes to heart what Jesus says about himself in John 14:6. He will not suppose that folk myths are of the same substance and significance as passages from Genesis. This cannot be a definitive answer to the issue of how these accounts are meant to be interpreted – and the issue was raised before the arrival on the scene of Bultmann with his theological pronouncements and his demand for demythologising – because religious truths themselves do not themselves constitute academic evidence.

In addition, religions always imply an *image of humankind*. This starts quite straightforwardly with notions of the human body, its anatomy and physiology, its make-up and functions. These notions may be markedly different from the anatomy and physiology familiar to European-Western science.

Also important are the statements originating from foreign cultures as to the nature of psychological manifestations and of people's intellectual abilities; the statements deal with how people distinguish themselves from animals, how people understand inanimate things, etc. All this needs to be known and included if we are seeking to understand that religions throughout the world in fact deal with strategies relevant in the broadest sense to all life's contexts for all mankind.

Ethnology has not yet processed its research results in this branch of study to the extent that development workers and church workers could benefit from them. It seems to me that not enough attention is being focussed on the image of humankind in the various cultures as is warranted. This neglect is particularly telling in connection with the development of teaching programmes and concepts useful for pedagogy and practice devoted to effective classroom teaching. For countries having a diversity of ethnic groups this provision is especially difficult, but nevertheless vital. At the present, of course, teachers bound for the Third World are still rarely, if ever, given proper training to teach pupils with a wholly different concept of self (cf. particularly chaps. 10 and 14).

13.2 Attitudes

Regarding his religion a person's attitudes are largely the product of the notions he cherishes (see above). By attitudes I mean the intentional and emotional responses to individual elements of belief: reverence, devotion, fear, ethical commitment, striving for control and mastery over powers which are considered to overshadow a person.

Among these attitudes two emotional areas play a particular role: honouring and reverence on the one hand, and dread on the other. These elements are present in so many religions that they are termed, in Latin, *fascinosum* (the awe-inspiring) and *tremendum* (the fear inducing), words that characterize the religious and the holy more generally.

Examples of the fascinosum are the impressions aroused on visiting a Gothic cathedral with its over-powering architecture or on observing a statue of a Thai Buddha as tall as a house in its temple twilight. Exemplifying the tremendum are the sacrificial practices followed by ancient American tribes (the high cultures of the Incas and the Aztecs) and by Polynesians who offered up human sacrifices to their gods: ceremonies at which hearts were ripped out of living bodies. In the Christian tradition an example of inspiring fascinosum partnering tremendum is the portrayal of the Last Judgment ("dies irae") in the requiems by Mozart and Verdi.

13.3 Actions

Religiously motivated actions are strongly influenced by attitudes couched in their emotional background. Yet even people's notions of what constitutes their religion have an impact on their religious actions.

There are actions which are designed to establish a link with higher powers. The most important of these are *prayer* and *offerings*.

Worshipful prayers contain elements of commitment and devotion, but also of submission. Most prayers voice a plea element implying that the petitioner is inferior in status to the one being petitioned.

Offerings are harder to describe. Several kinds can be distinguished, depending on the intention of the worshipper.

Firstly, there is offering as a gift or present. It is presented to a higher power with the intention of mollifying him in the event of his having been angered. The higher power's anger is recognizable from the affliction visited upon the petitioner which seems otherwise without explanation. The word "offering" could derive its meaning from the Latin verb *offerre* and the substantive *offerenda* (gifts and sacrifices), but its etymology (linguistic origin) is not fully confirmed.

Offerings in the form of gifts or presents are more commonly made to placate the higher power, even to oblige him to hear requests, with loss of face if they are not granted. This kind of offering occurs in cultures where somebody receiving a present feels obliged to reciprocate, the offering manifesting here as a form of manipulation with overtones of an act of magic. In this case the meaning of the word "offering" could perhaps derive from the Latin verb *operari* (to be busy with, to work), an etymology which is not confirmed.

The gift is thus an item handed over and committed to a higher power. In this definition the worshipper's intention must be considered; he may intend devotion and submission, but these can be mixed with a desire to manipulate. The cost of what is offered need not be high; sometimes the effort of procuring the offering, or meeting the transport costs of getting to the place of worship, is sufficient. Many actions which have little or no religious significance for us Europeans are, by contrast, seen as sacrificial by adherents of foreign religions.

If we, for example, take flowers to a grave, it is generally an act of simple piety, and certainly not an offering to our dead (differing slightly according to our religious denomination), not even a gift. People in traditional Indonesian cultures interpret a tribute like this as an offering. If we arrange for a flower-shop to place a wreath on a grave, local Indonesians think it meaningless. Flowers themselves are of course very suitable for acknowledging somebody has died, but not for their intrinsic value: we must make the effort to bring the flowers ourselves.

Numerous religions have a ***blood sacrifice***, where an animal or even a human is killed. The motives behind this act are various. The shed blood can indicate atonement for past sins. Behind the killings, though, can be a notion that the "soul" of the animal or person needs to be "released" from the body so as to access a higher power, or even to reach some kind of "other side". This type of blood sacrifice has the characteristics of an offering.

In this context there is a particular usage in German, where "Opfer" covers both meanings: offering and a blood sacrifice. In English and French the concepts are more clearly distinct: "offering" and "offrande" on the one hand and "sacrifice" on the other illustrate the two kinds unambiguously.

In pre-literate cultures the person making the offering is not particularly specified; anybody having a reason to do so can bring an offering, but it tends to be an elder or the head of a family. The more complex and multi-layered a society becomes, the more clearly defined is the office of a *priest*, and the more nuanced and detailed is the ritual.

The issue of the offering and its functions has spawned a host of publications and discussions, including in deep psychology and psychoanalysis (Sigmund Freud and his school). In addition there are numerous aspects of the concept of offering and sacrifice which cannot be fully considered here. The reader wishing to know more will find the relevant information in Thiel's study (1984). (The import of this ground-breaking book has been incorporated in many ways into the text of the present chapter).

A further realm of actions is to be seen in the *depiction of superhuman beings*, their deeds and experiences – events which are broadly known from the mythology or history of a religion. Among such depictions belong ceremonies with religious choreography where masks are worn to represent otherworldly beings. Performances like this may take on the character of mythical dramas where the action turns on how elements particular to their culture originated, for example the plants for their food. It can all seem rather intentional, as though specific events need to be performed regularly as a kind of theatrical spectacle or that the myth needs re-telling in order to guarantee the regular growth of the plants.

One example of a myth like this is familiar from an account of the South-East Asian and Melanesian mythologem of the coconut girl Hainuwele who was killed and later cut to pieces. From this crime there grew blessings: her buried body parts became food plants; her head became a coconut, her arms and legs became yams, etc. It is obvious that an event like this lends itself well to mythical drama.

Something similar can be observed in the mystery plays of the European Middle Ages right through to the passion play presented every ten years in Oberammergau, Bavaria.

Prayer, offerings and the acting out of myths all have special formats and contents. Additionally, they are bound to their period and other circumstances because they are events in a religious context. Their represen-

tation and sequencing follow guidelines that give little scope for modifi-
cations. We are dealing with very old cultural elements whose origins are
sometimes mysterious, often with accretions that are now beyond fathoming: aspects which tell especially of *tradition*. Their stylised form points
to a *rite* or *ritual*. (Remarkably both word forms exist, the first often used
as a singular, the second often as a plural).

Rites have as their prime aim to influence something. Four distinct
types can be seen, depending on the intended impact of each:

1) Actions to ward off evil are called *apotropaic rites* (from Greek
apotropein = to turn away). Evil can take on various forms. There are
rituals to prevent volcanic eruptions and rituals designed to ward off attacks by evil spirits. A similar apotropaic rite, once common in wine-
growing areas, involved making a noise whenever hailstones threatened: villagers rang the church bells or sent a posse of men into the
vineyards to fire guns; the noise was meant to deter the threat to the local economy.

In many cultures there are apotropaic rites against the *evil eye*. There
is a belief that with it many people can make humans and animals sick
and even cause death; and that sometimes one can be protected by holding one's hand in front of one's face.

2) Sometimes evil gets into an unexpected place or strikes a human
community suddenly and unexpectedly. In this case it has to be expelled.
Actions to ensure this are called *elimination rites* (from Latin *eliminare* =
to drive over the threshold, chase out of the house). One classic elimination rite is to load a community's sins on to a *scapegoat*, a practice we
know from the Old Testament.

The witch hunts of the European Middle Ages and of the early Modern Period were also elimination rites. The so-called witches represented
evil, present but hidden in society, which had to be got rid of by torture,
or by burning at the stake, or by other cruel means. One motivation was,
indeed, to punish those involved, but it was not the most important.

3) Ritual burnings are a transitional manifestation culminating in
cleansing rites which can be considered a specific form of elimination
rite. The distinction is helpful because cleansing rites do indeed eliminate
evil, but not so much from society as from the individual. If world religions are considered from this perspective, the impression is that the majority of rites are individual cleansing rites.

The notion of cleansing by fire to consume evil and profanity is rare in
pre-literate cultures, because in these cultures fire tends to be symbolic of
life and energy. By contrast, in high forms of religion fire is considered a
cleansing power. Notions of purgatory must be viewed in this context.

Water is a much more widespread cleansing agent than fire. For example, Hinduism presents the spectacle of ritual bathing on the banks of the Ganges where thousands may gather for this purpose. In Islam there are various acts of washing. In Christianity there is baptism and sprinkling of holy water. Water often serves as a symbol of life, particularly in desert areas of drought. Here water can acquire a further meaning of holiness, being then sometimes used even as a sacrificial gift.

Another ritual cleansing agent is salt. In many areas salt is so expensive that it is used as a currency and also as a sacrificial offering. As a symbol it stands for all that is imperishable and immutable.

Blood can also be given a ritual significance. Sometimes it is used in rituals to conclude a deal; for example in Africa, blood brotherhood is widespread: two men unrelated to one another symbolically mingling drops of their blood.

Yet another cleansing ritual is sometimes linked to abstinence, i.e. fasting, sexual abstinence, sleep deprivation, going without entertainment. In religions having holy scriptures, fasting is especially associated with preparing to meet the numinous (numinous = relating to the supernatural, divine). Many researchers in the field of religions explain abstaining from food and drink as symbolic of death. This seems rather exaggerated, but is nevertheless apt.

4) *Rites of passage*, as they are called, are very important for all cultures. Their significance was recognised and described systematically for the first time by Arnold van Gennep in his study published in 1909 (German version in Schmitz 1964). Rites of passage accompany a person's change of dwelling, or a change in a person's condition, social position or age: the coming of age to be married, the assumption of office (for example entering the priesthood), burial, etc.

Rites of passage are often manifest as *rites of initiation* (Latin *initiatio* = introduction). The novice moves from one status to another, mostly out of childhood into adulthood, thereby receiving the required status to be taken seriously by society and to be granted a voice.

Initiation into society often starts with a rite accompanying the mother's pregnancy, especially if she is pregnant for the first time. This ritual can be very complicated in its duration and its functions. Changes of status are considered particularly risky, because it is assumed that the novice is a prey to evil spirits. Young children are often considered particularly at risk of attack. For this reason rites of passage must involve other lesser rituals to counter such risks.

Time is often significant in rites of passage, because many are tied to particular moments or relate to astronomical events. The initiation festivals of the Yao people, an Islamised ethnic group of Tanzania, are held at full moon at the end of July or beginning of August. At this festival youths become adults.

The basis of the initiation ritual is a temporary *exclusion* or barring of the initiate from his or her community. The novice is first led from the village out into the wilderness where spirits or ancestors dwell.

At the end of the exclusion period there is often a ceremony of *circumcision* or *excision*, such as the extraction of a tooth, which is the outer symbol of initiation. This part of the ritual often comprises a test of courage; if the novice voices pain the ritual is not fulfilled.

Initiation rites can become traumatic experiences: circumcisions are generally conducted under difficult medical conditions, not merely regarding physical injury accompanied by terrible pain – poor hygiene leads to serious infections badly treated and slow to heal. The scar tattoos applied to young adults in New Guinea during the ritual are made particularly prominent by filling the skin cuts in the back with ash. These wounds result in scars; the more dramatic the better. Weeks of fever follow, which is the more bearable part. For the girls genital mutilation mostly results in lifelong sexual dysfunction.

When the agony is finally at an end, i.e. when the initiation rituals have been concluded in the time-honoured manner, the outcome is celebrated: new clothes are put on, there is feasting and dancing, and in many cases social norms are lifted, with sexual licence being condoned.

The person proceeding over his lifetime through a series of rites of passage ends each one with something hinting at a symbolic death. This is represented by separation from society, by suffering pain, illness and similar trials; the novice starts each new era with intimations of symbolic resurrection, represented by reinstatement into society, recuperation, new clothing, the presenting of objects and equipment, etc. Finally after actual physical death there is the passage into the next life as an ancestral spirit or other spirit.

The ritual accompanying this transition is generally the ultimate one. Sometimes it equates with the ritual of burial which in many cultures is very elaborate. The actual transfer to an existence as a spirit of the dead is often not completed until after a period varying from a few days to a year. Where the period is a year the person's body is exhumed, and the bones are washed and given final burial.

When this type of rite of passage is viewed from the perspective of the whole length of a person's life, one hidden but particularly interesting function of this institution becomes clear. In many pre-literate cultures the succession of rites of passage can be said to give structure to life. The rites order life's events into phases clearly marking beginnings and endings with festive occasions which participants will recall over a lifetime. A simple understanding of history is thus inculcated – a crucial perspective for pre-literate cultures. A similar staging of historical time was familiar to ancient Greeks; they named the periods between the Olympic Games after the winner of the games just ended. That is how other events could be fixed in time, e.g. the birth of a child occurring in the third year of the Olympiad of the winner Nikias.

Rites where the time factor is particularly prominent occur in agricultural communities. Sun, moon and the seasons are in cyclical relationship, so the solstices and phases of the moon are occasions for rituals, as are eclipses of the sun and moon. The Inuit hold more significant rituals at the onset of the Arctic winter night; for hunters it is at the beginning of the hunting season. New Year festivals are observed throughout the world.

Rites accompany the transition from one place to another and are observed when people cross from a profane territory to sacred territory, when they leave a tribal area, etc. An example of this was when in the ancient world a victorious army would march through a triumphal arch.

In many instances it is not clear how rituals arose. Where this is known one can sometimes infer that they were the outcome of problems occurring in everyday life and being solved, and that they originally testified to an emotion or stemmed from a specific event. In their final form as rituals they only contain the most important elements of the original occurrence which is then stylised in the ritual. Here are some examples:

In the past people in Germany were convinced that after death the person's soul in the form of a spirit-person left the body and the room where that person had died. A window needed to be open to facilitate the spirit-person's departure. In many rural areas this still happens today, even though the people concerned no longer hold to this notion of spirit. Opening a window has become part of the ritual accompanying a person's death.

A Muslim kneeling on the ground in prayer will repeatedly bend forwards and backwards; this can be explained as a physical expression of an emotion, the religious *mysterium tremendum* which has become formalised over time and now become a ritual.

One example of a specific event becoming highly stylised over the course of its ritualisation is the Last Supper in Jerusalem where Jesus met with all his disciples. From this occasion the eucharist or holy communion became the supreme example of ritual reduced to its most significant essence.

In no sense do rituals just take place in the sphere of a society's religion. Celebrations often run their course – even in a secular setting – in a way that is similar to rituals. Participants are offered guidelines and structures to help them find their bearings in the multiple complexities that make up a festivity attended perhaps by great numbers of people over several days.

In this respect Mischung (2003:217) is interesting, with his comment that in games of football each teams' fans exhibit ritualised behaviour by singing mocking chants at the opposing team.

13.4 Magic

Because in the structure of rituals there is no discernible relationship between its process and what is expected to flow from it, rituals can often seem completely irrational. Rituals of this kind are particularly likely to assume the character of *magic*.

A particular feature of many rituals is their explicit intention to intervene actively in processes where influencing by normal means (i.e. physically or naturally) is not usually possible – or desirable. Here is an example:

Thieves wanting to steal fruit from trees can generally be deterred by a sturdy fence or a wall. If this is too expensive or too time-consuming it is easier to impose a *taboo* – accompanied by some ritual – over the field or garden, threatening every thief or a member of his family with sickness or death. For the potential thief to understand what fate awaits him, visible signs can be placed at the boundaries of the plot, known as taboo signs. The taboo's deterrent effect is calculated on the basis that potential thieves share a common culture with those imposing the taboo; the thieves need to be convinced that the intended effect will indeed occur.

This kind of taboo is just one of many. Taking these others into account, we may define taboos as *prohibitions* or *bans* where noncompliance results in punishment. A person breaking a taboo is guilty and has to reckon with punishment. This may be meted out by a supposedly supernatural power, or may simply amount to the person being shunned by society. An example of a religious taboo in Christian circles is uttering God's name as a curse. An example of a social taboo is using the expletive "shit!", considered inappropriate in certain situations. The person using it deliberately can expect to be ostracised. On the Chuuk islands the concept of taboo is current in kinship terminology: a highly esteemed family member who deserves to be treated with respect is called "taboo above the others".

The impact of most taboos is said to be caused by a higher power, thought of either as a personal spirit being, or as something impersonal but *unusually effective* to be activated using rituals. This is known in ethnology as *mana*; it is crucial for somebody interpreting this kind of magic to understand its essential "force".

This force is given special significance in many religions, as shown by the fact that various languages have a term associated with it. Thus in the jargon of anthropologists mana is an *overt* category, unlike the concept "religion" which hardly ever is spoken about and so is a *covert* category.

This force is very often given a resounding name. The Irokese Indians call it "wakonda", the Algonquins use "manito". African Pygmies call it "megbe", many Bantu ethnic groups use "ndoki" and related expressions. Mana is the most well-known term, which is why it was adopted as the general name for all such forces. It is a word from the Austronesian (Oceanic) language group; it became the general term in ethnology because the concept was the object of particular research in ethnography.

In 1891 Robert Henry Codrington published a study entitled "The Melanesians. Study in their anthropology and folklore". In it he defined mana as follows: "Although an impersonal force, it is always connected with some person who directs it" (119). This definition, as we now know, is rather too narrow, but nevertheless captures its essence.

The following characterics of mana as a concept are those generally recognised in the Oceanic region. It should not be expected that the concept is fully comparable throughout; in the individual religions only some meanings from the full range possible are evident.

Mana is the term for an attribute of processes, things and beings; this attribute is the unexpected or the unusual. The term cannot simply be translated "force" or "power" as often happens; they only give a limited sense of its meaning. Mana is not just in evidence in the religious sphere, but also in the secular and ordinary circumstances of daily life. As well as "force" and "power" it can also mean in some cultural contexts "authority", "status", "good fortune" (in contrast to "bad luck") "wonder" and even "validity".

Mana is in itself a value-free concept, but viewed subjectively it is ambivalent. There is good and bad mana according to whether its impact is felt to be useful or harmful. A magical curse is considered by the person affected to be full of harmful mana.

It is not particularly obvious on the surface whether a process, thing or being has mana. Only its actual effects provide the evidence: they must be supplied with mana.

Things generally show that mana has been conferred on them by the fact that unusual effects can be achieved deliberately, even brought about against all expectations. This can occur in a variety of ways.

If a person is unharmed after falling from a tree or narrowly avoids being struck by a falling object bystanders tend to respond by saying, "Wow, man, you must be well endowed with mana today!" Europeans would presumably have commented in terms of the person being lucky.

A spear must have mana to be hitting the fish more often than other spears, or to be hitting bigger fish than other spears. In these circumstances this unusual effect can be caused by mana in the fisherman as well. That it is not here a feature of the spear but of the fisherman is proven if he manages the same unexpected feat with various spears as before with his own.

Not everything having an intended consequence or proving to be unusually effective achieves it through having mana. A tool which is easier to work with than others is just particularly "handy", not specially supplied with mana. Situations involving something evidently having mana are very unlikely to be successful without it; the smaller this likelihood, the greater the mana. This means that a spear does not merely show it has mana through being compared with other spears, but also, for example, by hitting its target many times in succession.

There are people who engender respect and obedience in others just by their presence. The *authority* of a personality like this resides in the mana conferred upon him and mirrored in that person's *spoken word*. The more people respond to him without hesitation the greater must be the person's mana. In addition to this meaning of "authority" the concept embraces "power".

Status and mana depend on each other. The person having mana enjoys high status. Conversely, a person endowed with status is assumed to have mana.

Mana in an authoritative person's speech can be dangerous, just like mana in other circumstances. If that person pronounces a curse over anybody who defies his will, that curse results in harm or even death to his victim.

In this form the concept of mana can loom quite large in the thinking of ethnic groups which have turned to Christ. When representatives of a church, or missionaries or indigenous priests merely indicate something sinful by name, any person who has committed the sin inevitably fears that he will fall victim to a curse uttered by the word of the authority figure.

On the other hand, mana mostly works as an advantage to church workers. It is generally expected that having a priest in the canoe or in the lorry cab makes an accident on the water or on the road unlikely, even if the means of transport is not in a very good state of repair.

When people are dealing with somebody whose mana can mean danger, they are forced to heed a whole range of behavioural guidelines. The person enjoying special status resulting from his authority (or not, as the case may be) is taboo: showing him due respect is vital; infringing this code is likely to bring bad consequences.

Mana even comes with emotions, with an impact to match. It is sometimes reckoned that the feelings of ill-will and hatred triggered in a person of higher status (or simply birthed in a wish to inflict punishment) engender consequences: these can bring calamity, illness or death upon whomever is targeted by these feelings. In many ethnic groups this leads to people seeking pardon for fear of the consequences meted out by a person of higher status; something that occurs even if people just suppose that they might possibly have offended that person. This is tantamount to people investing in reserves of reconciliation.

Everything that has been said about people and mana is also valid for spirits: the greater the mana of a spirit being, the greater its status vis-à-vis fellow spirits.

Processes that have no apparent explanation, events which could not possibly occur the way they have occurred, are often attributed to the effects of mana – which can emanate from humans or from things. A spirit being is often at work. In these processes mana means something that Europeans would understand as a *miracle*.

Spirits that are able to create things out of nothing by acts of will or word, and that are also able to hurl thunderbolts and cause floods, do so on the basis of their mana.

Most ethnic groups tending towards animistic beliefs are aware of reports of spirits having brought the world into being through mana. The physical powers that they use are usually called by another name.

The fact that processes, things and beings have mana needs to be confirmed. Mana is usually discovered through chance, as is loss of mana. Sometimes, however, things and even people can be provided with mana, or with even more mana. This occurs sometimes by their coming into contact with a thing or being that already has this attribute.

There is a widespread notion that mana arises or is passed on in the context of a *ritual act*, as for example the mana put into a medication during its manufacture (see chap. 15). In this case it is evident how closely the concept of mana is connected with *magic*. Magical processes are thus not exclusively defined by the use of a special form of words ("the spell") to give the magic effect to the process or outcome. In many cases compliance with a ritual is sufficient, i.e. complying with the correct sequence of recommended stages towards producing mana and its magic outworking. The sequencing of the stages may indeed take the place of any magic formula.

Procedures like these can be at work with **talismans** and **amulets**. These are used if they are discovered to have some unusual effect, and supposedly possess a type of mana, having demonstrated it already; or else it is assumed that the objects were empowered during the course of a ritual (such as an act of consecration) to create special effects.

In ethnology a distinction is made between amulets and talismans: amulets are effective by their ability to ward off evil and misfortune; talismans are thought to attract goodness and bring their wearers favour and fortune.

Fetishes are a special case; their effectiveness also resides in powers like those of mana. A fetish is a material object possessing impersonal force or power which is considered personal, and which can be activated and manipulated by gifts (offerings and sacrifices). Its potency can even be heightened. (This definition of the term fetish matches Thiel's formulation in his very readable introduction to this phenomenon, 1986). By contrast amulets, talismans, everyday objects and people equipped with mana have not generally acquired this by anything previously imparted to the objects themselves. Yet sometimes mana can be imparted by an offering integral to the ritual where the creation of mana is expected. The offering is then directed to a spirit being; people assume that this will bestow mana or increase it.

The most comprehensive treatment of fetishes (and so-called "holy" objects generally) is given in Kohl 2003.

Mana as a personality trait (such as authority) can hardly arise in the context of an action. Yet the action where a person is invested with an office – for example as a chieftain – releases increased mana as official authority in that person. Sometimes this happens by success in an exam.

This pattern of thought can even be traced in a characteristic way in Christian ethnic groups with a background of animism. The prayer of a church elder is sometimes considered more effective than the prayer of an ordinary member of the Christian community. This increased effectiveness is not the result of mana having been transferred *during* the act of blessing when his office was conferred; it is considered to have arisen *from* the very act of blessing.

Spirits can be involved when a person or thing receives mana, yet their cooperation is not absolutely necessary. Mana is, of course, always reckoned to be something unusual and out of the ordinary, but not for all that simply religious nor purely linked with the afterlife and transcendent beings. Evidence for this is seldom unambiguous by virtue of the fact that mana may or must have ultimately originated in the life beyond,

The extent to which the term mana can be separated from religious notions is nicely illustrated by an incident in Micronesia during my linguistic researches into mana and its meaning. I had given a local colleague a cheque in dollars for him to go shopping on a neighbouring island. In my haste I had forgotten to sign the cheque. My colleague came back the following day; his words to me were that the cheque without a signature didn't have the required mana to buy anything. As with other mana expressions in his language, this one contains no particular religious reference.

In summary, mana is essentially the unusual element implementing change in processes, things and beings, which may manifest as authority. Spirit beings have particularly effective mana depending on their status. Yet mana is not exclusively transcendent and linked to religion.

Moreover, the concept of mana is a classic problem for the ethnology of religion. In the history of research into mana there are two distinct phases. The studies up to the appearance of Friedrich Rudolf Lehmann's (1915) inclined towards speculation, caused by their lack of an adequate basis of raw ethnographical and linguistic data. This led in turn to unreliable generalisations and unbalanced views of mana as a concept. In his doctoral thesis Lehmann brought together all the available studies on mana up to 1915, compared them and reissued his augmented study in 1922. His assertion that linguistic principles play a significant conceptualizing role in understanding mana led in the period thereafter to a range of empirical studies. Of these, Raymond Firth's article (1970) may be considered exemplary.

Using the mana concept we can derive a definition of the term *magic*. This is a process where a person manipulates higher powers for his own use (or for harm to others): through strictly observed rites (correctly spoken formulae, correct sacrificial procedures, etc.) such powers can be coaxed and even compelled to hold sway over another person. One feature of magic is therefore the inevitable, automatic component. Those using magic suppose that whenever the ritual created or activated by mana is carried out exactly according to prescription, its impact is inevitable.

Magic can also be understood as the opposite of what could be termed "authentic religion", that is the handing over and subordination of self to higher powers. The practitioner of magic, on the other hand, does not subordinate himself to them; he takes possession of them.

Moreover, magic as a mental habit is not confined to pre-literate religions; it is omnipresent.

A somewhat different type of manipulation of higher powers is at work whenever a person tries to experience something obscure and hidden in the future. Items fall in such a way as to allow an interpretation of what lies obscure in the future: coffee dregs, playing cards, pebbles, bones and feathers deliberately thrown by local faith healers so they may determine how an illness can be treated. These procedures are called *divination* (Latin *divinus* = godly, according to the will of a god).

There is a whole range of divination types. The Romans recognized *omens* in nature which guided their actions: a black cat appearing suddenly on the left of the observer was considered a bad sign; from that moment onward for the rest of the day it meant having to be alert to anything unforeseen and harmful. For the Romans divination was carried out by special priestly officials called *augurs*. They interpreted the constellations, the flight of birds, and the state of the entrails of sacrificial animals to bring to light anything unknown.

A popular form of divination is when somebody picks off daisy petals to find out what may be hoped for in a boy-girl relationship ("he/she loves me; loves me not ...")

13.5 Ethics

It is right to mention here a final category of actions deriving from a person's religious beliefs and attitudes; these satisfy the appeals for a moral life in fulfilment of the commands and prohibitions of higher beings and powers said to watch over an individual. We mean the area of *ethics*.

All forms of religion place demands on a person to live life according to particular rules. Without adhering to such rules people would find it impossible to live in community. The injunction "thou shalt not steal" has to be stated and upheld universally. If everybody could just grab what somebody else had honestly acquired and owned, then the careful management of resources and organised labour – so attractive and vital for guaranteeing a decent human community – would fade. A similar fundamental tenet is the command "thou shalt not kill". Without demands for these to be kept, and without agents to enforce them, a community would destroy itself.

Observance of *ethical norms* like these is enforced in two ways: 1) by embedding them in the individual's conscience (superego) during the enculturation phase, and 2) by linking such demands with the will of a non-human authority, a higher power, which can threaten punishment if the norms are not met. In other words: breaches of the norms inevitably provoke anger in the non-human authority. The result is a state of sin in which the individual cannot dwell without suffering dire consequences. In pre-literate religions these do not – as a matter of principle – just affect the "sinner" but the group he belongs to: a father who spends all his wages on drink will be punished by something bad happening to him or one of his children. The fear of causing a catastrophe like that is intended to bring violations of the norm under control, if not prevent them completely.

The agent of non-human authority in this sense can be a Supreme Being. Where there is ancestor worship it tends to be the deceased family members who represent this authority. This can result in striking conceptual links evident during Christian mission work. It is mostly a surprise for the European church worker to realise that when locals become Christians from such a cultural background they still nevertheless attribute to the Holy Spirit the functions of a supreme punisher, who punishes sin with illness and early death.

Behind this pattern of thinking is the notion that sin does not lead to damnation in some kind of "after-life" or in "hell" but to punishment here and now, on this earth. In modified form, the principle can even be recognized in forms of religion where there is no doctrine of higher powers punishing a problematic lifestyle by sending disaster. Strictly speaking, Buddhism does not recognise gods, nor any punishment for sin in an after-life. A person leading a morally compromised life risks a different calamity: all the while he keeps sinning he will be continually reborn as a creature (reincarnation) from an ever more humble social level; this fate can lead him down to the level of the animals. Only if he manages to lead a blameless life is he freed from having to suffer the evil of a life on earth; he is released from existence. He reaches nirvana.

13.6 Religion and Securing One's Existence

As I said at the beginning of this chapter, the religions of the world have a great number of features in common, but also a great variety of differences. This fact must be repeated in conclusion, for an important reason. In all religions the economic make-up of a society and all the factors that influence it (such as geographical location, climate, etc.) play an important role. Thus in a culture where water is scarce but vital for agriculture and livestock rearing, the corresponding religion will be similarly distinctive: there will be a rain god, a series of rituals to cause it to ensure in due time the necessary rainfall or the rising of river levels; and there will be religious experts – rain magicians – entrusted with masterminding the proper rituals. Pre-literate religions apply themselves energetically to *securing existence*, overcoming forces of nature, and so on; the foreign visitor gets the impression that they are strongly *oriented towards the here and now*.

In European and Western cultures practical matters to counter the forces of nature seldom feature as issues of religious behaviour. In these cultures the emphasis is on *future orientation*. Whereas a person's current life can largely be made secure by means of modern technology, his future fate is still uncertain because future events are unknown. For this reason people in the West increasingly settle for allying themselves with powers that are said to watch over humans and with whose help the future can supposedly be experienced and influenced: *spiritism* (making contact with the spirits of the deceased), *forms of divination* (such as tarot cards), *astrology* (recourse to horoscopes), *fortune telling* (palmistry, etc.) and much else.

Religion in its broadest sense is always the expression of the fact that people in all cultures and societies observe the visible and measurable world, and that it does not satisfy them. Throughout the world they have this conviction that there must be more than what is immediately accessible and tangible. Their thirst for knowledge of a reality which lies "behind" – or might lie behind – cannot easily be suppressed. A person's need to comprehend what lies behind, to know the world beyond the natural one, to explore time after somebody's death, is evidently not just "the opium of the people" as Karl Marx called it; it is one of the basic human needs, which must be satisfied for a person to remain healthy in mind and soul.

More detailed introductions to this chapter's topic:

Mischung (2003) gives a very readable, succint and recent presentation of the discipline of ethnology of religion and its components. His bibliography is manageable and contains further significant studies. Greater detail on the topic can be found in Klass (1995), Rappaport (1999) and Belliger/Krieger (^{2}2003).

More on the topic of this chapter can be found in the following studies:

Beer, Bettina; Fischer, Hans (Hg.): Ethnologie. Einführung und Überblick. Berlin 2003. (This is Fischer's 5th ed. of 1983 in a new version).

Belliger, Andréa; Krieger, David J. (Hg.): Ritualtheorien. Ein einführendes Handbuch. Wiesbaden ^{2}2003.

Codrington, R. H.: The Melanesians. Studies in their anthropology and folklore. Oxford 1891.

Firth, Raymond: The analysis of Mana: an empirical approach. In: Harding 1970:316-333.

Gennep, Arnold van: Les rites de passage. Étude systématique des rites. Paris 1909.

Haekel, Josef: Religion. In: Trimborn 1971:72-141.

Harding, Thomas G.: Wallace, Ben J. (eds.): Cultures of the Pacific. New York 1970.

Klass, Morton: Ordered universes. Approaches to the anthropology of religion. Boulder · San Francisco · Oxford 1995

Kohl, Karl-Heinz: Die Macht der Dinge. Geschichte und Theorie sakraler Objekte. Munich 2003.

Lehmann, Friedrich R.: Mana. Eine begriffsgeschichtliche Untersuchung auf ethnologischer Grundlage. Dresden 1915.

Lehmann, Friedrich R.: Der Begriff des "außerordentlich Wirkungsvollen" bei Südseevölkern. Leipzig 1922.

Mischung, Roland: Religionsethnologie. In: Beer/Fischer 2003:197-220.

Rappaport, Roy A.: Ritual and religion in the making of humanity. Cambridge 1999.

Schmitz, Carl A. (Hg.): Religionsethnologie. Frankfurt am Main. 1964.

Thiel, Josef Franz: Religionsethnologie. Grundbegriffe der Religionen schriftloser Völker. Berlin 1984.

Thiel, Josef Franz (Museum für Völkerkunde, Frankfurt): Was sind Fetische? Frankfurt am Main 1986.

Trimborn, Hermann (Hrsg.): Lehrbuch der Völkerkunde. Stuttgart 1971.

Chapter 14
Animism

This chapter explains what animism is as an overall conceptual system and what elements it encompasses; what kinds of animism exist; and how it should be understood as a strategy for overcoming particular problems in life. Special emphasis is placed on animism being less of a religion than a worldview having a particular image of man as central.

Animism is one of the central concepts in the comparative study of religion and ethnology of religion. By animism in its most common form is meant the *belief in the existence and influence of spirit-like beings* manifest in human or animal form and having knowledge, power and abilities that humans do not have. In traditional, pre-literate, cultures it is not just *spirits* in the actual meaning of the word that feature among these beings, but also human *souls* – and occasionally also things which have something like a soul.

The origins and early forms of animistic religions lie in the dawn of human history. In ethnology of religion these days, academics consider it likely that animism represents the conceptual framework for the very earliest forms of religious activities. Over the course of the history of research on this issue a number of hypotheses were formulated; yet these were revealed as one-sided. Two of them have gained some credence, but in a fundamental way they are contradictory.

According to Tylor (1871) animism arose from *dream experiences*, where man is unconscious yet experiences himself as existing. From this, Tylor says, man decided that apart from his body there was at least one other being belonging to him whose experiences could be witnessed when dreaming. This conclusion led to the conception of a soul (Latin *anima*) which complemented the body and whose presence formed an indispensable requirement for the body's life. According to Tylor, the concept of soul that this notion gave rise to, and the accompanying belief in the existence and potency of spirits, was the starting point for human religious behaviour. After somebody's death his human soul was venerated as an ancestral spirit and later as a quasi-divine being. From among an abundance of highly esteemed spirits, a single one eventually became in people's thinking the Supreme Being. Thus, in a late phase of human culture, arose the doctrine of one God, *monotheism*.

As far as the current meaning and use of the term animism is concerned, Mischung (2003:206) has aptly remarked, "... the term animism and the adjective animistic are both in common use these days. But both have undergone a shift of meaning and no longer generally equate with Tylor's concept of an omnipresent animation or soul-stirring in nature; animism is mostly a general term for complexes of spirit notions that cannot be attributed to the high religions."

According to Schmidt (1926-1955) humans originally had a monotheistic concept of God, but then in the course of cultural history this notion faded to a belief in the activity of a number of very different spirits. This explanation is known in the relevant literature as the *degeneration theory*.

At the present moment it seems impossible to prove that one of the two approaches is the correct one.

We can start with the assumption that all existing indigenous groups these days have recourse to animistic forms of religion to solve specific problems of their existence. Since we are dealing here with cultures that are pre-literate or that have only recently become literate, their members' knowledge and competencies are essentially passed on to the next generation orally, without institutionalised teaching. (This is why in more recent publications they are known as traditional cultures.)

This orality and the absence of institutional teaching contribute to the fact that animism, against the generally held view, also has some part to play in Islam, Buddhism, Shintoism, etc. – particularly in rural communities and among the illiterate populations of the large cities of the Third World. We mean the forms of religion termed folk Islam, folk Buddhism, etc. with their basic animistic structures that cannot be ignored.

Animistic religions by themselves contain neither missionary nor militant characteristics in the way that Christianity and Islam do. Furthermore, a unified animistic theology does not exist. And since in the foreseeable future there will not be any more pre-literate societies or indigenous groups in the original meaning of the word, animism in its intrinsic form is bound to die out. In Afro-American forms of religion such as Voodoo or Umbanda it will, however, continue to maintain its enormous significance.

Characterising animism merely as a religion of traditional cultures is a rash oversimplification. For a start, the label "religion" here is problematic. It is better to view animism as a worldview with many different aspects. One of its basic concepts is the idea that alongside the material things and beings in the world there are not just innumerable *spirit-like beings* but also just as many *spirit-like things*. In many forms of animism people hold the view that for every single material thing and being there is a corresponding spirit-like thing assigned to it – a kind of invisible duplicate of what is material. With this concept of a *spirit double*, as Fischer (1965) correctly terms it, we have an animistic *picture of the world's make-up* which contains two aspects that mirror each other in behaviour: each thing exists in dual form, a visible material one and an invisible spirit-like one.

From a European perspective, the notion of a spirit double for things gives greater conceptual clarity than before to different religious terms like offering/sacrifice. When foods offered as gifts to ancestral spirits seem to the eye to remain untouched, this merely means that from an animistic perspective the food's material aspect has been untouched; what the ancestral spirits may have eaten is the spirit-like aspect. The material aspect can still be eaten by humans, but will have no nutritional value. Things without their spirit-like counterpart are considered limited in their ability to function. This applies also to humans, as we shall soon demonstrate.

Particularly in this respect animism shows itself to be not just a religion but a coherent – and simple – understanding and philosophy of nature: it attempts to respond to the issue of the essence of the world and of things.

One of the key elements of animistic worldviews is the conviction that there are spirit beings which significantly influence what happens in the world. These spirits are termed good or evil, depending on how their attitude to humans is viewed.

Many forms of animism do not merely exhibit a fear of evil spirits but also a devotion to good spirits (in their terms). These spirits may be deceased family members that people generally contact through *mediums* (intermediaries) to request advice or to express devotion. Animists find it hard to fathom when others call these spirits demons and react to them negatively, which is the tendency of Western and European Christians. In a special sense animists think of spirits of the dead as good spirit beings; for this reason animists have difficulty with the thought that the Bible forbids contact with them.

Animists describe evil spirits as basically animal-like in appearance (theriomorphic), often abnormal in physique and aggressive in nature. Their intelligence is reckoned to be rather low, such that people can deceive them and protect themselves from them in many ways. Here is an example.

In Hongkong people can be observed rushing across the road in front of a bus or a heavy lorry without any apparent reason other than to commit suicide. The astounding explanation for the risky behaviour is that they feel pursued by an evil spirit which needs to be run over and dispatched in this unexpected manner.

Evil spirits are almost powerless against good spirits. They are wary of light and wary of people. In view of anxieties shown by evil spirits, the Bible's metaphor of light and the value given to the notion of "community fellowship" in the New Testament both take on special significance for animists.

Therefore evil spirits cannot easily be identified with the demonic spirits in the Bible that are intelligent and powerful, and tasked by Satan to bring humans to ruin. It is clear that if in our Bible translations we rashly associate the evil spirit beings of animism with biblical demons, we shall end up in a theological tangle.

Evil spirit beings are generally seen as the **_originators of illnesses_**; dealing with them in animistic cultures essentially involves blocking and banishing these spirits. In addition, animistic thinking is practically always allied to an extensive **_medical theory_**. Yet this fact has been given scant attention in medical mission work and in medical development teaching programmes. For example, it can lead to doctors misunderstanding what patients from an animistic background mean when describing their symptoms (cf. chap. 15).

Illnesses and other harm can also be caused by spirits that are otherwise reckoned essentially good, for example when ancestral spirits punish living family members' misbehaviour with sickness or harm befalling somebody in the group. As we have mentioned before, in animistic religions sin is generally not considered punishable in the afterlife but in this life, by harm and hunger, illness and death. Notions of a hell are essentially foreign to animism.

Central to animistic forms of religion is their **_concept of what it is to be human_**. A human has a **_body_** and at least **_one soul_**. This soul is not directly linked to the body or contained in the body, but generally lives in proximity, and – crucially – leads its separate existence as a personality, having emotions and the will and power to think. This is why in the ethnology of religion the soul is referred to as "free soul", "dream ego" or spirit double – to name the most important (Fischer 1965; Käser 1977, 2004 and 2014).

The use of the terms "soul" and "spirit" in connection with animistic notions creates significant problems whenever representatives from Western society try to understand animistic concepts on the basis of Western concepts of soul and spirit.

Käser (2004), and in his recent book on animism, 2014, gives very accessible information on this. Klass (1995:96-105) also makes an interesting effort to resolve this problem of terminology.

The two main functions of these souls are to protect the body from harm, especially from attack by evil spirit beings, and to maintain normal life processes in the human body. This means that a person can well live for a certain time without his spiritual counterpart needing to be directly present. Only after a prolonged absence of the soul from the body do typical symptoms of impairment occur, such as defective circulation, unwillingness to work, depression, etc.; this results from the *loss of soul*. If the soul fails to return to the body in time, the person has a coma and eventually dies.

Hence soul does not imply the *seat of the emotions*, unlike its use in European and Western thinking. Animists usually assign the seat of a person's emotions to an *organ of the body*, such as the prominent organs: the liver, the heart, the kidneys, or other inner parts. Here, supposedly, is the hub of the intellectual processes also: thought, memory and the qualities of courage and discernment, etc.

It is not just the body that is home to the emotions and thinking, but the person's soul as well (free soul, dream ego, spirit double) constituting its individual personality. Spirit beings – good and evil ones – also mirror this make-up.

This typical animistic "psychology" and the "psychopathology" to match have together been a source and basis for European and Western cultures continually misinterpreting animism as a phenomenon. What is more, research into these matters is in its infancy.

The typically animistic idea of man's dual existence as body and soul give rise to a whole lot of other notions, not least in relation to his death. In the understanding of animists only his body, his temporal self, dies. His soul, his transcendent self, remains in its original form as a spirit being, albeit without a physical counterpart.

For this reason it is often not the case that the dead person's soul is thought to depart for some kind of "other world" familiar to those high religions possessing scriptures, because in the animist understanding of things this world and the next are not physically separate. True, there are places in the parallel world of the spirits where the souls of the departed willingly visit, or where they permanently dwell. Yet as a rule they can return to their earlier worldly existence at any time.

The Supreme Being that I mentioned in the previous chapter also lives in this transcendent world.

It should not be supposed that animism exhibits identical forms throughout the numerous ethnic groups on earth; this is only the case with some essential principles of animism. For example, revering deceased family members is not a *sine qua non* for those of an animist mindset. As regards animistic religions two fundamental types can be discerned: a) animism without ancestor worship and b) animism with ancestor worship.

Type (a) is dominant in non-sedentary hunter-gatherer cultures. In their culture people hold that after death a person's soul becomes an evil spirit being to be feared. They bury their dead without ceremony, and shun them and avoid the places of burial; they do not make offerings to their dead, nor do they seek any contact.

Shamans, not generally mediums, act as intermediaries between the imminent and transcendent worlds. The chosen form of contact with spirits is via *ecstasy*; in their opinion they are sending their soul (or one of their souls) on a *journey into the afterlife* or spirit world where it communes with so-called *auxiliary spirits* and is imbued with the knowledge needed by the shaman to enact his functions as a healer of sickness. The auxiliary spirits are not usually thought to be spirits of the dead.

Type (b) is almost always found in sedentary arable farming cultures (planters and cultivators). Here the thinking goes that after death a person's soul becomes a good spirit being that continues to behave like a family member and that can be relied upon for help and sympathy. Arable farmers therefore bury their dead close-by, and offer them gifts, and hold them in respect.

Their intermediaries between the two worlds are *mediums*, whose form of contact with the spirits is via *possession*. Supposedly, they are visited by the spirits of the dead from the life beyond; as mediums they then announce the spirits' intentions to the living.

There are some parallel structures between animism and Christianity. Both proceed from the thought that there is a material world (this life) and an immaterial spirit world (the life beyond), with many and various links between the worlds. In the past this has been a blessing for missionaries in their teaching, given that Christian content could be woven more easily into animistic thought patterns than into the structures of book religions. Nevertheless the differences between the two forms of religion are considerable.

Among animists (cf. chap. 13) the notion of God is not usually that of a loving father sacrificing his son to save mankind, nor that of a judge punishing people to make them take responsibility for their actions (although this last purpose is more likely).

Their notion of man reveals somewhat fewer differences, in that the arrangement of body, soul and spirit in biblical theology corresponds to an animist arrangement of body, spirit double and seat of the emotions.

In an animist understanding, sin is not first and foremost an infringement against the norms of a non-human authority, but against the norms ensuring the preservation of the particular group, or family, or whatever. This is why the ancestral spirits are also involved in upholding the norms; sin thus lodges in the animistic imagination by dint of its social manifestation.

It is an elementary misunderstanding to suppose that animism is identical to *occultism*. If this were so then groups with an animistic orientation would be incapable of forming their normal human communities, since people bowed down by occultism lead a joyless, self-destructing and essentially asocial existence. Whenever animistic cultures existed back in the early phases of human history (and there is plenty of evidence for this) they thrived for several thousand years at least. It is hard to imagine that their people were hounded by a dominant occultism. Yet it is vital to say that animists do not easily identify what borders on occultism; this is often then an issue when they become Christians.

Animistic thought processes are very hard to define by external evidence, for the concepts that result are hidden in people's minds. They are nevertheless discernible, because they have left traces in their language. A person intent on understanding a particular form of animism needs first to become immersed in the group's language. The shared language alone offers reliable access to what animists themselves mean by their animism. Only after several years of general exposure to the culture and lifestyle of animists can a researcher be confident of making a worthwhile evaluation of the pertinent features.

The knowledge that everything to do with an ethnic group's culture and especially its religion is also mapped in its language has given impetus to cognitive anthropology (cf. chaps. 12 and 19) as a recent research interest for the ethnology of religion. The processes and results of this research can be successfully implemented by church workers and development aid workers in foreign cultures. For this reason I wish to draw the reader's attention here to the seminal studies by Renner 1980 and 1983, and by D'Andrade 1995.

At the close of this chapter I want to emphasise that nobody should expect to be able to understand and feel fully comfortable with the thinking of people of an animistic world view by just absorbing experiences haphazardly – there is scarcely any area of culture where adopting such a learning process might make one more idly dependent on chance than in this area. Europeans can only achieve useful results, insights and effective work here if firstly they collate data systematically, and if secondly they make a clear distinction between what belongs to animism and what the Bible has to say. A researcher who muddles the two will obscure the path to any worthwhile understanding of reality. For further research I recommend a systematic catalogue of questions for one's own enquiries in Badenberg (2007, 2011, 2014).

More on the topic of this chapter can be found in the following studies:

Badenberg, Robert: Das Menschenbild in fremden Kulturen. Ein Leitfaden für eigene Erkundungen. Handbuch zu Lothar Käsers Lehrbuch Animismus. Nürnberg Bonn 2007. (French edition: La conception de l'homme dans les cultures étrangères. Guide d'investigation personnelle. Charols/France 2011. English edition: The Concept of Man in Non-Western Cultures: A Guide for One's Own Research. Handbook to Lothar Käser's Textbook *Animism – A Cognitive Approach.* Nürnberg: VTR Publications 2014

D'Andrade, Roy: The development of cognitive anthropology. Cambridge et al. 1995.

Fischer, Hans: Studien über Seelenvorstellungen in Ozeanien. München 1965.

Fischer, Hans (Hg.): Ethnologie. Eine Einführung. Berlin 1983.

Käser, Lothar: Der Begriff "Seele" bei den Insulanern von Truk. Diss. Freiburg 1977.

Käser, Lothar: Animismus. Eine Einführung in die begrifflichen Grundlagen des Welt- und Menschenbildes traditionaler (ethnischer) Gesellschaften für Entwicklungshelfer und kirchliche Mitarbeiter in Übersee. Bad Liebenzell und Erlangen 2004. French edition: Animisme. Introduction à la conception du monde et de l'homme dans les sociétés axées sur la tradition orale. Charols/France 2010. English edition: Animism – A Cognitive Approach. An Introduction to the Basic Notions Underlying the Concepts of the World and of Man Held by Ethnic Societies, for the Benefit of Those Working Overseas in Development Aid and in the Church. Nürnberg: VTR Publication 2014

Käser, Lothar: Diferentes culturas. Uma introdução a etnologia. Londrina/PR 2004.

Klass, Morton: Ordered universes. Approaches to the anthropology of religion. Boulder · San Francisco · Oxford 1995.

Mischung, Roland: Religionsethnologie. In: Beer/Fischer 2003:197-219.

Renner, Egon: Die kognitive Anthropologie. Aufbau und Grundlagen eines ethnologisch-linguistischen Paradigmas. Berlin 1980.

Renner, Egon: Die Grundlinien der kognitiven Forschung. In: Fischer 1983:391-425.

Schmidt, Wilhelm: Der Ursprung der Gottesidee. Münster 1926-1955 (12 vols.).

Sundermeier, Theo: Nur gemeinsam können wir leben. Das Menschenbild schwarzafrikanischer Religionen. Gütersloh 1988.

Tylor, Edward Burnett: Primitive Culture. Researches into the development of mythology and philosophy, religion, art and custom. 2 vols.
London 1871.

Chapter 15
Medicine

This chapter explains what being ill means for pre-literate cultures; what people think causes illness; what principles guide its treatment; and in what form this relates to religion. The chapter details the significance of the term medication, and its production and effectiveness. It explains the features which distinguish these practices from European-Western medicine.

In the chapter on religion as a concept I mentioned various contexts for the animistic concept of a human being: the human body, with the soul as an independent spirit-like person – each with the capacity for exercising emotions, will and intellect. The body as the human form of existence in this world emerged as that part of the individual on which "sin" avenges itself in the form of illness. This much makes it all too clear that animism as a world view contains a theory of medicine.

The foreigner from a European-Western background working in an environment like this needs to proceed from two basic principles if he wishes to investigate and understand the animist conception of medical practice: *illness* (meaning being ill) and *medicine* (meaning medication). In the languages of relevant cultures a word exists for each idea, because the concepts relate so intrinsically to human existence that each needs to be given voice. In addition there are two more terms closely linked with illness and medication; the term *diagnosis* is linked with notions of being ill, and the term *therapy* with notions of medication.

For people in pre-literate societies being ill is generally a great deal more momentous than for people in societies with scientific medicine and an effective national health service. In our system appendicitis can be swiftly diagnosed and operated upon, and even tooth ache occurring out of normal surgery hours can be treated without difficulty. Sunday opening and emergency treatment are both available almost round the clock even in the most difficult circumstances. When an emergency occurs off the beaten track the rescue service's helicopter can be called out. By contrast, on a remote island in the Pacific Ocean without a regular boat service or in an Amazon rainforest community hundreds of kilometres from the nearest hospital, a simple infection can mean certain death. Being ill in a situation like this brings with it a fundamental threat to human existence; it is easy to see that people in such communities are bound to have a different perspective than ours. This by itself is sufficient reason for their response to falling ill being different from that of us Westerners with our expectations.

The differences begin as soon as the question arises about what condition constitutes an illness. For Europeans, pregnancy and associated conditions are sometimes considered a malady because pregnant women and new born babies book in for medical check-ups, even if there is no direct medical necessity. In parts of the world where it is expected that pregnant women should continue their physical tasks – such as fetching wood and water until shortly before giving birth – their condition has nothing to do with the concept of being ill. Yet elsewhere, pains and aching muscles in the limbs resulting from additional physical exercise are viewed as ailments and quoted as reasons for being unfit for work, for taking life easy or for getting treatment from the doctor. Further, an aid worker needs to be alert to particular illnesses being classified differently than Europeans might expect: as we have seen in the chapter on language and culture, coughing and asthma belong for Chuuk islanders – for linguistic reasons – to diseases of the heart rather than of the lungs.

The causes of illness illustrate a particularly interesting pattern of thinking. There are indirect and direct causes of illness. Among the indirect ones are firstly *violations against cultural norms*. These may range broadly from aberrant behaviour (such as somebody not doing things in the traditional manner of their ancestors) through to *sins*, i.e. violations against the ethical norms governing community life. If somebody has committed a theft the consequence may be illness or other harm.

Violation against norms arouses the displeasure of powers thought to preside over humankind, such as ancestral spirits and deities. In their wrath they bring upon humans all kinds of affliction (illness, natural disasters such as earthquakes, droughts, plagues of locusts, famine and death). Yet the impact is not only interpreted as punishment for wrong behaviour; it is meant to prevent wrong behaviour in the first place by acting as a deterrent.

Illness-inducing sins or violations against norms are seldom drawn up in a fixed tariff where particular wickedness is equated with particular illness or harm. When a person falls ill or suffers a catastrophe for which there seems little obvious explanation, the attempt is made to find the originator by reconstructing who in the previous weeks and months might have been guilty of some violation or other. The effort to find somebody who may come under suspicion nearly always succeeds.

It must be emphasised that harm, illness and death as punishment for sins and violations against norms do not necessarily strike the infringement. It may strike somebody in his group or family, such as his children or parents. This is a facet of the group orientation which gives stability to the social structures of these cultures: the individual may endanger other members of the group through his behaviour. Falling ill and dying are typical dangers.

Ancestral spirits and deities make use of direct causes of illness to enforce adherence to the norms or to punish non-adherence. They either commission the evil spirits in league with symptoms of particular diseases to attack a person and make him ill; or else they take away his soul (his spirit double, his dream ego), the spirit being that partners the person, endowing him with full viability and competence, and defending his body against attacks by evil spirits intent on causing sickness. In this instance ethnology speaks of illness occasioned by *loss of soul*.

Loss of soul can also occur if a person suffers a shock or pain such that the person's soul (or one of several) hurries away from being near the body because it can no longer look upon suffering, for example that of a woman in labour. Among many, the relevant signs of illness could be mostly symptoms like debility, signs that might be diagnosed by scientific medicine as strokes, and coma-like conditions.

In the folk medicine of Central and South America an illness triggered by loss of soul is called *susto*. The word in Spanish and Portuguese means "fright". The symptoms can be caused by anything, from the usual shocks in life to deep traumatic experiences. To avoid susto people should only be aroused from sleep very gently. Nobody should hold a mirror to a small child's face, in case he takes fright and succumbs to susto. The symptoms of the illness are very varied: diarrhoea, running amok, schizophrenia, etc. There is scarcely any conceivable illness which cannot be traced back to susto.

The worker in a formerly animistic society that has not long espoused Christianity should reckon on God or the Holy Spirit sometimes being held responsible for both types of punishment for wrong behaviour. It is assumed that they commission evil-minded spirits to attack a person or that they themselves directly cause this loss of soul. The reason for this lies in existing thought patterns which – despite Christian teaching to the contrary – unwittingly make this connection seem so plausible that the corresponding notions are sustained over long periods and maintain their power to charm.

Among the indirect causes of illness is what is known as the *evil eye*, ascribed to some people who can work harm with it; the various kinds of *curses* also fit here. Ethnology sometimes calls these various influences *witchcraft*. In pre-literate societies and the like there are specialists whom people can call upon to harm a victim they wish to target for whatever reason; using a ritual the specialist will cause him to fall sick and even die. These are rituals which supposedly activate powers (mana!) or even spirits to make people ill in body or mind, or to harm them in another way. Both types of curses (the sickness-inducing ritual and the evil eye) are then said to be especially involved whenever a young person dies suddenly and without apparent reason.

There are ethnic groups in whose cultures this kind of magic is especially prominent, and considerable social tensions can result from it: a person suffering illness or harm immediately looks for suspects, whom he accuses of witchcraft – mostly those whom he or his family are already at odds with for other reasons. The accusations are seldom verifiable and mostly implicate weaker members of society, especially young women. Those presumed guilty are avenged, often in gruesome and bloody ways.

As well as indirect causes of illness, direct causes play a much more sophisticated role in animistic thinking, indeed the real role: ***contacts with evil, harmful spirit beings***. In order to fall ill a person need not have been in physical contact with a spirit being. It is enough to see or hear one. The Asheninca people of the *Pajonal* (grassland) of Eastern Peru are convinced that the sight of a rainbow – considered the work of demons – can lead to severe cases of diarrhoea.

Disabilities of all kinds belong under this category. Africans suffering from onchocerciasis ("river blindness") often attribute it to their treading on a demonic spirit's territory and being punished with loss of sight. Similar explanations are given for birth defects (birthmarks, deformities or missing limbs, etc.) interpreted as the result of an attack ("bite") by an evil spirit on the unborn baby. Depending on the severity of their defect, malformed children are often not considered human beings but as evil spirits and are labelled accordingly. Because they are objects of fear these children are neglected and mostly succumb to early death. This is one of the reasons why in these societies disabilities are seldom visible.

In medical systems with an animistic core structure one must reckon on every illness, more exactly every distinguishable symptom, having a specific spirit being; this is then accused of having caused the particular illness. The spirits are then tangible through their names, being referred to by the illness they provoke.

Here is an indication of a link between two conceptual patterns of thinking, a relationship which is quite alien to the European-Western mind: a pattern of illnesses corresponds to a pattern of spirits. The systems are considered to run parallel.

To the foreign aid worker, particularly with an academic training, any system of illness evidently relates to something scientific; on the other hand a system involving spirits is reckoned as the realm of religion or suchlike. This conceptual gulf seems to be one of the reasons why only a few doctors who are working or who have worked in the Third World have realised that the people they look after make close links between the two. The issue can be put starkly: a conceptual link between medicine and religion, something scarcely given credence by Europeans, is self-evident for animists. This can lead to significant misunderstandings between a European doctor and an indigenous patient.

Ideas like these about the cause and nature of illnesses are not by any means confined to what are termed animistic ways of thinking. Those without formal schooling lack our sophisticated knowledge of anatomy and physiognomy, which at least extends to the basic notions of the names and functions within the human body. This is why they sometimes have the strangest explanations for certain illnesses. One example is that mentioned before, the idea among the Chuuk islanders that the air they breathe goes into the heart, and that therefore to them coughing and asthma are not illnesses of the respiratory system but of the heart, treatable accordingly (cf. chap. 12). Indigenous practitioners are alert to thinking like this, European doctors are not. If their patients speak about their complaints in these terms and unwittingly think along these lines, misunderstandings are unavoidable.

From what we have said there is a need for the non-indigenous doctor or nurse firstly to learn at least the language of the locality they are working in. Secondly, they cannot avoid becoming familiar with the religion and the ideas of anatomy and physiology in their ethnic group. These are not strictly to do with animism as such, but they are really vital for understanding what patients say.

Local practitioners settle on a *diagnosis* in a variety of ways. The simplest is based on what is evident to the eye, or on what the patient says about his condition. Then the practitioner links the symptoms to a particular illness, as he has always done. The diagnostic process therefore is not basically different from that of scientifically-based medicine.

The stark contrast occurs when spirit beings (auxiliary spirits, ancestral spirits) are asked via a *shaman* or a *medium* for the possible causes of the illness. This procedure of drawing supposed medical knowledge from the life beyond is applied particularly where an unknown illness is concerned. Even *dreams* can offer some information, but often it is *divination* that supplies a diagnosis (cf. chap. 13).

Within the realm of *therapy*, the source presumably of the most serious misunderstandings between representatives of scientific medicine and patients from pre-literate societies, belongs the idea of *medication*. The misunderstandings stem from the fact that each facet links the idea with other attributes and embraces it conceptually under differing headings, such as the following:

In animistic thinking medication is not used to heal illness, but to *eliminate symptoms*. This means that the essential thing is reckoned to be a *single dosage*, and that the medicine can be discontinued when the symptoms have faded. Applying this thinking to scientific medicine can have fatal consequences for the patient. There are numerous diseases which require the patient to take medication even when his symptoms are no longer visible.

This may mean that a doctor has to coax or even compel a patient on a course of treatment to continue with medication if the disease requires it, even in the absence of symptoms. Sometimes the doctor needs to summon him, because the patient sees no reason from his own understanding of medicine why the treatment needs to continue.

Moreover, patients with an animistic mindset assume that a particular medicine is only affecting the single impaired organ being targeted at the time, without any side-effects on other organs. Patients often think it is self-evident that in scientific medicine there is for every conceivable ailment and disease, even for cancer, only one specific effective medication. Given these circumstances, the comment that smoking causes lung disease is brushed aside with the rejoinder that the hospital has a cure for everything.

In the thinking of a pre-literate society medication must be nasty to do good. Therefore a doctor from overseas will often be expected to administer an injection, or prescribe a medicine which tastes bitter or unpleasant, or which needs to be swallowed in large quantities.

In animistic systems of medicine the medication is principally *herbal*, but *animal body parts* can also feature. In some ethnic groups various *soils* or *minerals* are thought to bring healing. In this regard it is interesting that in any ethnic group's locality the number of plants categorised as medically effective roughly corresponds to the number of symptoms considered and termed ailments. These medicinal plants appear then also as elements of a concept/word field, supporting the thinking that the familiar plant world can be simply understood as "scientific".

We recognise here another link between conceptual structures alien to modern European-Western thinking and complementary to what is mentioned above: a (medical) system of illnesses corresponding with a (religious) system of spirit beings, and also with a (biological) system of plants, giving in fact three systems running in parallel.

There are important consequences of the fact that humans of an animistic background consider contact with evil spirits the most significant source of sickness. Their notion of medicine as a whole has an essentially religious basis. So the practitioner is always the specialist in religious matters, with methods that have a fundamentally religious character. From pre-history and archaeology we know that this was the case in early forms of culture, for example in the Mayan, Inca and Ancient Egyptian civilisations. The principle is at work even in the Old and New Testaments: the priest was involved in the treatment of leprosy patients (Lev. 13; Matt. 8:4).

Traditional medicines are not considered to work by virtue of their chemical composition; that is secondary, or irrelevant, because without a corresponding *magic formula* or *ritualistic preparation* along strict traditional lines there can be no effective healing. Without the formula or the "right" procedures, the right *mana* needed for an effective cure cannot be conjured up.

An indigenous healer will even take great care over collecting the required ingredients. If he makes a mistake in preparation he interrupts the process, burns what has already been prepared, and begins again. If he does not do this, the medicine with "wrong" i.e. dangerous mana can increase the patient's symptoms that need reducing and can trigger symptoms even in the healer himself, making him ill and killing him.

Here is the ambivalence of medication as a concept. It is supposed to heal, but can, paradoxically, also cause death. So in the languages of ethnic groups with this kind of understanding of medicine the word for the concept of "medication" is also used of chemicals, pesticides, disinfectant, and cleaning fluids.

According to these groups' thinking, certain conditions like a person's sexual attractiveness can be helped and enhanced through medical treatment. An appropriate medicine either increases the patient's own powers of attraction, or else releases in the other person feelings of love and sexual longing. Among the Kusasi people of Ghana and Burkina Faso, women who fear that their menfolk will abandon them often visit their practitioners for the kind of medicine that will dissuade them.

Medicines of this kind also get their mana during the preparation process, or through the accompanying magic formula, albeit with the risk of it backfiring if mistakes occur. The usual basic ingredients are sweet-smelling liquids made up as local cosmetics. Industrially manufactured and imported perfumes and scents can serve the same purpose, and are then also called "medicines". Included among these are cosmetic products having only an indirect effect, such as hair dyes, shampoo and even toothpaste.

In conclusion, there are in animism's practice of medicine a number of treatments which are believed to help alter certain psycho-intellectual conditions. They are used in a whole range of situations. If a person is noted for gloomy moods or a tendency to outbursts of raving madness said to stem from his contact with an evil spirit, then he is treated with medication that leads to a "cheering" of his heart.

Medication like this can be used by normal folk in situations requiring wisdom, a good memory, quick responses, and clear thinking and speaking: when planning a significant undertaking, or facing important decisions, or learning magic formulae that need to be recited by heart without mistakes, etc. Because "inspiration medication" like this is said to have positive effects on the emotions, people expect that it will raise their own will to achieve, their stamina and self-control. That is why people always use it against stage fright, or when they need courage or a peak sporting performance or, increasingly in this modern age, a good examination performance.

Because of its positive effect on people's intellectual capacity, this medicine is used particularly by craftsmen on difficult projects and by experts in the field of magic practices, specifically by boat builders working on South Pacific outrigger canoes, by African rain-makers and by local healers themselves, of course.

Mediums, who assist people still living to get into contact with their deceased group members, sometimes also take this medicine for additional mental and spiritual prowess; they do so if they want to – or indeed have to – fulfil their functions for their community particularly well. Only then is the medium considered able to report clearly and properly on the wishes and intentions, and various information and advice, given by the ancestral spirits being questioned.

Medicine like this is commonly held to be effective even when taken by spirit beings. It can therefore be part of the gift offered to the ancestral spirit to encourage clear information or to appease his anger and promote his friendly disposition.

Abnormalities of the spiritual and psychic kind, considered chronic or innate, cannot of course be removed by this kind of medical practice. People with related symptoms are generally not thought of as capable human beings but as evil spirits or as the offspring of evil spirits.

In none of these cases are psychotropic drugs involved, as they would be used in modern psychiatry, with their effective chemical basis. The indigenous preparations are medicines which are effective by *analogy* (e.g.

bright colour equates with enlightenment in spiritual and intellectual matters) or by the link with mana which they acquire as they are being prepared. Nor are these medicines comparable with drugs and narcotics taken by shamans to trigger their visions and ecstatic experiences which are interpreted as pertaining to souls liberated from their bodies. These show the effectiveness of chemical elements. They need not necessarily be classified as medication, given their rather different purpose.

It is not just the colour which makes a plant or a mineral the suitable basis for medication to treat a similarly coloured symptom. On many occasions it is assumed that the medication is effective because the shape is analogous. Put simply, a red swelling that resembles a tomato needs to be treated with a tomato or similar fruit, or at least with medication prepared from the fruit extract. The shape and colour of the plant aid the elimination of the symptoms, or – if the process is wrong – merely enhance the symptoms.

In animistic medical practice, even where no medication is called for (as with *massage techniques* – even on patients with tuberculosis!), the procedural techniques (quite besides their scientifically recognised benefits) are often embellished with the status attaching to the magic formulae so intrinsic to other medical conditions; the massage by itself is considered ineffectual as a way of alleviating health problems.

Medical staff trained in European-Western cultures are seldom, if ever, prepared for such eventualities before they begin their work overseas. Being unprepared like this makes for practical difficulties, because doctor and patient start from a different conceptual basis, and are unaware of the fact. Inevitably this leads to misunderstandings, because each party assumes that their counterpart shares the same agenda and explanatory framework. Expectations of the other party's viewpoint are adjusted appropriately, but they are not fulfilled. This makes for considerable long-term problems of cooperation.

The close pairing of religion and medicine in societies of an animistic mindset is not only a major problem in developmental aid, but also a danger – one that cannot be overestimated – for the culture. This occurs when scientific medicine is provided for a population in the context of development aid without taking into account prevailing habits of thinking; for example where an authority is responsible for a doctor being allocated to a largish district. Since the doctor works with completely different methods (unconnected with religion) from those of the indigenous healer, his presence will provoke conflict from the start. This conflict will even be inevitable if the doctor tries to graft the healer's methods into his own practices. From that point on at the latest, the healer will become in-

tolerable in the eyes of the colleague from the world of science, typically
where he attempts to heal and fails in the treatment of tuberculosis by
massage techniques and sacrifices to spirits, and where the doctor on the
other hand succeeds with an antibiotic treatment. The conflict between
the two is essentially a battle about authority with a great potential for
considerable reverberations in the existing culture. In this way not only
does the disempowered healer lose his authority as a fellow human, but
also – more significantly – the institution he represents loses credibility.
A doctor's activity in a culture with animism as its background strikes at
its foundations in a vital area, religion. If scientific medicine is consistently practised without regard for this aspect, then animistic cultures will
sooner or later lose one of their main supports, since nothing other than
scientific medicine with no link to religion is a substitute. Does the European doctor disrupt or even destroy cultures?

The question arises as to the justification of Western understanding of
medical practice as development aid or even humanitarian aid. If the aid
is viewed in this light of negative shifts in cultural practice, then any kind
of medical support for such societies is out of the question. Yet viewing
aid from this single standpoint brings one up against still more issues;
these are triggered when members of cultures like these are denied any
medical help for specific instances with the justification that withholding
treatment gives due credence to their culture. That inaction is tantamount
to sacrificing humans on the altar of their culture and incurs the accusation of failing to bring life support.

One final point: in European-Western societies there is a widely
shared belief that animistic medical practices like those highlighted in
this chapter amount to "nature's cures" which we have forgotten and to
which we need to "return" as swiftly as possible. I have serious reservations about such thinking. I am, of course, clear that our own scientific
medicine has obvious inherent flaws, in neglecting for instance psycho-
social factors relating to ill health in pre-literate societies. I am also ready
to admit that healers in ethnic groups with animistic tendencies have over
thousands of years gathered expertise in "herbal medicine" placing them
in the position to use plants for their chemical ingredients in treating illness successfully. It is, however, clear that this forms merely one aspect
of healers' therapies. The other consists of their using principles of analogy, relating the basic ingredients to the shape, colour, etc. of the particular symptoms. As a procedure this is just as way-out as those haphazard
diagnoses which healers pronounce with help from the principle of divination. Nobody can seriously wish to promote a "return" to a medical
practice where treatments are used because they represent "original wis-

dom" and because they are mentioned in the context of "ancient wisdom" in the hands of people said to be "living in harmony with nature".

The specialist term applied to the relations between illness and culture varies in ethnological literature. In older publications it is *ethnomedicine*. In recent times the term increasingly used in substantial studies is *medical ethnology*, from the usual term *medical anthropology*.

Lux (2003) goes into helpful detail on these and other matters of medical ethnology. Kippenberg/Luchesi (1978) is very informative on the notion of "magic".

More on the topic of this chapter can be found in the following studies:

Good, Charles M.: Ethnomedical systems in Africa. Patterns of traditional medicine in rural and urban Kenya. New York and London 1987.

Hinderling, Paul: Kranksein in "primitiven" und traditionalen Kulturen. Norderstedt 1981.

Johnson, Thomas M.; Sargent, Carolyn F.: Medical anthropology. A handbook of theory and method. New York 1990.

Keck, Verena: Falsch gehandelt – schwer erkrankt. Kranksein bei den Yupno in Papua New Guinea aus ethnologischer und biomedizinischer Sicht. Basel 1992.

Kippenberg, Hans. G.; Luchesi, Brigitte (Hg.): Magie. Die sozialwissenschaftliche Kontroverse über das Verstehen fremden Denkens. Frankfurt am Main 1978.

Krauss, Günther: Kefu elak. Traditionelle Medizin in Oku (Kamerun). Göttingen 1992.

Lux, Thomas (Hg.): Kulturelle Dimensionen der Medizin. Ethnomedizin – Medizinethnologie – Medical Anthropology. Berlin 2003.

Minz, Lioba: Krankheit als Niederlage und die Rückkehr zur Stärke: Candomblé als Heilungsprozess. Bonn 1992.

Pfleiderer, Beatrix; Greifeld, Katarina; Bichmann, Wolfgang: Ritual und Heilung. Eine Einführung in die Ethnomedizin. Berlin 1995.

Romanucci-Ross, Lola etc. (eds.): The anthropology of medicine. South Hadley, Mass. 1983.

Schiefelhövel, Wulf ; Schuler, Judith; Pöschl, Rupert: Traditionelle Heilkundige – Ärztliche Persönlichkeiten im Vergleich der Kulturen und medizinischen Systeme. Braunschweig and Wiesbaden 1986 (Curare-Sonderband 5.1986.

Sullivan, Lawrence E. (ed.): Healing and restoring. Health and medicine in the world's religious traditions. New York and London 1989.

Williams, Paul V. A.: Primitive religion and healing. A study of folk medicine in North-East Brazil. Cambridge 1979.

Zier, Ursula: Die Gewalt der Magie. Krankheit und Heilung in der kolumbianischen Volksmedizin. Berlin 1987.

Chapter 16
Animism and Christianity

This chapter explains what these two religions have in common and how they resulted in the basis for the development of typical mixed religions such as cargo cults, voodoo, Umbanda, Macumba and Candomblé.

Besides significant differences, there are a number of common features between Christian forms of religion and animistic forms, which can be understood as akin to parallel structures. When the religions came into contact during the processes of Christianisation, the effects were many and varied. The period of discovery, colonisation and Christianisation of foreign cultures by the Western world strongly influenced the history of pre-literate societies and their religions in the centuries of the modern era. It changed them radically, and led to particular developments.

Of all the many parallels in the make-up of Christianity and animistic forms of religion only a few of general significance can be mentioned here. Both have a similar *worldview* (though they differ in conception); both have a comparable view of *what a human is* (Christian: body, soul and spirit; animistic: body and one or more souls/spirit doubles); and both have a doctrine of the continuing *life of the personality after death* (Christian: according to the conduct of one's life, either in a state of eternal bliss or damnation; animistic: according to culture, either as an ancestral spirit or as an evil spirit of the dead).

The parallelism in basic structural patterns is one of the reasons, among many others, why the activity of Christian missions in societies with an animistic orientation (unlike activity in other societies) has experienced relatively little rejection. The central concerns of biblical doctrine are more easily grafted on to an animistic understanding of the world than they could be grafted on to the body of teaching of one of the book religions. This is evident conversely from the statements of church workers overseas talking about their personal experiences. When they compare them they are most likely to view their activity in animistic contexts as satisfying, rewarding and successful.

The fact that Christian doctrines are relatively easily integrated with animistic thinking does not mean that during the transmission process they come across exactly as envisaged. Christian concepts can be recognised in the target culture in unexpected places, but the theological relationships which arise are not without ramifications. The cause for this lies in the difference between the systems; these cannot simply be annexed, because they are not compatible in every aspect. As with all world views and patterns of thinking, animistic thinking functions through grids or matrices which require any new elements to adapt to its characteristic form when they meet. One can compare the process with that of superimposed geological layers. The substrate lying at the bottom influences through its surface structure and its chemical make-up the superstrate placed over it. Vice versa, the superstrate imposes some changes on the substrate, most notably where their surfaces touch directly. What exactly will emerge finally cannot be closely predicted during the process itself. Sometimes we find a concept in the foreign thought system made even more unfamiliar as to become unrecognisable. Thus the unforeseen must be taken into account, as in the following:

On one of the islands of Melanesia Catholic missionaries began their work by visiting the homes of the elderly who were sick or close to death, and baptising them. After a relatively short time most islanders did indeed take part in the regular Sunday church services that were being held, but – to the astonishment of the missionaries – refused for a long time to have their children baptised. The islanders' seemingly odd response had a simple explanation: their own world view included rituals where people could be made ill or even killed. Their own rituals and the foreigners' manner of conducting baptisms showed a number of parallels. Because most of those baptised at the outset of the missionaries' work died from their physical weakness soon after, the islanders concluded that baptism must amount to a *death magic*. Naturally they did not wish to subject their small children to such a thing.

This example makes it all too clear that elements of a culture to be meaningfully exported into another culture and embedded in a particular place cannot simply be transplanted like this; they need to find their milieu independently. The foundational structure of the substrate makes this a matter of necessity.

It is worth noting that the *form* of a cultural element is easier to adopt than its *substance*. This explains the theological difficulties experienced in many overseas churches surrounding the concept of offering (especially its meaning in the New Testament), even after more than a century of mission history and theological application within the local context.

In its ideas and its theology the notion of an offering is often firstly linked with that of a gift. An offering is defined as a gift offered – unlike other gifts – to a higher being; perhaps a gift intended to solicit a favour from an ancestral spirit. The problem lies in the fact that this kind of gift contains the obligation of a reciprocal gift, as is usual when an item is given in return for an artwork or for a home-cooked meal. In this way offerings to higher beings within a conceptual system like this are linked to the realm of commerce and services, something unimaginable in European Christian theology. It is therefore not surprising if theologians from an animist background make pronouncements that are at least rather disconcerting; it helps to clarify why even the most sincere indigenous Christians display time and time again through their behaviour that they are actually attempting to make themselves amenable to God through an offering made in this frame of mind, as the following shows:

A man found a job in a far distant town. On the Sunday before the beginning of the man's journey to the new job the head of his family required the relatives each to bring one dollar to the church service and place it on the altar as an "offering". By way of justification the family head announced that the man would then be protected from any accident.

It is clear from this example that there was no obvious problem with transferring the new form of offering (money as a gift of value, an altar instead of an ancestral shrine) into people's religious thinking. The new substance (an offering free of any intention to manipulate God) was not transferred.

An important reason why conceptual systems have a distorting effect like this is to be found in the fact that new ideas are largely transferred to other cultures via the spoken word. There is no other way to transfer the New Testament concept of offering except to use the word for "offering" in the target culture, into whose mindset the new concept is to be embedded. This word has specific features of its meanings, and a particular position within a semantic field. Its positioning defines its meanings; and because its semantic features are rooted in the unconscious these are remarkably stable elements. The substance of a word's meaning tends hardly to change. It would be naïve to suppose that one could prevent any wrong understanding of offering merely by supplanting the old meaning by substituting the "more correct" explanations of the new concept. Principles underpin the nature and function of culturally shaped patterns of thinking; they guide an intricate and protracted process whereby new meaning brings new substance to traditional word forms.

If one takes into consideration that every single culture (and the thought system within it) is made up of thousands of similar factors, then one gets some idea what role culture actually plays in the process of foreign elements being adapted and accommodated.

What can happen whenever a cultural substrate formed along animist lines is overlaid by one structured along Christian lines is exemplified by

a series of religious phenomena which are known as *cargo cults*. These
occur in specific guises throughout the world. In Melanesia they have
imprinted themselves on the consciousness of the general public and of
ethnologists since about the middle of the nineteenth century. There also
they have acquired the name which has become a conceptual term in academic use.

Cargo in English usage means goods freighted by plane and ships. For
this reason cargo cults are sometimes called by their less common name,
goods cults. Three elements form their basis: 1) the thought patterns of
animism and ancestral cults, 2) the revelation that the foreigners (Europeans, Americans and Japanese) occupying the Melanesian islands possessed abundant wealth and a prowess in technology which exceeded
anything previously imagined by locals (agricultural machinery, weap-
onry, radio sets and telecommunication, ships and aeroplanes), and 3) the
doctrines of Christianity.

Cargo cults and comparable phenomena are also called *millenarian*,
millenarianistic or *chiliastic* movements. The reason is their relation to
the thousand-year reign mentioned in the New Testament (Revelation
20), which John portrays as one of perfection and fulfilment. The millen-
nium referred to by the cargo cults is, of course, not thought of as comprising exactly one thousand years. Transformation and eschatological
myths are involved in many such movements, in their depiction of events
where a *saviour* appears, sweeping aside all kinds of unbearable situations and establishing a realm of peace and well-being (cf. chap. 13).
Cargo cults are for this reason also called *salvation movements*.

This ancestral cult movement (i.e. an essentially animistic pattern of
thinking) starts from the idea that well-being is ultimately guaranteed by
a person's ancestors, and thus has its source in the non-physical world.
The person possessing abundant material goods equal to his foreign rivals
was bound to have great mana – and thus powerful magic – at his disposal; he had obviously prompted his ancestors to share it with him liber-
ally. At the awarding of contracts to those perceived to be ancestral spirits
the behaviour of these foreigners (as witnessed by the indigenous Melanesians) was indeed impressive; in the locals' view it could only be understood as a manifestation of magic, especially during times of war: a
person in uniform spoke unintelligible words (in English, of course!) into
a gadget from which emanated equally unintelligible but audible replies.
A short while later ships or planes landed and unloaded spectacular quantities of cargo, yet only for use by the foreigners. The same happened
whenever a foreigner wrote strange symbols on paper that locals could
not read, and sent them off in an envelope. The Melanesians had no idea

where the goods came from nor how they were produced, nor how many people had worked to make them.

Their wish to possess wealth like this led them to behave in a way which we are already familiar with in relation to preparing medicines. Many ethnic groups cut landing strips in the bush and equipped them with dummy aircraft built on stilts. These were designed to attract the planes laden with the goods from the ancestral spirits. In many areas (for example on the islands of Vanuatu) local people adopted fantasy uniforms and held imitation military ceremonies following the foreigners' example. However, the thing that was decisive for the rise of the cargo cultures was the religious dimension: the doctrines, liturgies and rituals of Christianity that they associated with foreigners ran parallel in their thinking with their likely special influence on the will of ancestors who had passed into the afterlife.

The outcome was the manifestation of cargo cults, and cargo community members gathering on Sundays dressed in military uniforms on compounds in front of their churches. The cargo flag would be raised to the sound of whistles and parade ground commands before people marched into their actual service in church.

This rather up-front behaviour so typical of Melanesian cargo movements rests on structural patterns enabling them to be universally classified and interpreted.

The rise of a cargo movement begins with a *prophet* announcing a *cataclysm*, namely the imminent end of the world. According to this, ancestors will return to earth in the company of a liberating power that will create unhindered access to all those goods that people so desire. Next (according to the prophet and the cargo community) comes a realm of eternal happiness. All this involves preparations for the arrival of wealth, the laying of landing strips and building of store houses for the goods. An *organizing cult* is born to create norms directing the cargo community and its ritual of celebration. Yet while these preparations are underway vital necessities risk being overlooked. The care of livestock and small-holdings may get neglected, and money may be thrown to the wind on the assumption that it will soon lose its value.

The fact that the new cargo community has thus far had to go without the promised wealth is explained by the prophet and his disciples in a variety of ways. On the basis of the prevailing explanation two fundamental kinds of cargo movements are operating here.

The first kind explains the continuing absence of cargo with the reasoning that, ever since the arrival of the white foreigners, local people have neglected their own culture and religion. This has led to the demand that previous indigenous cultural practices (no matter what people sup-posed these to be) should be revived. This is why these cargo phenomena are called *revitalisation movements*; they are characterised by anti-colonialism, by a hostile attitude towards Christianity, and by a hatred of foreigners. An example of this is the Mau-Mau uprising in East Africa immediately after the Second World War.

The second kind seeks to explain the absence of cargo thus far by re-ferring to the lack of effort made by locals to draw closer to the foreigner. What emerges as a substitute is a demand for locals to be slavish imita-tors of the foreign culture and at the same time to push towards accultura-tion that speeds up the evolution in the culture and society. When this oc-curs cargo churches like those mentioned above take root.

Cargo cults are continually springing up in various places and linking effortlessly with charismatic Christian conceptions and movements. Yet as a rule they are generally short-lived, because most of their leaders' prophecies are so irrational that they cannot happen. One of the earliest and best documented cargo cults in Melanesia, called the Milne Bay movement, collapsed when its prophet forecast a date for the arrival of the cargo, and the day came and went with nothing unusual.

The early successes achieved on the basis of such irrational happen-ings are astonishing. The leader of the Mount Turu movement set up in 1970, Matias, managed 83% of the votes in his constituency; he had promised that all those who had paid their "membership subscription" promptly would be granted white skin on independence day.

Leaders of cargo movements, and more generally leading political figures in pre-literate societies and the equivalent are also successful. This may be explained by the way that – among other factors – their members are largely attuned to oral communication and can easily be won over by speakers with good rhetorical skills: what sounds insightful must be true; if it were not true, it could not sound plausible. If a degree of wishful thinking is added, persuaders have a captive audience.

In short, cargo cults are syncretistic religious movements trying to ac-cess by means of rituals the material wealth of foreigners who venture into their environment. A very good introduction to the history and the various manifestations of cargo cults can be found in Worsley (1973). Swatridge (1985) describes how even education can be understood as a cargo phenomenon.

Alongside cargo cults there is one other significant religious form, a mix of animism and Christianity: *Voodoo* (spelt variously). In its original form it came from West Africa, reaching the Caribbean, then North and South America through the slave trade. Voodoo's central concept lies in the veneration of spirits, and human communication with them. Among these spirits are reckoned a number of Christian saints, as well as the original African deities; and the most significant approaches linking with the afterlife are via the phenomena of ecstasy, trance and possession – cult members access this experience by their frenzied dances. Numerous rituals relate to the diagnosis of illnesses resulting from witchcraft and loss of soul, and their various remedies.

Over the past 200 years or so voodoo cults in their various guises have become powerful movements. They exist in Brazil and other countries of South America under the name *Umbanda*, *Macumba* and *Candomblé*; their adherents number millions. Voodoo communities exist in Haiti, Cuba, Jamaica, the Southern states of the U.S.A., and in the Black neighbourhoods of New York, Miami and Los Angeles.

One phenomenon of voodoo which is less well understood is that of the *zombie*; much popular nonsense has been aired about it. Linked to the zombie phenomenon is a specialist practitioner called the houngan. It is said that the houngan can poison people using a technique that means that they can be revived 72 hours after burial to a state of existence where these so-called reanimated zombies no longer possess will-power, but blindly follow the instructions of the houngan who gets them working slavishly for his purposes.

Remarkable pictorial evidence of Voodoo and an introductory essay are provided in Christoph/Oberländer 1995. For many years Davis (1988) has sought to clarify issues surrounding the phenomenon of zombies. I list other specialist studies below.

More on the topic of this chapter can be found in the following studies:

Bramly, Serge: Macumba. Die magische Religion Brasiliens. Freiburg 1978.

Christoph, Henning; Oberländer, Hans: Voodoo. Geheime Macht in Afrika. Cologne 1995.

Davis, Wade: Passage of darkness. Ethnobiology of the Haitian Zombie. London 1988.

Figge, Horst H.: Geisterkult, Besessenheit und Magie in der Umbanda-Religion Brasiliens. Freiburg/München 1973.

Gerbert, Martin: Religionen in Brasilien. Berlin 1970.

Hohenstein, Erica Jane de: Das Reich der magischen Mütter. Eine Untersuchung über die Frauen in den afro-brasilianischen Besessenheitskulten Candomblé. Diss. Frankfurt 1991.

Minz, Lioba: Krankheit als Niederlage und die Rückkehr zur Stärke: Candomblé als Heilungsprozess. Bonn 1992.

Swatridge, Colin: Delivering the goods. Education as cargo in Papua New Guinea. Manchester 1985.

Worsley, Peter: Die Posaune wird erschallen. Cargo-Kulte in Melanesien. Frankfurt/M. 1973. English edition: Worsley, Peter: The Trumpet Shall Sound. Cargo Cults in Melanesia. London 1957 (and later).

Chapter 17
Culture, Human Behaviour
and the Problem of Understanding

This chapter explains what we are doing when we observe human behaviour and attempt to make sense of it: keen to discover the intention behind a particular behavioural act, we take the shortest route between likely intention and behaviour. The chapter investigates errors of judgment that may result from this, and how they impact on our dealings with a foreign culture. The chapter suggests how we may lessen any harmful consequences, or avoid them.

After mentioning the most important aspects of what we call culture, namely those directly affecting the pragmatic worker in a foreign field, there remains one problem area to discuss, the one known in the pertinent literature as *cultural relativism* (Rudolph 1968).

This is the insight that human behaviour acquires its rationale and relevance essentially from its cultural context as a meaningful coherent system: everything humans undertake only ever makes obvious sense once it is understood in terms of a cultural system, with its all-pervading strategy for imposing coherency upon life; if this nexus is lacking then actual connotations are also lacking. People's actions and behaviour can only seem significant and reasonable when seen *in relation to the culture* surrounding them.

It follows that to describe human actions and all that arises from them (including the material goods and gains) without considering the depth of their cultural framework results in a partial and one-dimensional portrayal. Important issues – such as the treasure store of their concepts with their significance and all the values and intentions attaching to them – cannot be settled without reference to the cultural framework.

When we looked at the concept of culture (cf. chap. 4) we aired the issue of human behaviour not existing for itself, but always for the message one person wished to (or needed to) give another. If in a place of worship a person removes his hat, the action *may* convey the respect he desires to show.

However, there is no necessary, natural or absolute link between this action and its meaning. The action only signifies respect if this person is a Westerner or a Christian. It is the cultural frame which invests the behaviour with a special reverence. If the culture then changes to a Jewish one, the person taking his hat off signals the opposite.

The implication is that any act of human behaviour can signal a great variety of surprising, noteworthy and contradictory meanings, depending on the culture in which the behaviour is rooted. One other particular consequence is that the same behaviour can also convey the most diverse, surprising, noteworthy and contradictory meanings to those who are bystanders trying to draw inferences from outside. These observers have a perspective proper to their own culture, rather than one appropriate for the person they are observing – unless they happen to belong to the same milieu.

For this reason it is impossible to **understand** human behaviour (strictly speaking to **understand it correctly**) without first absorbing the culture which gives the behaviour its meaning. Therefore, by a correct understanding we mean: understanding the human behaviour we observe and experience in the same way that those of the shared culture and society understand it.

This definition of understanding must be phrased even more precisely, because even within one and the same culture and society any particular behaviour may be interpreted variously according to the **intentions** underlying it, as in the following example:

One day my wife and I were driving on the motorway when we were overtaken by a car occupied by a couple with two children. They had luggage on the roof of their car. It was summer and the weather was bright and sunny. From this we assumed that the family was going on holiday. When we stopped at the next service area we found we had parked near their car, and started chatting to the children. We remarked how lovely it must be to be going on holiday, and asked where they were heading. The children replied: "We are not going on holiday; we are going to our granny's funeral."

Evidently we had not understood the family's behaviour correctly, even though we were very familiar with their culture. This indicates that, despite the defined framework of observers sharing the same culture of life-strategies, human behaviour can be misunderstood. In attempting to select correctly from among several possible grounds for particular behaviour, people easily make wrong assumptions. Proper understanding, of course, requires knowledge of the culture, but also the **intention – the motive and purpose** – underlying a specific action.

By behaviour in this sense we mean every type of human activity: a person responding to a social group situation, or going hunting, or making a stone axe, or playing a musical instrument. Even actions like these have underlying intentions, motives and purposes that one needs to take into account in order to understand the overt behaviour correctly.

Wherever we encounter other people we are under an obligation to understand their behaviour properly, including interpreting their underlying motivation. We do this continually without being conscious of it, even when we are observing animals. Children even do so with regard to things, saying for example of a teacup lying on its side: "the cup is tired".

Behind this remark we recognise a principle worth following when we interpret behaviour: we take our own experience as our reference point. The child knows that when he is tired he lies down; therefore this must be true for the cup as well. When the observer has had similar experiences in a similar situation or would behave in the same way, then he supposes that the person he is observing is responding likewise. Because in this instance the link between observed behaviour and declared intention is easy to make, the observer is convinced that he has understood the behaviour correctly. The brilliant holiday weather, the family in the car and the luggage on the roof rack together provided such an easily constructed context and a meaning for it that the thought did not occur to us that under these circumstances there might be another reason for travelling than going on holiday. Our conclusion seemed so plausible that there was no doubt, even though at the very next stop on our journey we had a clear demonstration that doubt would have been more appropriate.

The way actual motives can be very different from those we envisage is illustrated by the following example. Some people sing while they work; in Italy farmers may sing operatically while picking tomatoes, and in Africa farmers have been known to sing while scattering seed. One could easily suppose that they are doing so from pure *joie de vivre*. What could be more natural, after all? In truth, though, only the jolly Italian farmer is voicing his musicality; the African farmer, by contrast, is intoning a magic spell as a plea for his plants to grow better, or for it to rain.

Our unthinking attitude which leads us to hasty conclusions when fathoming reasons for particular behaviour may stem from the fact that we are compelled to a specific chain of thinking whenever we attempt to make sense of things. Our first instinct is to observe an effect, namely behaviour. Only then can we immerse ourselves in the cause, intention and motivation driving the behaviour. Thus our understanding is based on a procedure which runs contrary to what we are hoping to make sense of. Understanding is thus always an ***attempt at reconstruction***, where the sequence forces us to uncover cause, intention and motivation by means of inferences.

This constitutes a multi-dimensional risk, one that gets riskier the further its cultural setting gets from where we feel at home. When we impute wrong motives for behaviour we are shown up at the very least as naïve or clumsy; we behave tactlessly or we blurt out a cheery remark (e.g. to the family in funeral mood and not holiday mode). In dire cases we make wrong decisions or even do our fellows a great injustice.

Let us suppose we are involved in a project somewhere in the Third World, such as a hospital or an agricultural cooperative where locals and Europeans are working in partnership. When the cash box is checked there is an imbalance; a sum of money is missing. Eventually the local project leader admits to having taken it as a temporary loan, without prior agreement with the overseeing committee, and without written approval. The European partners are aghast and mutter the word corruption. The locals, on the other hand, make no comment and wait to see what transpires, or else they play down the issue and declare that it is no great matter; it just needs discussing calmly and settling without fuss. The Europeans blatantly insist on calling it corruption. What had actually occurred was this:

The project leader had been asked by a higher-ranking relative to lend him some money from the project's funds, because a friend who lived a long way away had just died. The relative wanted to attend the funeral and also needed to buy an appropriate gift. He said that he would pay back the sum as quickly as possible.

In European eyes the case is clear-cut: a gift cannot be financed by asking a relative to take ready cash from his firm, even if he expressly says that he will repay the sum as soon as possible. (In many societies experience tells me that the phrase "as soon as possible" can equate to "after several years and repeated, strenuous reminders").

For the local project leader the case is also straightforward. If he refuses a request from a higher-ranking relative he is infringing his society's ground rule, which stipulates that authority structures need to be acknowledged. A person acting against them is behaving as an upstart in flagrant breach of etiquette, and will lose face; at the very least the talk will be of dereliction of family and social duty. In this specific instance the project leader would otherwise have committed a social lapse verging on blasphemy. He would have deprived a fellow human of the opportunity of paying his last respects to the deceased. He had no intention of bearing this personal burden, under no circumstances. Taking from the cash box seemed to him the lesser evil.

Corruption and support for a family member: two utterly different motives that can each be cited to explain the rationale behind the project leader's behaviour. For the man himself the second motive was valid. This is why his European colleagues did him an injustice by imputing to him the same motive as would have fitted their circumstances. (It goes without saying that no efficient business supervision is possible where the motivation is so close to home; any drive for strict oversight just adds to the potential for conflict in these cases.)

What, then, constitutes this special understanding we wish to apply to human behaviour? It is nothing more or less than *recognising the link between an effect* (the behaviour) *and a cause* (intention and motivation). Once we have established this link we can be said to have understood the relevant behaviour. The problematic aspect is that we can only take account of the behaviour; the causes, intentions and motivations are hidden in the minds of those whose behaviour we are observing.

Another issue is that human behaviour is seldom triggered by just one single intention. We can thus never really be sure in our quest whether we have found the relevant one, the one which in this instance really has motivated the person's behaviour. When we observe human behaviour we need to be alert: what we presume to be an obvious motive can turn out to be yet one more possibility among several others.

The more distinct the cultures of the observer and the observed are, the more relevant the above issue becomes. Consequently, when fathoming human behaviour our attempts must be all the more cautious the more the observed culture differs from our own and the more uncertain our understanding of it is.

This is significant for the development aid/church worker who is expected to take the initiatives available in foreign cultures. It means that he must swiftly get to know the target culture and all its strategies for making sense of human existence, and learn how to deal with them. In particular it means learning his fellow workers' local language. If he does not learn it, the motives behind their behaviour will remain a mystery, or else he will be imputing to them only such motives as he himself might have. The tension this leads to merely gets worse the longer he acts in this misguided way. Many projects have foundered from this, and the workers involved have been forced to abandon them.

Naturally the local partners have the equivalent issue: observing behaviour and inferring the correct intention behind it. They are equally likely to come to the wrong conclusions. However, it is often much harder for them to identify the workings of this mechanism – it would be expecting too much to suppose that such insights come naturally.

In order to counter any possible confusion the foreign worker has no other course of action than to keep adjusting his behaviour in a way to allow the host party with their own frame of reference to discern the foreign worker's motivation in each particular instance. This is a tricky process, but it is the only way of resolving incomprehension.

A further difficulty relating to the question of how to achieve understanding occurs when the overseas worker is finally back home or on
leave and is recounting to a committed audience his experiences of living
in the foreign culture. The words and pictures he uses to describe and illustrate his life embody the behaviour of the locals out there; his audience
here are all watching and expecting to be given plausible explanations to
make sense of the behaviour. In the hall they are proceeding on the assumptions prompted by their very own frames of reference – they are intent on finding the shortest route between motivation and behaviour. Precisely what the speaker has in fact experienced, namely a full picture of
"life working abroad", is quite a challenge for him to convey to the audience.

Mission workers struggle with a further issue. During their home assignment that they spend preparing talks and sorting Power Point presen-
tations they are also gathering the finances to ensure their work can be
continued. So they will take care to ensure that what they say has the correct framework for effective audience interpretation. If this is not possible
without making undue demands on their audiences, they will select those
aspects for presentation which enable full and easy comprehension.
Given that these are the circumstances, how can one manage to present
the "whole" truth? This truth must remain an aim for us to strive towards;
yet we may not be able to reach it.

More on the topic of this chapter can be found in the following studies:

Abel, Theodore: The operation called Verstehen. In: Albert 1964:177-
188. Albert, Hans (Hg.): Theorie und Realität. Ausgewählte Aufsätze
zur Wissenschaftslehre der Sozialwissenschaften. Tübingen 1964.

Fuglesang, Andreas: About understanding. Ideas and observations on cross-
cultural communication. Uppsala 1982.

Haferkamp, Rose-Anne: Untersuchung zum Problem des Verstehens
fremder Kulturen. Feldexperiment mit Schülern im Museum für Völkerkunde. Diss. Cologne 1984.

Herm, Bruno etc. (ed.): Werkbuch Mission. Lesebuch und Orientierungshilfe. Wuppertal [2]1986.

Rudolph, Wolfgang: Der kulturelle Relativismus. Berlin 1968.

Scheunemann, Gerlinde: Wenn ich "ja" sage, versteht sie "nein" – In fremden Kulturen leben. In: Herm etc. (ed.) [2]1986:57-70.

Chapter 18
Ethnology, (Church) Development Aid, Mission and the Problem of Cultural Change

This chapter explains why and how cultures change, what ethical questions arise if there are influences from outside to change or sustain a culture, and how in these circumstances an ethnologist's perspective may help evaluate the contribution of development aid, tourism, Christian evangelisation etc.

Whether their structures are simple or complex, cultures are far from being rigid constructions; they are all subject to a continual process of *change*. Therefore cultures have a history.

Changes, even significant ones, seldom affect all the constituent parts of a culture at the same time. Generally only a specific cultural nexus or a few elements undergo change. Yet no realms of a culture and their constituent elements function in isolation but in relation to one another, meshing like the cog wheels of a gear mechanism. Therefore changes in a particular area sooner or later affect elements in another area. For example, the introduction of state pension schemes has led to the extended family as an institution losing its significance for the support of older members who have retired from work. The result has been the so-called nuclear family taking its place and determining our social structures. A cultural change has occurred in religious life after it was recognised that bacteria caused infectious illnesses: in many church fellowships people taking holy communion no longer drink from the same cup; each uses a separate glass, for reasons of good hygiene.

Such procedures either arise from within a culture or are triggered from outside, i.e. from a foreign culture. Changes to a culture occur regularly, for example through a group of youngsters wishing to do things differently from those who are older, or wishing to be different – for example in the way they dress. Often changes come about through a discovery, e.g. that microbes cause sickness. However, cultural changes can occur through necessity, to remove abuses; such as in political trends, where power has accrued unfairly to particular sections of the population, who are thus able to accrue wealth and privileges at the expense of others consigned to poverty. Occasionally changes like these are violent, taking on the character of a revolution; one example being the feudal system in the European Middle Ages, which later led to the Peasants' War in Germany and the Reformation.

Cultural change arising from within is usually less dramatic; there is time for the individual elements to adjust, essentially because the change is stirred by members of the culture and society themselves. They are familiar with their culture; they live with it; and they alter it with greater judgment and patience than unknowing outsiders ever would. We may suppose that they are better judges of what is feasible, of what the impact might or might not be, even when less familiar elements are introduced from other cultures.

Yet this principle is not universally valid: it sometimes happens that attempts by insiders to graft foreign elements into their own culture bring about problems. Everywhere in the Third World there is an acute need for European-Western technology. People insist on using cars; and transporting goods by lorry is easier than by ox-cart. Where in societies with typically simple technology it seems helpful to introduce newer technology, it is sometimes clear that they lack elements essential for the effective use of advanced technology. For example, cars and ships need regular, careful maintenance, all the more so when the technology is complex. Yet maintenance is one element foreign to the technology of pre-literate cultures. The locally produced tools and implements of daily life are of simple design to allow for easy repair, and most are not worth spending time on to repair; people use them until they have become impracticable, and then replace them. More sophisticated tools and gadgets are treated in the same way, even though – with their various components – they are very prone to failure. They are used until a component breaks, e.g. the fuel injection pump in a car. If this cannot be repaired or replaced (as is often the case) the whole complicated, expensive motor is unusable. This is the reason why the lack of a "maintenance mindset" is costing the Third World a huge amount; to which is added the loss of thousands of lives, every year. The ferries they brought into service between the islands of South East Asia have highly complex technology and need to be checked and maintained carefully. Yet this is not happening. They perform well until the first defect. In the meantime all the other technical equipment has fallen into an advanced state of disrepair and the whole system collapses. Total catastrophe.

I do not mean to imply that the people are not able to understand the interconnectedness of things. The problem is that their cultures are not sufficiently attuned to their peoples' wish for new-style technology. They have not had enough time to develop a mind for maintenance.

I see some justification in supposing from this example that cultural change from outside creates greater problems than change triggered from within. This issue then leads to the question: how should the activities of outside agents working as foreigners in unfamiliar cultures and societies be viewed and evaluated?

Over the preceding 17 chapters I have taken it for granted that in foreign cultures and societies people can be engaged naturally in processes of change – or even in maintenance – according to the obvious local expectations and pressures. Yet at this stage I must pose questions about the risk incurred in this. Is the ethical reasoning sound enough to justify foreigners intervening as agents of change and maintenance in other peoples' cultures and societies? What right have we foreigners to get involved? Should we even be debating whether cultures, especially foreign ones, need altering? Should cultures not rather be viewed as entities needing to be preserved from change and decay like heritage artefacts curated by thoughtful human beings undertaking this guardianship as their self-evident moral duty?

For a variety of reasons the topic is difficult to discuss and even set out clearly. The difficulties are inherent in the topic, but they are also raised in abundance by those participating in the debate. Let us deal with the inherent issues.

The fact that they can be so fundamentally misinterpreted, that so many presuppositions abound, stems from the huge complexity of the notions "culture", "development aid" and "mission".

I have dealt in detail with culture to such an extent that it must have become clear that a single culture (even one as simple as an African pygmy group) consists of numerous elements requiring years of research and representation to collect and describe them all.

A second area presenting difficulties is the matter of defining "development aid". In biology the development of an organism involves a process of uninterrupted nuancing in an originally simple cluster of cells having the same form and function and becoming more and more specialised. Are cultures and societies requiring development aid to be equated with clusters of elements, in effect gaining the more they are subject to mutations or additions and the more they are encouraged to take a particular direction? Yes, indeed; at least in certain cultural realms, otherwise people themselves would not adapt their own culture in the way they do to meet their requests and requirements; and not continue developing it as they do. Yet: Should this occur through external change, through foreigners? Can foreigners ever determine what benefits an alien society, and what does not? Who knows best, the insider using his own culture or foreigners? Even if one concedes that the emotional and intellectual distance typical of foreigners gives them a sharper focus on many issues compared with an insider, the answer to questions like these is not straightforward.

Regarding the issue of foreigners working and causing change in an alien culture, any doubts become less significant if workers have been called to undertake the task by the foreign community itself. This usually happens in circumstances where the local commercial/economic enterprise or church community has requested specialists to help, such as teachers, doctors, nurses, kindergarten staff etc. They will have been asked to share their professional expertise and commitment. In this instance the motive for change comes not from outside but from within, from locals whose home-grown strategies for shaping existence will alter in the process. If foreign workers did not accept an invitation, and said their reason was that nobody should ever alter, or even wish to alter, anybody else's culture, they might be guilty to the charge of failing to care.

Given these circumstances, it is not easy to answer the question of how to assess the work of missions. For somebody assessing this without having experienced how the work happens on the ground an aspect of mission activity comes to the fore which development aid in his opinion does not possess. For him mission undertaken by foreigners in foreign cultures is an alien initiative, an example of how *not* to do mission. This perspective on the issue is only true to a limited extent. Foreign initiatives taking place within the foreign culture are all initiatives carried out without first involving the express permission of the local people. In the early days of mission the initiative was mostly from outsiders. Nowadays this is hardly ever the case. Whenever local church organisations are actively engaged in mission within their own environment the term alien initiative is inappropriate. The issue is a complex one, and before one can presume to come to any useful judgment about it, a number of factors need to be considered.

The difficulties start as soon as we wish to define what should be understood by the term mission. This is because it can involve groups motivated by extreme fundamentalist persuasion, by charismatics, Catholics, Protestants, all of evangelical outlook, right through to organisations tending more towards development aid. Sometimes their understanding of what constitutes mission will be very varied, and their teams' impact on the local cultures where they are working will also be very varied. Development aid organisations, both secular and church-based ones, are mostly intent on avoiding the impression that they are on mission. Their teams, however, generally have a typical outlook on life which cannot help but impact the foreign society. Quite apart from the difficulties intrinsic to the issue of cultural change and mission, we are dealing with people whose make-up and tendency makes any simple judgment about the moral justification of changing a community's culture rather difficult, because there are clearly diverging opinions and assessments among those involved on the issue of "foreign culture", especially on what "mission" should or should not mean.

Chiefly involved among these people are missionaries themselves. Their enthusiasm is of a pragmatic kind. Theorists are in the minority. Until quite recently, most Protestant missionaries were qualified in a trade or profession, an essential requirement for surviving the difficult circumstances of living overseas. Their background as skilled workers meant they represented one particular segment of society, the middle classes. They passed on their Christian teaching with their norms and values without greatly pondering over the issues. Today things have changed somewhat; people are more positively self-critical, it seems to me, but not different in a fundamental way.

Younger missionaries, in particular those at the outset, are quite commonly deeply convicted that the gospel as they understand it does not merely mean the salvation of their own people in their home environment, but also – unreservedly – in the foreign environment. Initially most of them tend to overestimate the scope, and particularly the speed, of their influence. This is nothing unusual, since even novice doctors and development aid workers and others of an altruistic temperament working in the Third World also tend to miscalculate like this. When missionaries get more experience they view things more soberly, and return home to their familiar environment with greater self-knowledge; yet they rarely see themselves as destroyers of cultures even though they are often confronted with this accusation, and even address the issue pointedly to themselves. Both younger and older missionaries have in common an experience of living the Christian life as a model which satisfies them in a profound way and which – with their vocation – gives their life fulfilment and meaning; so they consider this as a model for others as well.

A further group which we shall mention now are those we might term the "general public" here in Europe and in other Western societies. Their picture of foreign cultures and of mission work is typically straightforward, reflecting the man in the street: missionaries are extraordinary individuals with a lifestyle of gentle utopian piety. They set off overseas to care for the souls of simple folk, something that is not at all bad, but they end up preaching against the lifestyle out there of natural harmony and other delights; these preachers would do well to stop. According to this view, missionaries are in the job of disturbing people's habits, but not of destroying their cultural habitat.

"Missionaries destroy cultures" is an accusation made by people representing two factions whose intellectual stance gives them some influence over the general public. On the one hand there are the proponents of leftist political ideologies and on the other the proponents of ethnology. Sometimes they combine to form one. Some of them raise the charge of cultural destruction in a blanket fashion, in a blunt and occasionally biased manner. For such critics, missionaries are agents and perpetrators of mischief. Indeed, it is possible to speak of a conflict: the mission societies versus both groups – a conflict which sometimes simmers under the surface, and sometimes boils over.

Missionaries are often at the mercy of this combative debate, because they do not feel in a position to match their opponents' arguments, because they are only familiar with the specialism "foreign cultures" through their personal experience and attitude rather than through the claims and aims of theory. On the other hand, ethnologists rarely have a notion of what living as a Christian means for a missionary, something that is also not easy to convey.

Nevertheless certain nuances must be highlighted, for there are considerable differences among ethnologists in their critique of churches and missions. Recent studies about this controversy have brought interesting things to light (Salamone 1986). In simple terms, women ethnologists are much less opposed than men ethnologists to church and mission; women find it easier to access the ethnological sources via the missions (such as archives of mission societies, and mission stations overseas).

The most outspoken critics of missions are clearly younger men working in ethnology, particular those having no experience of fieldwork in ethnology, those having poor language skills when it comes to the ethnic group they are studying, those who are under-financed and those who are worried about not having enough material for their thesis by the end of their fieldwork period (Salamone 1986:66). On the other hand, older researchers who have spent four or more years in field research and have extensive knowledge of how missions and church organisations operate are generally willing to admit that the activity of these agencies does not inevitably destroy cultures, and that the agencies can contribute meaningfully within the environment and sometimes even help to maintain cultures.

In discussing mission, people often overlook the fact that mission workers in foreign cultures – whether in the sprawling cities of the Third World or the villages of indigenous inhabitants of the Philippines – are the only foreigners with no commercial, touristic, or sexual agendas. I mention the last point expressly because I wish to denounce it as a disgrace and because I get irate that those who warn about cultural destruction only mention the impact of churches and missions, who are busy attending to these same physical and spiritual needs which that kind of agenda for exploitative contact with civilisation causes and promotes.

Furthermore, there are a whole lot of other misunderstandings circulating among cultural experts and other critics as to what cultures are, and what mission is, specifically today.

There were times when missionaries used military power as a means of promoting the spread of the Christian faith. We need only consider the events surrounding the Spanish conquest of America in the 16th century. Such behaviour by the church and missions has long since disappeared. No missionary these days bursts upon a foreign culture by his own self-anointed authority. He would not have an opportunity to carry out his goal. Public opinion, however, is less clear that missionaries and church workers never compel anybody in any way whatever to become a Christian. The missionary these days is no longer hailed as a "faith hero", which was the way he was perceived in the first half of last century. Many missionaries and church workers are now lecturers, advisors, Bible translators, European partners of indigenous organisations and interest groups. The public imagination still hangs on to a picture of the mission worker which gives the impression that he alone was responsible for the horrors of the European conquests and colonialism – this colonialism to serve which the missions supposedly first beat a path into foreign habitats, making themselves available as willing agents for the colonial oppressors' political, military and commercial goals.

Even if the churches and missions made mistakes over the course of history, it would be quite unreasonable to slander them as present-day destroyers of culture and to demand that they should stop their work. What would we make of somebody asserting that available healthcare was harmful to public health and should cease to exist, just because over the course of its development medicine had made mistakes and taken a few blind turns (such as blood-letting to treat anaemia!)?

Nobody who has not experienced it first-hand can appreciate the extent of the trust which people from ethnic groups place in missionaries and church workers. The Asheninca people of Eastern Peru sell their products (for example coffee) to Peruvian traders who do business in the area; and because few Asheninca Indians can read, write and add up, they are at the mercy of these traders, who dupe them by not paying the proper price for their products. To avoid being cheated, the Asheninca ask their mission workers or other church workers to accompany them to the traders, because only then do they know that they will not be cheated.

This relationship of trust goes unmentioned when the work of churches and missions is judged and then condemned. If critics recognised the broad application of this trust they could hardly persist in this mindless assertion that purveyors of Christianity are forcing it upon the locals or conning them as the accusations and sound bites claim.

A convincing proof to the contrary is provided by the history of Christian mission work in the Pacific islands. Without the relationship of trust between the representatives of the missions and the islanders themselves the evangelisation could never have happened within the short space of 55 years.

Large-scale whaling operations beginning in the second half of the 18th century had brought to the islanders the first profound influence of the cultures of the West. After the discovery of sandalwood in Hawaii in 1789 there was a kind of wood rush among Australian and American merchants, which led to deforestation everywhere: 50 years later there was no more sandalwood in the Pacific region. The clearing of forest had dramatic consequences for the islanders and their culture, but the subsequent intensifying contact with the whalers became a catastrophe. The impact of this contact on the islanders was devastating. Imagine the whaling crews – who had spent months suffering meagre ship's rations, strict discipline and back-breaking work in the cold sea mists of the North Pacific – coming across the population of a Polynesian settlement. In panic the indigenous men endeavoured to bring their womenfolk to safety. That was only possible in the larger more mountainous islands with deep valleys and thick undergrowth. Venereal diseases spread, and there were measles outbreaks and smallpox epidemics.

The next to land on the Pacific islands were American and European church representatives, whose behaviour was in stark contrast to the whalers' and the sandalwood traders'. These recent arrivals had come with no commercial interest, and they were energetic in confronting the excesses of the white traders, often taking the side of the local "Kanaka" (as the indigenous were nicknamed by the white traders) even against the governments of their own countries of origin, in the declared endeavour to keep national politics away from the islands. The word quickly got around the localities. Many islands whose population had succumbed to the traders sent representatives to where mission stations had already been established and begged desperately for "their own" missionary; they well knew that the sandalwood traders and the captains of the whaling ships were afraid that the crimes of their men would become known to the home country courts via the missionaries' reports. This prospect did indeed compel the captains to intervene and discipline their crews. The often repeated accusation that missions undertook their activities merely to mask their own colonializing endeavours in the Pacific region is not borne out by the facts (Koskinen 1953; Jaspers 1972).

Because the representatives of the churches and missions on the islands argued the case for the islanders' rights consistently and with conviction, they won the trust of the title-holders, i.e. the local political leadership. Not surprisingly, these locals did not oppose the new teaching and did not reject it. In these circumstances it was not a case of missionaries having to win them over by fair means or foul.

Behind the charge against church organisations that their activities destroy cultures we can discern the false insinuation that foreign cultures and their structures are one hundred per cent wholesome and beneficial for all concerned, that they manage life's problems in an ideal way, at least better than any supposed solution in other cultures, and even better than the one Europeans might suggest. The inference from such unproven speculation is that arrangements and structures in place should not be changed; that locals quite properly want these arrangements and structures to continue – so goes the unproven assumption. By dint of this delusion a simplistic image of culture is held up for our approval: a shining example of what is said to be most appropriate for the population to maintain. It is easy to conclude from this that nothing ever needs altering, and nothing should be altered. The logical extension of this is that foreign cultures are all the more untouchable the more exotic they are, like holy cows unblemished by sacrilegious contact with reality.

The behaviour of the people themselves who use foreign cultures to shape their existence contradicts this hallowed image. They would willingly remove elements from their cultures, disregard them and espouse new elements if the need arose (a change in life's circumstances, in the climate or the school syllabus, or whatever), for example if this took the stress out of work practices or if this just appealed to them (new technologies such as the mobile phone). We Europeans relentlessly update our cultures, eager and ever faster, with the latest versions (still) proving inappropriate and unsatisfying. I shall return to this theme later.

It is astonishing how people can declare without thinking twice that in foreign cultures, at least in pre-literate ones, the population once lived in a paradise of relaxed social structures and circumstances, before churches and missions inevitably wreaked their destruction. This sort of commentary has since acquired all the qualities of a myth. Robert Edgerton (1992, 1994) has shown how little justification there is for it.

Also, it has been forgotten or deliberately ignored that cultures and their processes can work against people and their interests and the needs of mind and soul. All cultures – even the so-called civilised ones – have these aspects and elements in them.

In general we need to say that it is not only the ideal situations but also the blatantly awful crimes people are ready to commit which are shaped by the respective culture and its rules. The concentration camps of the Third Reich are one example, with their rituals, uniforms, insignia and experiments in cruel social and scientific ideology. Cultures and their religions can lead to a dead-end, from which there is no exit for anybody because they are unable or unwilling to admit their own fatal position.

We should not be blind to the issue that some individuals and groups throughout the world experience traumatic violence perpetrated via hidden structures in their own culture and social system. There are even forms of religion – or at least individual aspects within them – which mean grave psychological distress for those affected. One example of this is the anguish for tens of thousands of women suspected of witchcraft in the European Middle Ages until the Renaissance and the Early Modern Period, and who went to their deaths after unspeakable physical and emotional agony. In some societies this is occurring even today.

In many South American Indian groups their religion teaches that a person's soul at his moment of death becomes a demonic spirit-being which attacks those left behind; its aim is to pull them down to the same fate. This creates among the surviving population a fear of being present at the death of a relative or of having him die at home. The fear can drive people to carry a dying person into the woods and abandon him there. It is impossible to fathom what kind of hopelessness lurks in existential crises for people who believe that life after death offers nothing but an existence as a demonic spirit which threatens continual mortal danger for those still living.

An awful example of cultural and religious elements being stacked against people and their requirements is as follows: in numerous African ethnic groups every year there are tens of thousands of girls who undergo female genital mutilation in the name of religion. They are thereafter incapable of sexual fulfilment, to say nothing of the health risks of the alarming unhygienic procedures (the use of pieces of glass and razor blades) involved in the circumcisions (Lightfoot-Klein 1989). In a (modern) Christian setting this outrageously shocking ritual and many others besides (such as the burning of widows) are unthinkable; critics of the work of churches and missions choose to ignore this fact when decrying and demonizing Christian sexual morality.

In chapter 15 on medical work in pre-literate cultures I mentioned among other issues whether medicine with its "traditional knowledge" can be equated with "natural healing", or whether it requires at the very least supplementary, scientific medicine. The following case is self-explanatory:

A young Indian woman from the South American Chaco (Paraguay) had given birth at home. During the difficult birth there had been complications, and she had suffered heavy bleeding. As it got worse her relatives took her to the local healer, the shaman. Following his ritualistic medicine routine, the shaman sprinkled ash from a wood fire into her wound and instructed the relatives in a further procedure: to tie her legs together at home and allow her nothing to eat or drink for a fortnight. When the patient seemed on the point of dying from this drastic treatment she was brought to the local Mennonite compound's clinic (where I met her and heard her story). After a few weeks she was able to return home healed. We can suppose that she for one did not think that the scientific medical treatment disturbed or destroyed her culture.

The situation of women and the efforts made to give them equal rights yet again constitute classic examples of hotly debated cultural change. It can be assumed that from a world-wide perspective, and at least in the non-industrialised countries where most of the mission and church activity goes on, women do 80% of the routine work but own just 20% of what is produced. This state of affairs is underpinned and approved by the norms and values of the cultures themselves. I cannot see why this should amount to grounds for classing discrimination against women as "worth maintaining" merely because it is a publicly guaranteed outcome of social structures! Somebody wishing to alter the situation would inevitably be involved in thorough and possibly destructive cultural change.

Critics of mission and church work tend not to view intervention in these areas as reprehensible. Measures to eliminate these abuses readily gain approval among the public in Europe and the West; they are easily understood under "development aid". This is perhaps because, as in the case above, discrimination against women can be measured objectively in percentage terms and is not directly linked to religious structures. Anybody who is opposed at least seems more justified than somebody opposing hidden abuses which are wrapped up as discrimination against women in the structures of a foreign religion and which come to light less often. Yet, where changes in religious forms are necessary to remove such discrimination, the critics tend to be vocal in attacking the supposed culturally destructive work of churches and missions – whose declared aim is to promote such changes. The two types of changes being sought are not at all dissimilar in principle.

We just need to realise what happens if we intervene in a social process to bring about any changes, to give girls and women the opportunity to achieve emancipation, for example in their education and access to higher education. The consequences are sometimes far-reaching: the resulting conflicts between the sexes and generations alter family ties and authority structures in general. The consequences can entail the affected society being destabilised by the inevitable outworking on its economy, because the economy essentially is based on women being discriminated against. Amazingly, in this context nobody talks in terms of destruction or raises so much as an objection against cultural change; it is called giving help to encourage self-help. However, things are not that simple in reality.

Further examples where culture can appear to be brutally inhuman are where young men in many South-American ethnic groups are made to undergo initiation rites. On these occasions they can be buried awhile up to their neck in an ant heap, or tied up directly above a hornets' nest. This can indeed show that somebody is a man displaying no audible pain. But is it also clear that the taking of a man's life is being condoned here, perhaps even in the name of a deity who might be angered if the ritual was neglected. In our culture this would be an instance of premeditated harm, to be brought before a court. Is the ritual to be maintained just because it is part of a foreign culture?

In this point it is right to mention a group of people who cannot participate in the discussion about the work of churches and mission, or who simply have not been asked. I mean those overseas in the Third World who are on the receiving end of development aid and mission and thus directly involved. If asked for his view, nobody in my experience who is living in a culture now impacted by Christianity ever wishes himself back in the old ways.

In many areas of the world indigenous church organisations are operating in the wake of initiatives by mission societies. They are becoming aware of increasingly vital tasks in countless hopeless and helpless situations. What they are achieving is the opposite of cultural destruction: many are concentrating on removing the scars of destruction that others have inflicted. Third world Christian organisations are known to be less prone to corruption – and they have their own internal structures which can be maintained even where conflict is undermining political and central administration; these indigenous church organisations with their aid programmes are not forced to stop, even where nothing else is functioning on a state level.

There is a further reason to call into question whether the activity of church organisations can be viewed from the sole perspective of a culture being destroyed, which is the focus of the argument these days. Even when one considers that somebody like the apostle Paul did not mince his words but dared to speak boldly against Greek culture, or that the first missionaries to the Germanic tribes sometimes brutally took a sharp axe to the roots of their religious symbols, even then the accusation of cul-

CHAPTER 18: ETHNOLOGY, DEVELOPMENT AID, MISSION ...

tural iconoclasm is problematic. Can one really only speak of destruction here, when sublime cultural achievements such as our gothic cathedrals, or Michelangelo's paintings in the Sistine Chapel, the works of Shakespeare or Bach's Mass in B Minor resulted from it? There are a whole lot of cultures and languages which without the endeavours of Christian organisations would either have disappeared long ago or would not have survived in the first place.

For a start, the term "destruction" is fundamentally incorrect. In the life of a people there is scarcely anything *more* stable than the thought structures which determine behaviour and hence culture. If a group like this has a large enough number of individuals then its culture as such is not generally endangered: it cannot be destroyed in the usual meaning of the word, and certainly not by church workers or missionaries. That accusation would be overstating somewhat the church's ability and influence!

Of course, there have been occasions when foreigners have indeed destroyed cultures, even though they were acting with the best of intentions. The stone axe played a significant role as an authority symbol for the Yir Yoront people of Australia (mentioned already in chap. 7). The first foreigners arriving in the ethnic area were Australian cattle farmers, not church workers or missionaries. They introduced them to the steel axe by using it as their way of paying for tasks. The steel axe brought about a sudden cultural change, which within a very short time led to the collapse of the social system and values of the relatively small ethnic group. Yet such cases are rare. Cultures are solidly built systems and have a natural inertia against very rapid changes, and they are resilient against collapse.

Just how absurd the charge of cultural destruction can appear when applied one-sidedly to church organisations and missions is evident in the following. If in a culture the sun and moon are being worshipped as deities, a church worker would comment and refer to relevant Bible passages and say that such behaviour was to be rejected. A comment like that would result in our colleague being criticised for destroying the local culture. However, a teacher explaining to local pupils the basic notions of astronomy such as the movement of the sun and the moon, and when dealing with the topic of sun and moon calling them physical astronomical phenomena, is not in principle doing anything different from the church worker; but it does not count as cultural destruction, just educational support.

This kind of criticism lacks logic and conviction in arguments about the processes of cultural change affecting other contexts as well. With the development of modern agricultural techniques the typical Black Forest farm, for example, has undergone radical change. Many tools that in the past were hand-made and repaired by the farmer (such as the threshing flail) are no longer employed. If an animal falls sick, it is no longer treated with holy water or the rituals of magic medicine as it would have been universally only a few decades ago. These days the farmer rings the vet, who can get to the farm – even in winter – because nowadays the roads have all been cleared of snow, unlike in the past. Technical "development" has brought an end to these things and this thinking, and has extinguished Black Forest culture in many areas of life. Yet nobody calls this cultural destruction; they call it progress.

I would like to take the issue to the limits of the absurd by asking what a young Black Forest farmer would say if he were forced to follow his grandfather's routines of business and animal husbandry on the grounds that it was vital for maintaining the Black Forest farming culture!

In support of this comes a revealing anecdote. Perhaps some aspects did not quite happen as the story goes, but its core message is helpful. Once upon a time an ethnologist was talking about the work of a church colleague with an elderly Indian. The ethnologist said pointedly that the Indian would do better to stick to ancestral ways and think, decide and act like his grandfather. This prompted the Indian to ask why the ethnologist himself did not live like his own grandfather.

For this reason I can fully endorse Girtler (2004:81) who says "It is not the task of the field researcher to advise the groups and cultures in question for nostalgic reasons or for reasons of foreign tourism to go back and adopt old life styles."

Yet this should not mean that the otherness of foreign cultures can rightly be swept aside as soon as possible by the foreigners called to work there. Their endeavours – which I trust I have recognised and clarified in the previous chapters – are defined by their ethical parameters, making them responsible for the changes brought about. It would also be naïve to believe that people in foreign cultures just need the gospel, to solve all their problems, or indeed for their problems to have been solved already. Yet it should mean that without exception all foreigners engaging with a society's foreign culture are agents of change; and that they should not be labelled simplistically at the outset on the basis of their particular activity as good agents or bad agents. The fact that somebody is a church worker or a missionary does not automatically make him into a culture wrecker. In partnership with locals he is an agent of change endeavouring to achieve change that locals wish for; this kind of change is not to be crudely vilified as destruction. Incidentally, this is sometimes the view of ethnologists – even eminent ones like, for example, Ward Hunt Goodenough. At the beginning of his substantial investigation (1963) on issues to do with changes to cultures caused by development aid and other aid Goodenough underlines the similarity in principle of all agents of change, and lists church workers and missionaries in the same breath as engineers, mechanics, teachers and so on.

If change were equated with destruction then no tourist should ever visit a developing country, and no emergency and development aid should be undertaken. I draw particular attention to this last point because such aid does not merely cause considerable change, but is offered with the declared intention to bring such changes about; this is a claim that churches and missions (together) do not assert with the same self-confidence.

The view that cultural change by itself is not fundamentally destructive has been supported even by Leighton (1980) in a study which examines the relationship between cultural change and mental illness.

More on the topic of this chapter can be found in the following studies:

Edgerton, Robert B.: Sick societies. Challenging the myth of primitive harmony. Toronto et al. 1992. [German edition: Trügerische Paradiese. Der Mythos von den glücklichen Naturvölkern. Hamburg (Kabel) 1994.]

Girtler, Roland: 10 Gebote der Feldforschung. Vienna 2004.

Goodenough, Ward Hunt: Cooperation in change. New York 1963.

Harding, Thomas G.; Wallace, Ben J. (eds.): Cultures of the Pacific. Selected readings. New York (Macmillan) 1970.

Jaspers, Reiner: Die missionarische Erschließung Ozeaniens. Münster 1972.

Koskinen, Aarne A.: Missionary influence as a political factor in the Pacific Islands. Helsinki 1953.

Leighton, A. H.: Kulturwandel und psychische Erkrankungen. In: Pfeiffer/ Schoene 1980:247-256.

Lightfoot-Klein, Hanny: Prisoners of ritual. An odyssey into female genital circumcision in Africa. New York and London 1989.

Pfeiffer, Wolfgang M.; Schoene, Wolfgang (Hg.): Psychopathologie im Kulturvergleich. Stuttgart 1980.

Salamone, Frank A.: Missionaries and anthropologists: An inquiry into their ambivalent relationship. Missiology 14.1986:55-70.

Sharp, Lauriston: Steel axes for stone-age Australians. Human Organization 11.1953:17-22. Also in: Harding/Wallace 1970:385-396.

Chapter 19
Fieldwork in Ethnology

This chapter explains how ethnological facts can be collected using simple procedures and how conclusions can be drawn. A central issue is how to find informants for specific cultural topic areas, how one should interact with them, how to ask them questions and note their answers, and how to classify and evaluate the results.

19.0 Introduction

A person seeking to get acquainted with a foreign culture or at least with some of its aspects cannot reckon to succeed simply by spending time *in situ* taking in what he sees and experiences. If he is an attentive observer, learning from what he is observing, he will spot a whole number of cultural phenomena. Yet experience shows that much of importance nevertheless gets overlooked, especially the cultural areas hidden in peoples's minds as thought structures. Chance discovery is a very meagre resource for the person intending to work competently and effectively in a foreign culture: his work gains in quality once he grasps the foundational methods and procedures used by ethnologists in what is termed field research.

The aim of field research is *ethnography*, i.e. a systematic description of a culture or of one of its elements, usually in printed form. The basis for this description is a *data collection* (also termed *corpus*) which in an ideal case contains all the details of the cultural area to be researched.

In fact there are two collections of data which ethnography is based on: besides his ethnographical corpus the conscientious field researcher has his *logbook* for storing his own subjective sightings and experiences of the foreign culture and the events which occur around him and which he is drawn into. The logbook and the collection of data are fundamentally different, but complement one another, in that the former reveals the ethnocentrism of the culturally naïve observer-cum-researcher and the latter the ethnocentrism of the members of the foreign culture themselves.

Keeping a logbook requires self-discipline and consistency. It only has value for the later extrapolation of results if *observations are written regularly*. If the researcher is writing in the evening when he is routinely weary, quite a lot of unimportant material may get included. It is better to write observations the following morning. By then events will have become clear and the less important ones will perhaps have already vanished.

Moreover, regularly written logbook entries are a rich source for newsletters sent back to friends and relatives at home. The reverse can happen: regularly written newsletters can become a kind of logbook, whose vivid descriptions can even be distilled into manuscripts, given that publishers are easier to find for these logbooks than for formal ethnographies (see Käser 1972, 1989 and 1990).

One can only achieve a thorough cultural knowledge by proceeding *thematically*. The best way is to concentrate on those cultural areas where one's own professional interests lie. For church workers the whole realm of religion is on offer: perceptions of God, of the human soul and of man, etc. Doctors and midwives become involved with how local healers think and operate. A worker responsible for literacy and reading programmes collects material by listening to local story-tellers, etc.

19.1 Participant Observation

An important method for fieldwork in ethnology is *participant observation*. This can always be used if one witnesses a social event in a foreign culture, for example as a guest at a wedding, as a doctor in a vaccination project, as a customer in the market place or as a midwife attending a birth. Participant observation can be broadened to include photography, video-film, audio recordings or personal sketches.

It is usually not possible to actually make notes *during* an event of this kind. A Bedouin host would be disconcerted if, having invited a guest for tea in his tent, he found him making constant jottings into a notebook! For this reason it is common practice to draft detailed *minutes from memory*, after the experience. A series of reports of similar kind about similar events, for example weddings, may then be *compared*. From their *similarities* and *differences* the strategies underlying them can be deduced and used successfully later.

It is also possible to *learn a language* by this means. The researcher needs to be alert during events involving him, to prioritize their linguistic aspects, and listen to the way people around him express themselves; he should attempt to recognise words and associate them with meaningful contexts. I shall give an example from my own field work among the Chuuk islanders of Micronesia.

Saturday is a particularly good day of the week for meeting lots of people working outdoors. If one walks into the neighbouring village late morning, one can see that beside nearly all the houses great quantities of taro roots and breadfruit are being boiled over open or semi-enclosed fires. This is how one finds out that it is not just the women who cook but the men as well, a simple but important fact in the local culture, and evident from direct observation.

In front of one house an instructive scenario is being played out. A man has filled a bowl with boiled taro roots and is about to hand it to his wife. The wife takes the bowl and says loudly and clearly: *"kinissow!"*

"Aha!" thinks the participant observer, concluding that he has just found out the islanders' word for "thank you". This could be called a *hypothesis*, because the deduction is not necessarily correct, only likely. Only after a larger number of similar situations with the same outcome would a (likely) hypothesis become a (firm) *theory*.

A quarter of an hour later the observer comes across a group of women whose husbands must also have been cooking; in a bowl each is carrying on her head is a pile of delicious-looking golden yellow slices of breadfruit. Because the path is too narrow for two people abreast, the foreigner takes one step aside into the bushes to allow the group to walk past without breaking their rhythm. As they walk by, one of the women accidently bumps against the foreigner and calls out with a start: *"kinissow!"*

At this he is surprised. Only a few moments ago *kinissow* seemed to mean something like "thank you". Yet now he has heard it in a context implying "sorry!" His previous hypothesis cannot have been completely wrong, because from it emerged a meaning. Yet the hypothesis needs to be phrased differently or augmented.

The active observer is convinced from this experience that the meaning "thank you" which he associated with *kinissow* from his first encounter is not the full meaning an islander can attach to it. Without observing actively in both contexts where the word was employed, he would not have reckoned he should use it to mean something else in its range of meaning – for example, to excuse himself for being careless. From this he also deduces the proper way of learning a foreign language: not by proceeding from his mother tongue but from the foreigners' spoken language, because in a language words get meaning from their situational usage. (Leisi 1975 has written very vividly on this topic).

For that foreign active observer the two situations he has just witnessed are notionally very different. In his own language he would therefore have had separate replies: a thank-you for a present and a sorry for an act of carelessness. For the islanders, though, the two situations clearly share features; otherwise they would not be able to respond with the same linguistic form. The foreigner must then try to discover these shared features by participant observation.

In this case it is not difficult. In both experiences there is an element of indebtedness: when receiving something one feels obliged to say thank you, and when inconveniencing somebody one feels obliged to make an apology or make amends. When saying *kinissow* the islanders are expressing this indebtedness. This is the **conceptual frame** for the shared linguistic expression, a frame which conveys the impression of appropriateness to the local speakers; our active observer cannot share this impression because his own language here falls outside the frame.

Behind this issue are hidden a number of others, for example: which of the two realms of expression is the more logical. There were times when such observations harboured value judgments. Foreigners, Europeans, ethnologists and even missionaries would all claim rather bluntly that their own language formulations could convey a chain of thought properly, whereas the islanders' language was strange, irrational, primitive, at best "pre-logical". It did not occur to them when making this claim that islanders are aware of similar curiosities in foreigners' language. For example, a German naturally says "danke" to say thank-you when receiving something, but he also says "danke" when he declines something, e.g. food if he has already eaten enough. "Danke" in this situation seems equally strange and illogical to the islanders as *kinissow* does to a foreigner faced with the two situations described above. Making a kind of value judgment about it is nonsense; and claiming that some languages are "primitive" loses all justification against the backdrop of these and many other experiences.

The active observer establishes both events in his notebook, and he notes their linguistic aspects under the heading *kinissow* in his store of ethnographical data, the corpus. Over the years he collects a profusion of words each with their situation. Through this association the foreign language words gradually adopt in the observer's thinking precisely the meaning they have for local speakers.

This method of language learning achieves quick and intensive access to its characteristic, idiomatic usage. However, it only allows the learner to get close to "mastering a language". A perfect match of a word with its range of meanings only occurs if the speaker or listener has absorbed a language as a child at the tender age of language acquisition. Only then is it no exaggeration to talk of mastering a language. Talented adults may sometimes by sheer hard work learn to speak languages fluently, yet the goal of mastering them fully remains unattainable.

Active observing can be applied everywhere, anytime; sooner or later certain cultural topic areas derived from numerous details begin to crystallise – they prove of greater significance than some other areas for the foreigner developing his expertise. They can be made still more substantial and specific with the help of a further method: the *survey technique*.

19.2 The Process of Questioning

Hardly any culture exists these days on which somebody or other has not reported or published. Sometimes it amounts to a few sketchy or unreliable remarks, especially if the descriptions predate 1950 or are not by ethnologists. Nevertheless information of this kind can be decidedly helpful if we need to engage more directly with the culture: for the English philosopher Thomas Hobbes truth is easier to tease out from error than from absence of evidence. For even if somebody has only commented once on a phenomenon, we at least have a reference point – perhaps even a departure point – from which to delve further into the realms of a foreign culture, and *test* the statement against the truth.

Any statement can be of value even if it turns out to be false. In any case, firstly, it is always better than nothing, because it may blaze a trail to unimaginable treasures, and secondly because we need not commit the same mistake again; our predecessors have already seen to that.

In both cases – with false statements and true ones – we proceed by *doubting* their truth, then by formulating them as a *question* to a member of the relevant culture, our *informant*; I shall say more about him later. Meanwhile we need to find out how to cast doubt on the available facts (whether printed, or overheard by chance, or logged from our own active observation) and how to rephrase them as questions. Furthermore we must really learn how to ask questions in a foreign culture, knowing which are the essential questions (and how we should *not* phrase them) in order to achieve worthwhile results.

There are indeed wrong questions. I mean ones which cause or oblige the person to give us meaningless answers. In South Asia there are ethnic groups with animal deities such as snakes, cattle, elephants and rats. Let us suppose that we are investigating a group's religion where among its most exalted deities there is one in the form of a rat. At that stage we have heard nothing about a rat, but only know we are dealing generally with deities as animal creatures. Because we have heard in the past that deities take on animal forms as holy cows or as snakes, we now ask whether the deity under discussion looks like a cow or a snake. Our local informant now compares his notion of the rat with the two objects suggested. After some hesitation he thinks that the rat, by its habit of living close to the soil, is more like a snake than a cow; so he says that the deity is more like a snake. We can only imagine what kind of conclusion we could draw from this. Presumably the deity of our description will differ somewhat from the various depictions of a rat! The fault for this lies in our wrong questioning technique.

There is a great potential for asking the wrong questions. Let us consider just one simple example of how to devise a sheet of questions. In a short introduction to ethnology in South America by Haekel/Lukesch there is a (very) brief section on the Aché people, also called Guayaki (1972:130-131). Mention is made, among other things, of them collecting honey. Nothing further is said about this. If we wish to describe this cultural feature more closely we need systematic questioning. So we draft some questionnaires. We begin with the so-called *wh-questions*: who (men, women and children), what (tools and processes), when (season and time of day), where (holes in the ground and in trees), why (food, medicine) and how often (daily, every fortnight, when one comes across a nest), etc. We just note down systematically whatever occurs to us to ask.

If in the conversation with our informant it turns out that only men collect honey, we ask a further "why", and perhaps even devise more questions. Because a person when collecting honey from bee nests sometimes needs to climb tall trees, a considerable feat of strength, most ethnic groups consider it an activity for men.

New issues then arise, leading to new questionnaires relating to the difference between men's work and women's work. Questions and questionnaires become more substantial, like snowballs gathering weight and dimension as they are rolled downhill. Meanwhile our knowledge about the culture becomes substantial, not just our know-how about honey. We soon learn – sometimes quite incidentally – that this activity links with other strategies of coping with life. Without deliberately being asked, the locals often give us various clues which emerge haphazardly "between the lines" and become meaningful to us. Over time we move from being amateurs to experts, which allows us to formulate a theory about the cultural realm we are studying.

Regarding the honey collecting, we may happen to ask the wrong question, but one that is interesting nevertheless, such as: "What do you do if somebody is stung by a bee?" However reasonable this sounds to a European, to a South-American Indian in the rain forest it can seem bizarre or incomprehensible, because in tropical forests some species of bee are stingless; only nests of stingless bees are removed. So it is not surprising that our informant looks puzzled; to our mind the question seems sensible, to his mind it makes no sense.

We jot down the questions and number them on an *A4 sheet* of paper. The answers (for which we have an additional sheet) have matching numbers. Writing always only on one side for clarity, we restrict the questions to 10 per side, otherwise our answer sheet will not be big enough. When we ask our local informants, they give so many additional items of information and answers to our follow-up questions that we risk running out of space and muddling our notes. If for one set of questions on a single sheet there are several answer sheets, then their final evaluation proves more difficult than when one question sheet faces its matching answer sheet.

I recommend storing the question and answer sheets in a stiff-covered *ring-binder* (questions on the left, answers on the right), giving a solid surface for note-taking. This is especially important if we are visiting an older or less mobile person in his home, where we can expect some inconvenient working conditions: needing to crouch near the fire for light, away from the growling dog that does not like us and from hens and goats sharing the living space. Tables and chairs are scarce, and writing is difficult without something firm to press against.

The question and answer sheets, numbered, should have a brief thematic heading. On the answer sheet we should also put the name of the person who has supplied the information and the date of our interview. Later this can be helpful in two respects: men and women sometimes give surprisingly different answers, and not everybody we ask will be equally familiar with the culture. There may also be differences reflecting the age of those we ask: younger ones have less experience than older ones. At a later stage it is good to be able to identify from the name on the sheet the particular informant and to evaluate his information. That way it is easier to check for anomalies from the various responses.

Similar issues arise from the date of our interviews which should be written on the answer sheet. Questions and answers which we have asked or noted at an early stage in our research will be less reliable and precise because our general knowledge of the relevant cultural situation will not be as extensive as later on.

Our questions will become more exact and nuanced over the course of our research. Particularly, though, they will get more systematic, reflecting our greater familiarity with what counts as relevant for the foreign culture and what does not.

Ethnological inquiries, whatever their kind, gain in quality when we are not working alone. A researcher in the fortunate position of having a partner with shared interests should use this advantage; two people drafting the questions and interpreting the answers always come up with more than twice as many ideas as one person. On some occasions at least, a field researcher requires a discussion partner to steer his ideas, review his overhasty conclusions, reveal the mistakes that he would be blind to on his own, and also to share the joy when he makes an interesting discovery. Marriage partners play this role particularly well; at the outset it is often the only way for mothers with young children to get to know the culture they are living in. A partner writing fair-copies of question sheets, for example, will come to know about the topic area that the other is working at with a local informant and can add ideas that have not occurred to the other partner. He or she has, after all, similar levels of knowledge, is up to date and – in short – a competent fellow-worker. Moreover, there are areas of cultural inquiry which require the researcher and the informant to be of the same sex. Activities exclusively done by women or which are taboo for men (e.g. in the areas of hygiene, intimacy and love magic) can generally only be appreciated with the required delicacy by female ethnographers. This is particularly true in societies where women are considered subordinate to men.

Without input from an informant it is impossible for a researcher to get to know a foreign culture thoroughly with all its patterns of thinking. Only a local has the knowledge of its innumerable details and access to the many hidden minutiae which otherwise would remain hidden to the outsider, despite his careful application of professional strategies. The informant is deeply knowledgeable about his culture, just as we are with ours; he, too, has been immersed in it from childhood (cf. chap. 9).

19.3 Informants

There are a few facts relating to working with a local informant, male or female, that we should be aware of. Failure to appreciate the issues can make our work rather more difficult.

We should not expect close friendship with locals at the outset of our work; they will be good sources of information, but friendship in my experience takes time and patience. We must first initiate a relationship, but it will not happen overnight. A good relationship usually develops through sharing together, doing things together or relying upon one another. People often become our informants because they live alongside us in the community, selling us our vegetables or seeking our help if they fall sick.

It is noteworthy that those in the foreign culture whom we get to know quickest are generally the *marginal figures* in that society. By this we mean individuals whose behaviour differs somewhat from the norm. As a result they are viewed as outsiders, and their status among peers is thus slight. Because we as foreigners are also marginal figures with similar divergent behaviour and yet usually gain high prestige as members of European-Western culture, the so-called "marginal natives" (Freilich 1970) generally like approaching us to complement their own lack of prestige.

If we do not notice this happening – and it is often quite difficult especially at the beginning – we can find ourselves as isolated as the marginal folk themselves; then other important potential contacts start distancing themselves from us. Moreover, the marginal figures – because of their situation as misfits – are not as familiar as we would like with many aspects of the culture. What is more, they are occasionally outsiders, having been *acculturated*, i.e. by having had experience of another culture, for example by working for some time in a bigger town. They may therefore speak a second language, such as English; this makes it easier for them to approach us confidently. But the fact that they have been acculturated brings the risk that foreign influences will easily mar their statements, something that does not help us, nor the quality of our researches.

At the beginning of our residence it can be difficult to attract an informant because nobody is familiar enough with our *role* to understand what we want; we may well be suspected of being a kind of spy. Ethnologists interested in kinship relations, or in the apportioning of jobs or in ownership of land in a community might well be mistaken for officials in disguise passing on information to the government about local incomes, leading to rises in taxes. It is easy to imagine that against such a backdrop of suspicion our questioning might not bring the most reliable results!

As a rule, members of pre-literate societies experience difficulty assigning a meaningful role and purpose to a resident foreigner. Particularly they have difficulty defining a role for unmarried foreign women, whether development aid workers or missionaries; they find it inconceivable that a woman could travel so far from home, that she could still be unmarried at her age, or that she could be living without the reassuring presence of a responsible male relative like a brother, cousin or uncle. There are societies where the native men cannot introduce themselves to an unmarried woman unless a male relative of hers is present. If this situation persists for some while the local women occasionally seek to solve the issue by urging the foreign woman to marry one of their menfolk. This solution seems the best to the local families, but less than ideal to the European woman. To resolve the problems surrounding the issue, it often suffices for a male relative or two to come out to visit her.

In the recent past it was still considered a (rather simplistic) rule of thumb that people in the Third World always reckon there are two kinds of (white) foreigners living among them: the ones that are beardless but smoke are considered government officials and development aid workers; the ones that have a beard but do not smoke are church workers: especially trustworthy they may be, yet still quite irksome to deal with. The fact that they ask questions is not what distinguishes the two kinds of whites. The problem for the indigenous folk is more to do with how the whites react to specific aspects of the host culture.

As we might expect, church workers are intensely interested in the local religion, especially as regards its magic and occult aspects. Apart from the fact that the knowledge is secret or is economically beneficial to the family and thus cannot just be declared to strangers, there is a further reason for not sharing this knowledge openly: it is the locals' common experience that the strangers have a marked dislike of anything to do with magic and the occult, that they oppose it and confront those involved with it.

This behaviour is considered judgmental; it threatens their status – something the local people fear, especially as the word of a church worker is supposedly reinforced with mana and likely to provoke consequences (cf. chap. 13). This is why an ethnologist can acquire this kind of relevant information more easily than a missionary or a church worker; but nonetheless the latter both urgently need it to be able to work coherently and effectively. A great deal of tact is required. The church worker who seeks to oppose too readily, even with all the best biblical quotations, can be sure that he is blocking the very flow of information he seeks; so effectively indeed that people will avoid him and impede his work.

It is sometimes hard to gain the confidence of a specialist informant to explain things relating to a craft or technique; this is because his knowledge, like occult knowledge, is usually not something he has personal ownership or authority over; it is often the preserve of his wider family. Sometimes it is the source of their livelihood. So it is that local healers are paid for their treatment of patients in cash or in kind. The informants or their families fear that the foreigner asking the questions may be a competitor; the knowledge he is getting from them as the local specialists can be used to his economic advantage over theirs. If we wish to win over an expert we need to be patient, and presumably we shall need to pay him properly for sharing his knowledge.

After some time and experience it becomes clear to us whom we might consider as potential informants. We make an arrangement to meet them as regularly as possible for our sessions where we can work through our list of questions and queries. Sometimes older informants are rather frail, which means that we need to visit them in their homes; this is to our advantage, because they are available at any time of the day. Younger folk can only be contacted late afternoon or in the evening, because during the day they are working in their fields, or with their cattle, or out hunting.

Working with older informants is more irksome because they cannot hear so well or because, with no teeth left, they cannot articulate clearly. The researcher analysing speech and establishing phonemes under these conditions will need patience and staying power to avoid giving up on his informant despite his special intellectual insights.

Sessions with an informant (or occasionally with several) require considerable efforts of concentration from both parties. Tracing a careful mental plan, the interviewer picks his way through complex issues or thinks of situations which shed light on them. At the same time he needs to write down his informant's answers, which are seldom at a convenient dictation speed. While doing so, he also has to insert extra questions in response to something unexpected he has heard; and still he needs to work towards the next – rather weightier – question so that the interview can proceed with due momentum.

Full concentration when interviewing is vital for a further reason; not infrequently it occurs against a background of disturbance: a group of boisterous children as "participant observers", wanting to get a bit of the unusual action, or a pack of quarrelling dogs.

For this reason it is advisable not to prolong the interview, especially at the beginning, given that the situation is also rather unfamiliar for the interviewee. He is, of course, used to spending hours chatting informally with his own people about anything under the sun, but not used to a structured interview where there may even be an interpreter.

However intelligent our informants, they need to acquire skills to help us effectively. At the outset they will not be aware of our needs. If our questions concern everyday things that any child knows about, their information will be rather lacklustre or lacking in incisive details. Since Europeans in pre-literate societies are often held to be of superior intellect, our informant may well assume that we know the answer and are just testing him; this may come across as a rather humiliating experience for him.

If we are working with shame-oriented informants we sometimes hear answers which turn out on closer inspection or at a later stage to be fictional. The reason stems from the shame orientation of our contacts' way of thinking which dictates that they owe a plausible response to us interviewers to avoid any loss of face. These inventions are often quite revealing of the culture we are researching, but firstly we need to recognise them as invented material. The likelihood that we have been conned is quite high. (Freeman, 1983, describes a classic case of this). So it is vital to clarify yet again at the beginning of the venture that it is no disgrace if our informant says he does not know the answer. It is very useful, if applicable, to point out that somebody else will be interviewed as well. This gives him an incentive to be cautious and open; after all, a statement plucked from the air would unmask him and discredit him in the eyes of his fellows.

The best way of getting round the problem of our informant not realising why we are insisting on such obvious everyday details is as follows: describe to him very simply the equivalent matter in our own culture before asking him how things stand in his. In this way we trigger a relaxed response of recognition (the "aha" effect) and he can see why we are asking, and that our questions are genuine, and that we really do not know the answer to them. Over time he will become aware that he is truly the only person who can deal with our queries. This kind of pre-questioning is satisfying for another reason, since through our collaboration he gets to know an unfamiliar culture. To an intelligent communicator we are imparting discussion points of interest, both to him and his circle; and the points will be fully aired when we are not present!

If we use this method consistently for a while, a proper learning process emerges which to some extent "turns the informant around"; somebody who at the beginning was passively fielding questions gradually becomes more of a teacher, alerting us by his own initiative to various things and supplying information that we have not inquired about, either because we have overlooked matters, or because we have been unaware of them.

We must certainly show appreciation to our informant for all his work. If we are making use of his help regularly over a long period, as with a local mother-tongue helper in a literacy programme or in a bible translation project, he is entitled to the local rate of remuneration, not least because while he has been collaborating with us he has been unable to work in his field or go fishing or hunting. He may even have been obliged to pay for support for his family.

Informants with whom we have made only brief or occasional contact can be recompensed in kind, by a grateful gift of an item of clothing which they could not otherwise obtain, or of a tool or of a supply of medicine.

We must at all costs avoid the impression that our informants are different from their peers in being granted a special status. That just creates envy, and isolates both them and us.

What we are actually accomplishing by all our interviews is so inexplicable for those who are not immediately involved; the wildest rumours can start and do the rounds. This may cause concerns which can harm us. Not much can be done about them. Our best course of action is to be open with people about our purposes; at least this can form the basis for an active counter-rumour. We can be said to have succeeded in allaying these concerns if our aims are accepted as kind and coherent, and result in people being able to recognise by their own indigenous cultural frame of reference the genuineness of our intentions.

Their supposition that we shall be writing a book has become so commonplace that scarcely any ethnic group thinks otherwise. What is more, they consider that writing a book will make us extremely rich indeed. It does not help much to state that those publishers who accept research by ethnologists require a wad of ready money before they are willing to take on printing a manuscript. The idea that an author earns little more than pocket money is beyond their belief.

19.4 Cognitive Ethnology

Using the questionnaire method and with good informants, personal experience in the society concerned, plenty of patience and dogged persistence, a researcher can even study those aspects of an ethnic group's culture which cannot be observed directly, being mostly hidden in people's heads. By this I mean the thought structures (the mental matrix) underlying not only all the material objects of a culture, their use, and the behaviour of its members. These – objects, usage and behaviour – are generated by these thought structures. These are the rules vital for a person to know if he wishes to behave in such a way that the members of his culture can recognise his behaviour as typical. I mean the strategies for winning the struggle for existence and shaping life thereafter, i.e. those strategies which go to make up the primary ethnic culture.

By the so-called *cognitive methods* it is possible to comprehend what things, processes, circumstances and characteristics are conceptually interdependent; in other words, which elements in the environment of an ethnic group are significant for it, and how they are defined and integrated within a conceptual framework. An example from German (or English): people have legs, but so do dogs, birds, beetles, tables and much else. Examining a list of various kinds of legs, we discover there is considerable variety in the legs of people, beetles and tables. Nevertheless we classify all of them similarly: legs. We class them as belonging together even though they exhibit recognisable notional differences. The classifying can look rather different in other cultures. For a Frenchman, his legs are *jambes*, his animals have *pattes*, as do his elephants, storks and flies (in fact all his animals, except horses). On the islands of Micronesia, insects manage very well with fingers (*éwútún*) and so do crabs, whose pincers are called thumbs (*éwútúnapan*); in that culture fingers relate also to human toes, clock hands and sunbeams.

Different classifications for concepts, such as these, are not primitive or naive; they are just different from our expectations. At least, they are not predictable. A person working in a foreign culture should always reckon on encountering the most curious, surprising and interesting combination of terms imaginable. But this is what one must be familiar with if one wishes to talk about things and relate to things in the way the locals do. It is particularly important if one is teaching children.

The fact that one needs to speak "correctly" about things is a sign that the notional structures in which they are embedded must indeed have something to do with language. In actual fact they are so closely integrated into the local language structures that they can be deciphered, described and learnt with the aid of language and with analysis of their grammatical forms. To facilitate this, ***three basic questions*** are advisable. They can be supplied by somebody who already knows the relevant language, then learnt by heart as quickly as possible, even if the significance of each word of the sentence is not fully understood. The first question is:

What is the name for this thing, process, quality or circumstance?

In answer to this question, our informant says a ***word*** in his ***mother tongue***. This prompts the follow-up question:

What else does the word mean?

There then follows (ideally) all the things, processes, qualities or circumstances which one can denote by this word. In this way the informant communicates everything from his culture that he feels is conceptually integral to the word.

If the researcher has worked with these two questions for a while and has acquired some experience in handling the foreign language, it is time to introduce the third question, namely:

What kind of thing, process, quality or circumstance is this?

The reply to this question is the ***generic term*** under which the things, processes, qualities or circumstances are classed as being related. The generic term is important; it is recognisably the term to which what is being identified belongs on the next level up within the word field. Only when one knows what superordinated generic term gives the thing, etc. an identity can one finally use the new thing etc. "correctly" in speech, i.e. "classify the concept correctly".

This question technique is called *eliciting*. One of its great advantages is that the informant quite straightforwardly takes the measure of a concept in his own culture without digressing via the ethnographer's thought structures. The informant keeps *within* the context of his own culture, thereby conveying exclusively the *emic* aspects of the topic being discussed. (By emic we mean those features of a cultural element which are exclusively significant for its function *within* the system of which it is a part. Its other features are its *etic* aspects. Emic and etic, a contrasting pair, describe one of the fundamental concepts of the modern theory of culture).

Here is a graphic illustration of working with the three basic questions in real life. Let us suppose that we wish to know about a beetle's legs. We point them out on a live example or a picture to our informant:

Ethnographer: "What is this part of the body called?"

Informant: *"éwútún"*.

Firstly we just copy the word *phonetically*, just as we have heard it. Over the course of time we alter our transcription because we are learning how to distinguish the sounds and their nuances which in the language of our informants are unimportant (etic) from those which are significant (emic). Eventually we write the *phonemic* version, i.e. just that which is essential for distinguishing the various meanings of words.

Ethnographer: "What else does the word *éwútún* mean?"

Informant: Instead of a verbal reply he (probably) now points to his fingers, toes, the hands of his watch and the rays of the sun or other light source.

Within this group of things there is a problem, the fact that not all have the same notional emphasis. It is very likely that one of them carries the main emphasis or *focus* of the term. We must identify this so we can use the word properly. Of course, we should not just go ahead and ask the informant about its focus; that question would be too tricky. Whenever we raise this issue as a question in an accessible form and are patient, we get worthwhile, practical answers, even for complicated realms of meaning. An accessible question would be the following: "Which of the things that you have just indicated do you think of first when you hear the word *éwútún*? If he promptly says that "fingers" occurs to him first, then we have identified this as the focus of the semantic field he is describing by the form *éwútún*.

If we now ask the third question about the generic term ("What kind of thing is this?") then our informant says *kifetin inis*, meaning simply "body part". There is even a minor problem here: the generic term is not valid for all allied meanings, not for the rays of a light source, for example. I only mention this to show that in practice cognitive methods can raise surprising difficulties. We should not be discouraged, however, but just make allowances for the frustrations, and not suppose that everything can be answered down to the very last question. We can, however, note that systems of language and thought may embrace very many nuances of form.

In different examples the question about the generic term leads to fewer complicated issues, but ones that are nonetheless revealing. Let us say that we wish to find out the range of meanings for calabash, the vine plant called a bottle gourd. For Europeans it is a container. If we have elicited the word (*ruume*) and have got other "receptacles" such as bottles and cans from our related follow-up question, we then proceed to asking about the generic term. We find out that every *ruume* is a kind of *waa*, and suppose that *waa* must mean something like a container or storage space. Because we have learnt in the meantime not to take anything for granted but rather check everything, we ask what else *waa* can mean. We are now in for a surprise: *waa* can be a boat, car or aircraft, so not actually a "container" but a "means of transport" (cf. English "vessel"). Thus in this culture calabashes and bottles are stored in conceptually distinct areas, somewhat different from those a foreigner might expect. This applies also to the focus of the term. Informants admit that when they hear the word *waa* the first thing they think of is boat.

When eliciting information the researcher must always have in mind that when various informants classify a concept their answer may not always be identical, and not just as regards the smaller details. The reason is that the links between actual existing phenomena and their linguistliccum conceptual structures allocated by humans are not governed by laws; there is seldom a single possible link for a phenomenon.

The cognitive method for understanding conceptual structures is not just applicable to the visible, material elements of an ethnic group's environment (such as animals and plants) but also to the invisible and intangible realm embracing areas of psychic and intellectual activity, such as emotions (anxiety, joy, grief, love) and personal qualities (courage, decisiveness, patience, etc.). These particular areas also have interesting and instructive conceptual structures which reveal that the divide between thinking as an intellectual activity and feeling as an activity of the psyche or "heart" is not universal (Käser 1977).

As beginners we should, however, prioritize the visible for some while. We need to learn the procedures for asking our questions, and evaluate the informant's response to them and his occasional need for help in understanding our intentions. This is one of the main problems we confront; and in the realm of the intangible the challenge is all the more daunting. Sometimes it is only possible to understand non-material phenomena in specific situations. Relevant responses to "jealousy" as a concept can only be expected if we ask our informant to discuss situations where jealousy is evident: such as where one dog is stroked and the other is not, or where two men have fallen in love with the same woman. To be able to think up such scenarios requires a certain experience of living in the culture; the need to speak the informants' language really well is paramount.

In any case the cognitive method is the best for learning a *language of a pre-literate culture*. The method has advantages: one can manage with a relatively simple set of questions; one can thus begin with collecting facts, even if one's knowledge of the language is still rather limited; and with this method one cannot avoid conceiving of linguistic issues as directly related to cultural issues.

Allied to this is a very lovely side-effect: serendipity; one keeps happening upon surprising conceptual relationships. The *joys of a genuine discovery* are a peerless reward for tiresome researches and *motivate one to continue* whenever the pleasures of work (and ethnology) threaten to seep away. (A few other soothing herbs have grown up as antidotes; see my next chapter).

There are very good specialist studies on the methodology of fieldwork in ethnology. Schott's essay (1971) is recommended as a general introduction. What he writes about fieldwork is described in the context of ethnology's general objectives. His bibliography contains numerous further titles of interest to a field researcher. Other useful short introductions are Fischer (1983) and Beer/Fischer (2003). Those needing to tackle the sociology of an ethnic group or requiring insights into sociology and its fieldwork methods will find much of importance in Strecker (1969) and Girtler (2001). Freilich (1970) and Spindler (1970) are written in a very vivid and graphic style. More extensive portrayals of relevant procedures are to be found in works by Jongmans/Gutkind (1967) and especially Pelto (1970); this work has some of the best writing on this topic in general and on the cognitive method in particular. A more gradual access to the topic is Spradley's handbook (1979 a), with its absorbing twelve steps. In the same year he published his introduction to participant observation (1979 b; ²1980). Ideas to assist with planning field research are given in Crane/Angrosino (²1984).

The titles I have mentioned are just a small selection from the vast number of introductions and other studies on occasionally very specialist areas of fieldwork. These are listed in the bibliographies at the back of the publications here, and particularly in the short overview by Wassmann (2003) on what is meant by cognitive ethnology, and also in the very readable history of cognitive anthropology by D'Andrade (1995).

More detailed introductions to this chapter's topic:

Illius (2003) gives a clear and vivid portrayal of fieldwork, with an accessible bibliography of other significant publications.

More on the topic of this chapter can be found in the following studies:

Beer, Bettina; Fischer, Hans (Hg.): Ethnologie. Einführung und Überblick. Berlin 2003.

Crane, Julia G.; Angrosino, Michael V.: Field projects in anthropology. A student handbook. Prospect Heights, Ill. ²1984.

D'Andrade, Roy: The development of cognitive anthropology. Cambridge et al. 1995.

Fischer, Hans: Feldforschung. In: Fischer 1983:69-88.

Fischer, Hans (Hg.): Ethnologie. Eine Einführung. Berlin 1983.

Freeman, Derek: Liebe ohne Aggression. Margaret Meads Legende von der Friedfertigkeit der Naturvölker. München 1983.

Freilich, Morris (ed.): Marginal natives – anthropologists at work. New York 1970.

Girtler, Roland: Methoden der Feldforschung. Wien Köln Weimar 2001.

Haekel, Josef; Lukesch, Anton: Einführung in die Ethnologie Südamerikas. Wien 1972.

Illius, Bruno: Feldforschung. In: Beer/Fischer 2003:73-98.

Jongmans, D. G.; Gutkind, P.C.W. (eds.): Anthropologists in the field. Assen 1967.

Käser, Lothar: ... und bliebe am äußersten Meer. Bad Liebenzell 1972.

Käser, Lothar: Der Begriff "Seele" bei den Insulanern von Truk. Diss. Freiburg 1977.

Käser, Lothar: Durch den Tunnel. Bad Liebenzell 1989.

Käser, Lothar: Pauti. Berneck/Schweiz 1989, ²1990.

Leisi, Ernst: Der Wortinhalt. Seine Struktur im Deutschen und Englischen. Heidelberg (5. Auflage) 1975.

Pelto, Pertti J.; Pelto, Gretel H.: Anthropological research: the structure of inquiry. Cambridge ²1970.

Schott, Rüdiger: Aufgaben und Verfahren der Völkerkunde. In: Trimborn 1971:1-36.

Spindler, George D. (ed.) : Being an anthropologist. Fieldwork in eleven culturesNew York 1970.

Spradley, James P.: The ethnographic interview. New York et al. 1979(a).

Spradley, James P.: Participant observation. New York 1979(b), 1980.

Strecker, Ivo: Methodische Probleme der ethnosoziologischen Beobachtung und Beschreibung. Diss. Göttingen 1969.

Trimborn, Hermann (Hg.): Lehrbuch der Völkerkunde. Stuttgart 1971.

Wassmann, Jürg: Kognitive Ethnologie. In: Beer/Fischer 2003(a):323-340.

Chapter 20
Ethnology – Some Less Serious Moments

This chapter supplies the evidence that ethnology is not always a deadly serious business. I explain what can be done if all the cheerful fun has, nevertheless, gone out of it ... There are a number of ethnologists who get an intellectual buzz not just in describing the humour in the culture they are studying, but also in discovering the comic, off-beat, and downright ludicrous aspects in the discipline itself, and presenting them with a bit of a twist. What is particularly attractive about this habit is the unintentional comedy which is so freely available in print; so available that one has to wonder why it has not yet been subjected to systematic treatment, given there is enough material for a postdoctoral thesis.

It sometimes happens that the topic one embarked upon with such gusto and optimism – and which one is actually quite happy to be involved with – is simply getting too onerous; one cannot face tackling it ever again. One's sense of a fearful burden mostly results from an obsession, a dread that the limited time for field research will not suffice to accomplish all one has in mind, or from a slavish adherence to a lopsided schedule of poring over books and bibliographies, extracting gems from articles, and questioning informants. The other fascinating worthwhile or essential things of life have been consigned to oblivion. If a researcher has reached this state then it is high time to leave work in the field and head for a holiday. What is needed is a "Return to Laughter". This is the title of Elenore Smith Bowen's (Laura Bohannan's) famous anthropological novel (1954, 1964 etc.) describing in detail the mindset of a field researcher in Africa who lost all sense of fun and who needed to regain it.

There are many ways to rekindle one's laughter. One of them is, paradoxically, to look for books where ethnology is seen under a notably different light from the one that has been making life so unbearable.

It is a marvellous truth that everything earnest also has its curious, comic and off-beat aspects. Ethnological writing is no exception.

Scenarios of the ethno-ridiculous *genre* are of two kinds: the unintentionally funny ones, and the ones where the reader is deliberately entertained with zany distortions of cultural lore; with parodies describing fictitious ethnic groups and cultures, random myths and manners; or with scenes of fieldwork comedy featuring authoritarian officials, odd informants, or yours truly being clumsy.

A classic parody is the paper written by Horace Miner (1956) on the cleanliness rituals of the Nacirema. The very name of the group is a brilliant touch; reading backwards gives the clue. The (sober!) theoretical follow-up from the fun article can be found in Müller (2001).

Of similar style, but less successful than Miner's, is Heinrich Böll's satire "Im Lande der Rujuks" (1992) ("In the Land of the Rujuks").

With more than a hint of unintended comedy, some anthropological descriptions ape articles in ethnic studies periodicals of the early twentieth century, like those written by Buntaro Adachi (1937) on racial types and their characteristic body odours.

One's therapeutic odyssey back to the land of laughs ought to start with the various adventurous field researches by the English ethnologist Nigel Barley. It is amazing what he experienced between 1978 and 1981 living with the Dowayo tribe of northern Cameroon. Since 1983 his two volumes of inimitable tales have, unsurprisingly, appeared in numerous editions with various publishers, including in German. The Penguin editions (1986 and 1987) have made his writings very accessible.

Barley's report is, of course, exaggerated, yet basically it reflects accurately the way anyone experiences life as a traveller in Africa.

Equally highly readable is Barley's third book of this kind, his experiences among the Toraja of Indonesia (1988). It is no longer surprising that the author – even in his serious publications – chooses to reveal his subtle humour, for example in the neat punning title of his study on elegant African pottery in the British Museum ("Smashing Pots – feats of clay from Africa" 1994). Even his own ethnic group, the English, are the object for some gentle, between-the-lines humour (1989), just like Fox (2004).

Stories of time spent in field research make for good yarns among ethnologists. Philipp DeVita edited three collections (1990, 1992, 2000) of vivid authentic accounts of field work, with references to Barley's. Particularly effective is Ward H. Goodenough's "Did you?" (i.e. "Did you manage to go?"). The author describes how he learnt to give the correct answer to this question when he was living on the Onotoa Atoll (Kiribati, formerly Gilbert Islands). When a person comes back from the beach where the toilet shacks are, this is the exact question used as a greeting. The "proper" answer is best referred to privately in Goodenough's book.

Similar enjoyment is to be gained from Girtler's commentary (2004), a supplement to the 10 commandments of fieldwork he published in 2001. We must also include among parody-writing ethnologists the insightful and talented Epeli Hau'ofa (his tales, 1988), who died in 2009.

Son of a Tongan missionary couple working in New Guinea, he belonged to the academic circle of ethnologists. His tragi-comic tales bring out grotesque and far-fetched details of the lives and behaviour of South Sea islanders in their religious, business and official circles. His skilful recourse to witty self-mockery makes for great entertainment. Yet this is not his sole intention; the author demonstrates how these communities are affected by cultural change. Other publications of his appear to have a similar light tone and serious intent.

Deloria wrote an amusing satire (1969) on ethnologists at work researching particularly the Indians of North America. According to Deloria, the Indians are convinced that ethnologists must have been active in all the old cultures of the Middle East because these have all become extinct. Columbus must have had ethnologists accompanying him; otherwise how could his great sat-nav blunder have occurred that led him to America?

There is humour to be found in ethnological literature's suggestive titles. Oscar Wilde's play "The Importance of Being Earnest" is variously represented in alien guise, namely in Allen Bryant's "The Importance of Being Equal" (1990), an essay on the influence of colonialism in New Guinea. In 2006 Nicholas Fraser published "The Importance of being Eton".

Charles Dickens' "A Tale of Two Cities" prompted Lowell Holmes to title his study on the so-called "Mead versus Freeman controversy" "A Tale of Two Studies" (1983), included in Caton (1990). Gerson calls his study of tradition and modernity in Palau (Micronesia) "A Tale of Two Cultures" (1989).

A famous classic of ethnology, Ruth Benedict's "The Chrysanthemum and the Sword" is reflected in R. Whiting's "The Chrysanthemum and the Bat" (1977). Shakespeare's "Hamlet" is echoed in J. H. Teilhet-Fisk's "To Beat or Not to Beat, that Is the Question" (1991), in "To Be or Not to Be Accompanied by a Child" by Charlotte Frisbie (1975), in "To Be an Uzbek or Not to Be a Tajik" by Peter Finke und Meltem Sancak (2012), or in Richard A. Goodman's "Something is Rotten in Anthropology" (1991), a critique of the "Mead versus Freeman controversy". (The attributed quotation mentioned in the main text is a reference to Shakespeare and runs: "Something is rotten in the state of American anthropology".

The title of Alan Sillitoe's famous novel about the resocialisation of a young delinquent criminal "The Loneliness of the Long-Distance Runner" is parodied by Ambrose (1978) in his study of the island traders in the Bismarck Archipelago ("The Loneliness of the Long Distance Trader in Melanesia") and by Langemann (1997) in a study about problems in translating texts from the Far East into Indo-European languages. ("The Loneliness of the Long Distance Translator").

Bible texts figure extremely rarely in titles of ethnological studies, yet 1 Corinthians 13:13 is behind Marcus (1994).

Godelier (1994) uses a well-known line from a fairy-story in the title of his study into the future of ethnology: "Mirror, mirror on the wall ..."

The contrasting terms emic and etic which are key to describing cultures (cf. chap. 19) are humorously satirised by Berreman (1966). He renames them "anaemic" (weariness caused by blood imbalance) and "emetic" (causing vomiting).

Care must be exercised when hunting for parodies; not everything is as it seems! The study by Herwig Wolfram and Walter Pohl (1990) on ethnogenesis and the Bavarians does not belong in this chapter, nor does Edward Sapir's study (1938) on the issue of why ethnology needs the psychiatrist.

The ethnologist Richard W. B. McCormack describes the Bavarians in particular (1991) and the Germans in general (1994) through his keen eye and sharp wit. Here are two samples: At election time in Bavaria, in the constituencies where a majority vote for the ruling party in the Landtag (Parliament) cannot be taken for granted, the pencils in the voting booths are tied on such a short string that voters can only reach the top name on the list for their cross (1991:25). Regarding Germans, the author describes the ostentatious gift-giving festivity called potlatch held in Indian ethnic groups on the North West coast of North America where hosts at festival time destroy their own valuables in a demonstration of how wealthy they are, in a bid to gain prestige. McCormack compares this manifestation with German cultural trends, finding echoes of the potlatch tradition in the German gastro pile-up, namely the cold buffet, or the fatal foggy motorway auto pile-up (1994:42).

Larson's book (1985) has a similar intention. The preface was penned by none other than the erstwhile Stuttgart *Oberbürgermeister* Manfred Rommel. Quotation "A pig which is afraid of the butcher will never produce a decent schnitzel".

In 1969 there appeared in the United States a bestseller which went into new editions every few weeks, David Reuben's "Everything You Always Wanted to Know About Sex (But Were Afraid to Ask)". This popular title occurs in James D. McCawley's "Everything that Linguists Have Always Wanted to Know About Logic, but Were Ashamed to Ask" (1981). Between the (plain) covers is a witty but thorough introduction to the relationship between language and thinking. The author was professor of linguistics and oriental languages at Chicago University. Ethnologists with a special interest in languages will enjoy his other delights (1974, 1976, 1979, 1982).

In older ethnographic works, passages that earnestly described an ethnic group's body shape are nowadays highly amusing and sometimes also rather off-putting. In the quest for academic rigour, men and women would be lined up and meticulous measurements taken (for example, between their nipples) and categorised under a range of graphic phrases.

The comic effect stems from these authors' insistence on aspiring to professional thoroughness; an insistence which confers upon individuals' physical features a totally misplaced significance. Much of this is trivial, yet it still stands – inflated into something important and downright embarrassing. These days descriptions of this kind are condescending and discriminatory. I shall refrain from quoting any. Those who wish to know more should read the book by a sergeant in the imperial protection force for German East Africa, M. Merker (1904). Similarly, the work by J.V. Zelizko (1935/36) on the climbing ability of indigenous people is just bizarre. Readers interested in issues of environmental protection and waste management in early cultural history should turn to Ron Wallace; the key chapter 32 is called "Fouling the nest" (1991:115-117).

Sooner or later when a researcher is working on early theories about the origin of religions he comes across Sigmund Freud's "Totem and Taboo". Ethnologists tend these days to reject this famous work because it interprets cultural phenomena in rather a simplistic way. Thomas Gladwin (1962) poked fun at it in a short but sparkling essay, in which he investigates teenage girls' obsession with horses and teenage boys' obsession with cowboys for signs that this impulse derives from generic traumatic experiences at an earlier stage in mankind. Wonderful, spirited stuff from a renowned ethnopsychologist!

For some decades now an American "academic" periodical called "The Journal of Irreproducible Results" has been the forum for scientists to indulge in harmless self-mockery. They either publish scientific nonsense originally penned in all seriousness, or else present their own scurrilous imaginings togged up in donnish regalia. An anthology of the best parodies has been edited by George H. Scherr (1989; German edition 1986).

Anybody wanting more would do well to read R. C. Rist (1980) on blitzkrieg-ethnography; and K. J. Hollyman (1984) is very informative on the Gallic origins of the Polynesian peoples!

One final *genre*: ethno-crime fiction. An interesting example is Keita (1984): In an African capital city a series of powerful and corrupt men who have got rich on black-market selling of emergency relief aid are struck down by a mysterious bowman ...

More on the topic of this chapter can be found in the following studies:

Ackermann, Peter; Schulz, Evelyn (eds.): Diversity, change, fluidity – Japanese perspectives. Asiatische Studien LI 1 (Sondernummer). Bern et al. 1997.

Adachi, Buntaro: Das Ohrenschmalz als Rassenmerkmal und der Rassengeruch ("Achselgeruch") nebst Rassenunterschied der Schweißdrüsen. Zeitschrift für Rassenkunde 6.1937:273-307.

Ambrose, W. R.: The loneliness of the long distance trader in Melanesia. In: Specht/White 1978:326-333.

Barley, Nigel: Native land. New York 1989 (Viking Penguin).

Barley, Nigel: The innocent anthropologist. Notes from a mud hut. Harmondsworth, Middlesex, England, et al. 1986 (Penguin). Deutsch: Traumatische Tropen. Notizen aus meiner Lehmhütte. Stuttgart ; 1991 (Klett-Cotta).

Barley, Nigel: A plague of caterpillars. A return to the African bush. Harmondsworth, Middlesex, England, et al. 1987 (Penguin). – Deutsch: Die Raupenplage. Von einem, der auszog, Ethnologie zu betreiben. Stuttgart ²1990 (Klett-Cotta).

Barley, Nigel: Not a hazardous sport. London et al. 1988 (Viking Penguin). – Deutsch: Hallo Mister Puttyman. Bei den Toraja in Indonesien. Stuttgart 1994 (Klett-Cotta).

Barley, Nigel: Smashing pots. Feats of clay from Africa. London 1994.

Barley, Nigel: Dancing on the grave. Encounters with death. London 1995.

Berreman, Gerald. D.: Anemic and emetic analyses in social anthropology. American Anthropologist 68.1966:346-354.

Borofsky, Robert (ed.): Assessing cultural anthropology. New York et al. 1994.

Böll, Heinrich: Im Lande der Rujuks. In: Böll 1992:144-148.

Böll, Heinrich: Nicht nur zur Weihnachtszeit. München 1992.

Bowen, Elenore Smith (later editions: Bohannan, Laura): Return to Laughter. London 1954 (New York 1964 etc.; German: Bohannan, Laura; Stagl, Erika: Rückkehr zum Lachen: ein ethnologischer Roman. Berlin 1984.

Bryant, Allen: The importance of being equal. The colonial and postcolonial experience in the Torricelli foothills. In: Lutkehaus et al. 1990:185-196.

Caton, Hiram (ed.): The Samoa reader. Anthropologists take stock. Lanham et al. 1990.

Deloria, Vine : Custer died for your sins. An Indian manifesto. New York 1974.

DeVita, Philip R. (ed.): The humbled anthropologist. Tales from the Pacific. Belmont, CA 1990.

DeVita, Philip R. (ed.): The naked anthropologist. Tales from around the world. Belmont, CA 1992.

DeVita, Philip R. (ed.): Stumbling Toward Truth. Anthropologists at Work. Prospect Heights, Ill. 2000.

Finke, Peter; Sancak, Meltem: To Be an Uzbek or Not to Be a Tajik? Ethnicity and Locality in the Bukhara Oasis. Zeitschrift für Ethnologie (Berlin) 137.1.2012: 47-70.

Fox, Kate: Watching the English. London 2004.

Fraser, Nicholas: The importance of being Eton. London 2006.

Freeman, Derek: Liebe ohne Aggression. Margaret Meads Legende von der Friedfertigkeit der Naturvölker. München 1983.

Frisbie, Charlotte: Fieldwork as a "single parent": To be or not to be accompanied by a child. In: Frisbie, Theodore R. 1975:98-119.

Frisbie, Theodore R. (ed.): Collected papers in honor of Florence Hawley Ellis. Papers of the Archaeological Society of New Mexico. No. 2. Norman, OK 1975.

Gerson, L.: A tale of two cultures: the conflict between traditional and modern institutions in Palau. Pacific Islands Political Studies Association Conference Proceedings. Hawaii 1989.

Girtler, Roland: Methoden der Feldforschung. Wien Köln Weimar 2001.

Girtler, Roland: 10 Gebote der Feldforschung. Wien 2004.

Gladwin, Thomas: Latency and the equine subconscious. American Anthropologist 64.6.1962: 1292-1296.

Godelier, Maurice: Mirror, mirror on the wall … The once and future role of anthropology. A tentative assessment. In: Borofsky 1994:97-112.

Goodenough, Ward Hunt: "Did you?". In: DeVita 1990:25-28, 1992:112-115 and 2000:253-256.

Goodman, Richard A.: Something is rotten in anthropology. In: Caton 1991:274-275.

Hau'ofa, Epeli: Kisses in the Nederends. Auckland 1987 (Penguin).

Hau'ofa, Epeli: Rückkehr durch die Hintertür. Satiren aus Tonga. Nürnberg 1988.

Hau'ofa, Epeli: Tales of the Tikongs. Auckland 1988 (Penguin).

Hollyman, K. J.: Le sottisier savant ou spécimen exemplaire des preuves irréfutables de l'origine française des Océaniens. In: Société des Océanistes (éd.): Sociétés et cultures océaniennes. Paris 1984:135-137.

Holmes, Lowell: A tale of two studies. American Anthropologist 85.1983:929-935. Also in: Caton 1990:133-135.

Keita, Sounkalo Modibo: Der Bogenschütze. München 1991 (French original: L'archer Bassari. Paris 1984).

Langemann, Christoph: The ferry boat and the passenger, or: The loneliness of the long distance translator. In: Ackermann/Schulz 1997:219-250.

Larson, Bob: Getting along with the Germans. Esslingen München 1985.

Lutkehaus, Nancy et al. (eds.): Sepik heritage. Tradition and change in Papua New Guinea. Durham 1990.

Marcus, George E.: After the critique of ethnography: Faith, hope, and charity, but the greatest of these is charity. In: Borofsky 1994:40-45.

McCawley, James D.: On identifying the remains of deceased clauses. Language Research (Seoul, Korea) 1974.9/2:73-85. Auch in McCawley 1979:84-95.

McCawley, James D.: Notes from the linguistic underground. New York 1976.

McCawley, James D.: Adverbs, vowels, and other objects of wonder. Chicago 1979.

McCawley, James D.: Everything that linguists have always wanted to know about logic, but were ashamed to ask. Oxford 1981.

McCawley, James D.: Thirty million theories of grammar. London and Canberra 1982.

McCormack, Richard W. B.: Tief in Bayern. Eine Ethnographie. Frankfurt/M. 1991.

McCormack, Richard W. B.: Unter Deutschen. Porträt eines rätselhaften Volkes. Frankfurt/M. 1994.

Merker, M.: Die Masai. Ethnographische Monographie eines ostafrikanischen Semitenvolkes. Berlin 1904.

Miner, Horace: Body ritual among the Nacirema. American Anthropologist 58.1956:503-507.

Müller, Ernst Wilhelm: Ethnologie und komplexe Gesellschaften. In: Müller 2001:41-52.

Müller, Ernst Wilhelm: Kultur, Gesellschaft, und Ethnologie. Aufsätze 1956-2000. Münster et al. 2001.

Reuben, David: Everything you always wanted to know about sex, but were afraid to ask. New York 1969.

Rist, R. C.: Blitzkrieg Ethnography: On the transformation of a method into a movement. Educational Researcher 9.1980:8-10.

Sapir, Edward: Why cultural anthropology needs the psychiatrist. Psychiatry 1.1938:7-12.

Scherr, George H. (Hrsg.): Journal der unwiederholbaren Versuche. Band 1: Unwahrscheinliche Untersuchungen & unerfindliche Funde. Frankfurt/M. 1986.

Scherr, George H. (Hrsg.): Journal der unwiederholbaren Versuche. Band 2: Nie gesuchte Erfindungen & einfallsreiche Patente. Frankfurt/M. 1989.

Specht, Jim; White, Peter J. (eds.): Trade and exchange in Oceania and Australia. Mankind 11.1978.

Teilhet-Fisk, J. H.: To beat or not to beat, that is the question. A study on acculturation and change in an art-making process and its relation to gender structures. Pacific Studies (Laie) 14.1991/2,3:41-68.

Wallace, Ron: The tribal self. An anthropologist reflects on hunting, brain, and behavior. Lanham et al. 1991.

Whiting, R.: The chrysanthemum and the bat. New York 1977.

Wolfram, Herwig; Pohl, Walter: Typen der Ethnogenese unter besonderer Berücksichtigung der Bayern. Berichte der Kommission für Frühmittelalterforschung, 27.-30. Oktober 1986, Stift Zwettl, Niederösterreich. Teil 1: Historische Beiträge. Berlin 1990.

Zelizko, J. V.: Kletterfähigkeit der Naturvölker als atavistisches Merkmal der Urzeit. Mitteilungen der anthropologischen Gesellschaft in Wien 66.1935/36.

Postscript

May I presume that in your own researches you have already encountered (or will soon encounter) similar examples of calculated mockery of our discipline – or perhaps a genuine howler of ethnic proportions. Nothing would delight me more than to receive notice of suchlike, if possible with full bibliographical references.

I would also be grateful if you care to highlight mistakes or suggestions for additional material. I am, of course, willing to refund postage should you wish. Please write to: Lothar Käser, Ob der Hohlen 26, 79227 Schallstadt, Germany

Alternatively, send an e-mail: lothar.kaeser@ethno.uni-freiburg.de, or contact my publisher.

Bibliography

Ackermann, Peter (ed.) (1998): Diversity, change, fluidity – Japanese perspectives. Bern: Lang (Asiatische Studien, 51,1 : Sondernummer).

Adachi, Buntaro (1937): Das Ohrenschmalz als Rassenmerkmal und der Rassengeruch ("Achselgeruch") nebst Rassenunterschied der Schweißdrüsen. In: Zeitschrift für Rassenkunde, Jg. 6, S. 273-307.

Albert, Hans; Abel, Theodore (1964, ²1972): Theorie und Realität. Ausgewählte Aufsätze zur Wissenschaftslehre der Sozialwissenschaften. Tübingen: Mohr (Siebeck) (Die Einheit der Gesellschaftswissenschaften, 2).

Ambrose, W. R. (1978): The loneliness of the long distance trader in Melanesia. In: Specht, Jim; White, Peter J. (eds.): Trade and exchange in Oceania and Australia (Mankind, 11), S. 326-333.

Anderson, Atholl (1984): The extinction of moa in southern New Zealand. In: Martin, P. S.; Klein, R. G. (ed.): Quarternary extinctions. Tucson, Arizona, S. 723-740.

Bachofen, Johann Jakob (1861): Das Mutterrecht. Stuttgart.

Badenberg, Robert: Das Menschenbild in fremden Kulturen. Ein Leitfaden für eigene Erkundungen. Handbuch zu Lothar Käsers Lehrbuch Animismus. Nürnberg Bonn 2007. (French edition: La conception de l'homme dans les cultures étrangères. Guide d'investigation personnelle. Charols/France 2011. English edition: The Concept of Man in Non-Western Cultures: A Guide for One's Own Research. Handbook to Lothar Käser's Textbook *Animism – a Cognitive Approach.*

Bakhtiar, Mansour (1994): Das Schamgefühl in der persisch-islamischen Kultur. Eine ethnopsychoanalytische Untersuchung. Berlin.

Bargatzky, Thomas (1986): Einführung in die Kulturökologie. Umwelt, Kultur u. Gesellschaft. Berlin West: Reimer (Ethnologische Paperbacks).

Bargatzky, Thomas (1997): Ethnologie. Eine Einführung in die Wissenschaft von den urproduktiven Gesellschaften. Hamburg: Buske.

Barley, Nigel (1986): A plague of caterpillars. A return to the African Bush. [Deutsch: Die Raupenplage. Von einem, der auszog, Ethnologie zu betreiben. Stuttgart ²1990 (Klett-Cotta)]. Harmondsworth: Penguin Books.

Barley, Nigel (1986): The innocent anthropologist. Notes from a mud hut. [Deutsch: Traumatische Tropen. Notizen aus meiner Lehmhütte. Stuttgart 1991 (Klett-Cotta)]. London: Penguin Books.

Barley, Nigel (1988): Not a hazardous sport. [Deutsch: Hallo Mister Puttyman. Bei den Toraja in Indonesien. Stuttgart 1994 (Klett-Cotta).]. London: Penguin Books.

Barley, Nigel (1989): Native land. New York: Viking (A Channel 4 book).

Barley, Nigel (1994): Smashing pots. Feats of clay from Africa / Nigel Barley. London: British Museum Press.

Barley, Nigel (1995): Dancing on the grave. Encounters with death. [Deutsch: Barley, Nigel; Enderwitz, Ulrich (2000): Tanz ums Grab. Ungekürzte Ausg. München: Dt. Taschenbuch-Verl. (dtv, 12795)]. 1. publ. London: Murray.

Barley, Nigel; Enderwitz, Ulrich (2000): Tanz ums Grab. Ungekürzte Ausg. München: Dt. Taschenbuch-Verl. (dtv, 12795).

Barloewen, Constantin von (1986 and later): Japan und der Westen. Originalausg. Frankfurt am Main: Fischer-Taschenbuch-Verl. (Fischer-Taschenbücher, 6554).

Barnett, Homer G. (1953): Innovation. The basis of cultural change. New York, NY: McGraw-Hill (McGraw-Hill paperbacks : Problems of civilization).

Baur, Isolde (1951): Die Geschichte des Wortes "Kultur" und seiner Zusammensetzungen. München, Univ., Diss., 1951.

Beals, Ralph Leon; Hoijer, Harry (1959): An introduction to anthropology. 2. ed. New York: Macmillan.

Beer, Bettina (2003a): Ethnos, Ethnie, Kultur. In: Beer, Bettina; Fischer, Hans (Hg.): Ethnologie. Einführung und Überblick. Neufassung, 5. Aufl. Berlin: Reimer (Ethnologische Paperbacks), S. 53-72.

Beer, Bettina; Fischer, Hans (Hg.) (2003a): Ethnologie. Einführung und Überblick. Neufassung, 5. Aufl. Berlin: Reimer (Ethnologische Paperbacks).

Beer, Bettina; Fischer, Hans (2003b): Wissenschaftliche Arbeitstechniken in der Ethnologie / Bettina Beer; Hans Fischer. 2. Aufl. Berlin: Reimer (Ethnologische Paperbacks).

Belliger, Andréa (Hg.) (2003): Ritualtheorien. Ein einführendes Handbuch / Andréa Belliger, David J. Krieger (Hrsg.). 2. Aufl. Wiesbaden: Westdt. Verl.

Berreman, Gerald D. (1966): Anemic and emetic analyses in social anthropology. In: American Anthropologist, Jg. 68, S. 346-354.

Beuchelt, Eno (1983): Psychologische Anthropologie. In: Fischer, Hans (Hg.): Ethnologie. Eine Einführung. Berlin: Reimer (Ethnologische Paperbacks), S. 345-361.

Bock, Philip K. (1988): Rethinking psychological anthropology. Continuity and change in the study of human action. New York: Freeman.

Böll, Heinrich (1992): Im Lande der Rujuks. In: Böll, Heinrich (Hg.): Nicht nur zur Weihnachtszeit. Erzählungen. 2. Aufl. München: Dt. Taschenbuch-Verl. (dtv, 11591), S. 144-148.

Böll, Heinrich (Hg.) (1992): Nicht nur zur Weihnachtszeit. Erzählungen. 2. Aufl. München: Dt. Taschenbuch-Verl. (dtv, 11591).

Borofsky, Robert (ed.) (1994): Assessing cultural anthropology. New York: McGraw-Hill.

Bowen, Elenore Smith (later: Bohannan, Laura): Return to Laughter. London 1954 (New York 1964 etc.; German: Bohannan, Laura; Stagl, Erika: Rückkehr zum Lachen: ein ethnologischer Roman. Berlin 1984).

Bramly, Serge (1978): Macumba. Die magische Religion Brasiliens; 4 Gespräche mit der Macumba-Priesterin Maria-José Mae de Santo aufgezeichnet 1972-1974 in Rio und Paris. Freiburg i. Br.: Bauer.

Brewster, E. Thomas; Brewster, Elizabeth S. (1977): LAMP. Language acquisition made practical. Field methods for language learners. 2. Aufl. Colorado Springs.

Bryant, Allen (1990): The importance of being equal. The colonial and postcolonial experience in the Torricelli foothills. In: Lutkehaus, Nancy; Kaufmann, Christian (eds.): Sepik heritage. Tradition and change in Papua New Guinea. Bathurst: Crawford House Pr., S. 185-196.

Burling, Robbins (1984): Learning a field language. Ann Arbor, Mich.: Univ. of Mich. Pr.

Cain, Horst (1975): Persische Briefe auf Samoanisch. In: Anthropos, Jg. 70, S. 617-626.

Casimir, Michael J. (2003a): Kulturökologie. In: Beer, Bettina; Fischer, Hans (Hg.): Ethnologie. Einführung und Überblick. Neufassung, 5. Aufl. Berlin: Reimer (Ethnologische Paperbacks), S. 341-360.

Caton, Hiram (ed.) (1990): The Samoa reader. Anthropologists take stock. Lanham: Univ. Pr. of America.

Christoph, Henning; Oberländer, Hans (1995): Voodoo. Geheime Macht in Afrika. Orig.-Ausg. Köln: Taschen.

Codrington, Robert H. (1891): The Melanesians. Studies in their anthropology and folklore. Oxford: Clarendon.

Crane, Julia G.; Angrosino, Michael V. (1984): Field projects in anthropology. A student handbook. 2. ed. Prospect Heights, Ill: Waveland Press.

D'Andrade, Roy G. (1995): The development of cognitive anthropology / Roy D'Andrade. Cambridge: Cambridge University Press.

Davis, Wade (1988): Passage of darkness. The ethnobiology of the Haitian zombie. 2. [print.]. Chapel Hill: Univ. of North Carolina Pr.

Deloria, Vine: Custer died for your sins. An Indian manifesto / by Vine Deloria.

DeVita, Philip R. (ed.) (Calif : Wadsworth 1990): The humbled anthropologist. Tales from the Pacific. Belmont, Calif.: Wadsworth (The Wadsworth modern anthropology library).

DeVita, Philip R. (ed.) (Calif : Wadsworth 1992 [appeared] 1991): The naked anthropologist. Tales from around the world. Belmont, Calif.: Wadsworth (Wadsworth modern anthropology library).

Duranti, Alessandro (1997): Linguistic anthropology / Alessandro Duranti. Cambridge: Cambridge University Press (Cambridge textbooks in linguistics).

Ederer, R.: Zur Begriffsbestimmung von "Kultur" und "Zivilisation". In: Mitteilungen der geographischen Gesellschaft in Wien (Horn), Jg. 115.1985, S. 1-34.

Edgerton, Robert B. (1992): Sick societies. Challenging the myth of primitive harmony. [Deutsche Ausgabe: Trügerische Paradiese. Der Mythos von den glücklichen Naturvölkern. Hamburg (Kabel) 1994.]. New York: Free Press [et al.].

Egli, Werner; Krebs, Uwe (Hg.) (2004): Beiträge zur Ethnologie der Kindheit. Erziehungswissenschaftliche und kulturvergleichende Aspekte. Münster: LIT-Verl. (Studien zur Ethnopsychologie und Ethnopsychoanalyse, 5).

Feest, Christian F. (2003a): Materielle Kultur. In: Beer, Bettina; Fischer, Hans (Hg.): Ethnologie. Einführung und Überblick. Neufassung, 5. Aufl. Berlin: Reimer (Ethnologische Paperbacks), S. 239-254.

Figge, Horst H. (1973): Geisterkult, Besessenheit und Magie in der Umbanda-Religion Brasiliens)Univ., Diss. Freiburg im Breisgau 1972) Freiburg im Breisgau: Alber.

Finke, Peter; Sancak, Meltem: To Be an Uzbek or Not to Be a Tajik? Ethnicity and Locality in the Bukhara Oasis. Zeitschrift für Ethnologie (Berlin) 137.1.2012: 47-70.

Firth, Raymond (1970): The analysis of Mana: an empirical approach. In: Harding 1970:316-333. In: Harding, Thomas G.; Wallace, Ben J. (ed.): Cultures of the Pacific. Selected readings. New York: Free Press [u.a.], S. 316-333.

Fischer, Hans (2003a): Ethnologie als wissenschaftliche Disziplin. In: Beer, Bettina; Fischer, Hans (Hg.): Ethnologie. Einführung und Überblick. Neufassung, 5. Aufl. Berlin: Reimer (Ethnologische Paperbacks), S. 13-31.

Fischer, Hans (1965): Studien über Seelenvorstellungen in Ozeanien. Zugl.: Tübingen, Univ., Habil.-Schr. München: Renner.

Fischer, Hans (1983): Anfänge, Abgrenzungen, Anwendungen. In: Fischer, Hans (Hg.): Ethnologie. Eine Einführung. Berlin: Reimer (Ethnologische Paperbacks), S. 11-46.

Fischer, Hans (Hg.) (1983): Ethnologie. Eine Einführung. Berlin: Reimer (Ethnologische Paperbacks).

Fischer, Hans (1983): Feldforschung. In: Fischer, Hans (Hg.): Ethnologie. Eine Einführung. Berlin: Reimer (Ethnologische Paperbacks), S. 69-88.

Fischer, Hans (1996): Lehrbuch der genealogischen Methode. Berlin: Reimer (Ethnologische Paperbacks).

Foley, William A. (1997): Anthropological linguistics. An introduction. 1. publ. Oxford: Blackwell (Language in society).

Fox, Kate: Watching the English. London 2004.

Fraser, Nicholas: The importance of being Eton. London 2006.

Fox, Robin (1967): Kinship and marriage. An anthropological perspective. Harmondsworth: Penguin Books (Pelican books).

Freeman, Derek (1983): Liebe ohne Aggression. Margaret Meads Legende von der Friedfertigkeit der Naturvölker. München: Kindler.

Freilich, Morris (1970): Marginal natives. Anthropologists at work. New York: Harper & Row.

Frisbie, Charlotte (1975): Fieldwork as a "single parent". To be or not to be accompanied by a child. In: Frisbie/Ellis 1975:98-119.

Frisbie, Theodore R.; Ellis, Florence Hawley (eds.) (1975): Collected papers in honor of Florence Hawley Ellis. Norman, Okla.: Publ. for the Archaeological Soc. of New Mexico (Papers of the Archaeological Society of New Mexico, 2).

Fuglesang, Andreas (1982): About understanding. Ideas and observations on cross-cultural communication. Uppsala: Dag Hammarskjöld Foundation.

Gadamer, Georg; Vogler, Paul (Hg.) (1972): Neue Anthropologie. Stuttgart: Thieme (dtv, 4070).

Gadamer, Hans-Georg (Hg.) (1973): Psychologische Anthropologie (Neue Anthropologie, 5).

Gell, Alfred (ed.) (1992, 1996): The anthropology of time. Cultural constructions of temporal maps and images. Oxford: Berg (Explorations in anthropology).

Gerbert, Martin (1970): Religionen in Brasilien. Eine Analyse der nichtkatholischen Religionsformen und ihrer Entwicklung im sozialen Wandel der brasilianischen Gesellschaft. Berlin: Colloquium-Verl. (Bibliotheca Ibero-Americana, 13).

Gerndt, Helge (1981): Kultur als Forschungsfeld. Über volkskundliches Denken und Arbeiten. München: Beck.

Gestrich, Christof (2001): Christentum und Stellvertretung. Religionsphilosophische Untersuchungen zum Heilsverständnis und zur Grundlegung der Theologie. Tübingen: Mohr Siebeck.

Gipper, Helmut (1972): Gibt es ein sprachliches Relativitätsprinzip? Untersuchungen zur Sapir-Whorf-Hypothese. Frankfurt am Main: S. Fischer (Conditio humana).

Girtler, Roland (1979): Kulturanthropologie. Entwicklungslinien, Paradigmata, Methoden. Originalausg. München: Dt. Taschenbuchverl. (Dtv dtv-Wissenschaft, 4311).

Girtler, Roland (2001): Methoden der Feldforschung. 4., völlig neu bearb. Aufl. Wien: Böhlau (UTB für Wissenschaft Soziologie, 2257).

Girtler, Roland (2004): 10 Gebote der Feldforschung. Wien: LIT.

Gladwin, Thomas (1962): Latency and the equine subconscious. In: American Anthropologist, 64.6:1292-1296.

Gladwin, Thomas (1964): Culture and logical process. In: Goodenough, Ward Hunt (ed.): Explorations in cultural anthropology. Essays in honor of George Peter Murdock. New York: MacGraw-Hill, S. 167-177.

Godelier, Maurice (1994): Mirror, mirror on the wall ... The once and future role of anthropology. A tentative assessment. In: Borofsky, Robert (ed.): Assessing cultural anthropology. New York: McGraw-Hill, S. 97-112.

Good, Charles M. (1987): Ethnomedical systems in Africa. Patterns of traditional medicine in rural and urban Kenya. New York: Guilford Press.

Goodenough, Ward Hunt (1963): Cooperation in change. An anthropological approach to community development. New York: Russell Sage Foundation.

Goodenough, Ward Hunt (ed.) (1964): Explorations in cultural anthropology. Essays in honor of George Peter Murdock. New York: MacGraw-Hill.

Goodenough, Ward Hunt (Calif : Wadsworth 1990): "Did you?". In: DeVita, Philip R. (ed.): The humbled anthropologist. Tales from the Pacific. Belmont, Calif.: Wadsworth (The Wadsworth modern anthropology library), S. 25-28.

Goodenough, Ward Hunt (Calif : Wadsworth 1992 [erschienen] 1991): "Did you?". In: DeVita, Philip R. (ed.): The naked anthropologist. Tales from around the world. Belmont, Calif.: Wadsworth (Wadsworth modern anthropology library), S. 112-115.

Goodman, Richard A. (1990): Something is rotten in anthropology. In: Caton, Hiram (ed.): The Samoa reader. Anthropologists take stock. Lanham: Univ. Pr. of America, S. 274-275.

Göttner-Abendroth, Heide (1989): Das Matriarchat. 2. Aufl. Stuttgart: Kohlhammer.

Haekel, Josef (1971): Religion. In: Trimborn, Hermann (Hg.): Lehrbuch der Völkerkunde. 4., neubearb. Aufl. Stuttgart: Enke, S. 72-141.

Haekel, Josef; Lukesch, Anton (1972): Einführung in die Ethnologie Südamerikas. Wien: [Stiglmayr] (Studia culturalia, 1).

Haferkamp, Rose-Anne (1984): Untersuchung zum Problem des Verstehens fremder Kulturen. Feldexperiment mit Schülern (11-14 Jahre) im Museum für Völkerkunde. Univ., Diss.-Köln, 1984. Köln (Spiegelbild, 1).

Hallpike, Christopher Robert (1979): The foundations of primitive thought. Oxford, New York: Clarendon Press; Oxford University Press.

Hansen, Klaus P. (1995): Kultur und Kulturwissenschaft. Eine Einführung. Tübingen: Francke (UTB für Wissenschaft : Uni-Taschenbücher).

Harding, Thomas G.; Wallace, Ben J. (ed.) (1970): Cultures of the Pacific. Selected readings. New York: Free Press [u.a.].

Harris, Marvin (1968): The rise of anthropological theory. A history of theories of culture. London: Routledge & Kegan Paul.

Harris, Marvin (1989): Kulturanthropologie. Ein Lehrbuch. Frankfurt/Main: Campus-Verl.

Hau'ofa, Epeli (1987): Tales of the Tikongs. Auckland: Penguin Books.

Hau'ofa, Epeli (1995): Kisses in the Nederends. Honolulu: Univ. of Hawaii Press (Talanoa).

Hau'ofa, Epeli; Gizycki, Renate von (1988): Rückkehr durch die Hintertür. Satiren aus Tonga. Nürnberg: Tolling (Reihe Literatur des Pazifik).

Helbling, Jürg (2003a): Sozialethnologie. In: Beer, Bettina; Fischer, Hans (Hg.): Ethnologie. Einführung und Überblick. Neufassung, 5. Aufl. Berlin: Reimer (Ethnologische Paperbacks), S. 125-156.

Helmig, Thomas (1993): Verwandtschaft. In: Schweizer, Thomas; Schweizer, Margarete; Kokot, Waltraud; Johansen, Ulla (Hg.): Handbuch der Ethnologie. Berlin: D. Reimer, S. 145-174.

Henke, Winfried; Rothe, Hartmut (1994): Paläoanthropologie. Berlin: Springer.

Herm, Bruno u. a. (Hg.) (^{2}1986): Werkbuch Mission. Lesebuch und Orientierungshilfe. Wuppertal.

Hinderling, Paul (1981): Kranksein in "primitiven" und traditionalen Kulturen. Norderstedt: Verlag fuer Ethnologie.

Hirschberg, Walter; Fries, Marianne (Hg.) (1988): Neues Wörterbuch der Völkerkunde. Berlin: Reimer (Ethnologische Paperbacks).

Hirschmeier, Johannes (1987): Grundlagen des japanischen Arbeitsethos. Die Firma als Schicksalsgemeinschaft. In: Barloewen, Constantin von; Werhahn-Mees, Kai (Hg.): Japan und der Westen. Orig.-Ausg., 7.-9. Tsd. 2 Bände. Frankfurt a.M.: Fischer (Fischer-Taschenbücher, 6554), S. 270-285.

Hohenstein, Erica Jane de (1991): Das Reich der magischen Mütter. Untersuchung über die Frauen in den afro-brasilianischen Besessenheitskulten Candomblé. Univ., Diss.-Frankfurt (Main), 1991. Frankfurt/M.: Verl. für Interkulturelle Kommunikation (IKO-Wissenschaft und Forschung, 18).

Hollyman, K. J. (1984): Le sottisier savant ou spécimen exemplaire des preuves irréfutables de l'origine française des Océaniens. In: Société des Océanistes (Hg.): Sociétés et cultures océaniennes. Ouvrage collect. publ. par la Société des Océanistes (Musée de l'Homme, Paris), en hommage au R. P. Patrick O'Reilly. Paris: Ed. Anthropos (Journal des océanistes, 74/75), S. 135-137.

Holmes, Lowell (1983): A tale of two studies. In: American Anthropologist, Jg. 85, S. 929-935. (Also in Caton 1990:133-135).

Illius, Bruno (2003a): Feldforschung. In: Beer, Bettina; Fischer, Hans (Hg.): Ethnologie. Einführung und Überblick. Neufassung, 5. Aufl. Berlin: Reimer (Ethnologische Paperbacks), S. 73-98.

Ingold, Tim; Riches, David; Woodburn, James (eds.) (1991): Hunters and gatherers. New York: Berg (Explorations in anthropology).

Janata, Alfred (1989): A tale of two cultures: the conflict between traditional and modern institutions in Palau. Hawaii (Pacific Islands Political Studies Association Conference Proceedings).

Janata, Alfred (Hg.) (1999): Technologie und Ergologie in der Völkerkunde. 4., grundlegend überarb. Aufl. Berlin: Reimer (Ethnologische Paperbacks).

Jaspers, Reiner (1972): Die missionarische Erschließung Ozeaniens. Ein quellengeschichtlicher und missionsgeographischer Versuch zur kirchlichen Gebietsaufteilung in Ozeanien bis 1855. Zugl.: Münster/Westf., Univ., Diss., 1970. Münster, Westfalen: Aschendorff (Missionswissenschaftliche Abhandlungen und Texte, 30).

Jensen, Jürgen (1983): Wirtschaftsethnologie. In: Fischer, Hans (Hg.): Ethnologie. Eine Einführung. Berlin: Reimer (Ethnologische Paperbacks), S. 91-119.

Johnson, Thomas Malcolm; Sargent, Carolyn Fishel (1990): Medical anthropology. A handbook of theory and method. New York: Greenwood Press.

Jongmans, Douwe Geert; Gutkind, Peter Claus Wolfgang (eds.) (1967): Anthropologists in the field. Assen: van Gorcum [et al.] (Samenlevingen buiten Europa, 6).

Kaplan, Bert (ed.) (1961): Studying personality cross-culturally. Evanston, Ill.: Row Peterson and Co.

Karim, Wazir J. (ed.) (1990): Emotions of culture. A Malay perspective. Singapore: Oxford Univ. Press (South-East Asian social science monographs).

Kasdorf, Hans; Müller, Klaus W. (Hg.) (1988): Bilanz und Plan. Mission an der Schwelle zum dritten Jahrtausend ; Festschrift für George W. Peters zu seinem 80. Geburtstag. Bad Liebenzell: Verl. der Liebenzeller Mission (Evangelische Missionslehre. Vorträge und Aufsätze, 81).

Käser, Lothar (1972): ... und bliebe am äußersten Meer. Bad Liebenzell: Verl. der Liebenzeller Mission.

Käser, Lothar (1977): Der Begriff Seele bei den Insulanern von Truk. Univ., Diss.-Freiburg i.Br., 1977. Hohenschäftlarn: Renner.

Käser, Lothar (1989): Pauti. Mit einer Missionarin der Schweizer Indianermission bei den Campa-Indianern in Peru. Berneck: Schwengeler (TELOS-Bücher TELOS-Paperback, Nr. 2328).

Käser, Lothar (1990): Die Besiedlung Mikronesiens. Eine ethnologisch-linguistische Untersuchung. Zugl.: Freiburg (Breisgau), Univ., Habil.-Schr., 1987 u.d.T.: Käser, Lothar: Zur Besiedelung Mikronesiens. Berlin: Reimer.

Käser, Lothar (1990): Durch den Tunnel. Die Geschichte der Übersetzung des Alten Testaments in die Sprache der Truk-Inseln in der Südsee. Bad Liebenzell: Verl. der Liebenzeller Mission (TELOS-Bücher, 2343).

Käser, Lothar: Animismus. Eine Einführung in die begrifflichen Grundlagen des Welt- und Menschenbildes traditionaler (ethnischer) Gesellschaften für Entwicklungshelfer und kirchliche Mitarbeiter in Übersee. Bad Liebenzell und Erlangen 2004. French edition: Animisme. Introduction à la conception du monde et de l'homme dans le sociétés axées sur la tradition orale. Charols/France 2010. English edition: Animism – a Cognitive Approach. An Introduction to the Basic Notions Underlying the Concepts of the World and of Man Held by Ethnic Societies, for the Benefit of Those Working Overseas in Development Aid and in the Church. Nürnberg: VTR Publications 2014.

Käser, Lothar: Diferentes culturas. Uma introdução a etnologia. Londrina/PR 2004.

Keck, Verena (1992): Falsch gehandelt – schwer erkrankt. Kranksein bei den Yupno in Papua New Guinea aus ethnologischer und biomedizinischer Sicht. Zugl.: Basel, Univ., Diss., 1991. Basel: Wepf (Basler Beiträge zur Ethnologie).

Keesing, Roger Martin; Keesing, Felix Maxwell (1971): New perspectives in cultural anthropology. New York: Holt Rinehart and Winston.

Keita, Sounkalo Modibo (1991): Der Bogenschütze. Aus dem Franz. von Carola Gerlach. München: Kyrill-und-Method-Verl. (französisches Original: L'archer Bassari. Paris 1984).

Kippenberg, Hans Gerhard; Luchesi, Brigitte (Hg.) (1978): Magie. Die sozialwissenschaftliche Kontroverse über das Verstehen fremden Denkens. 1. Aufl. Frankfurt a.M.: Suhrkamp (Theorie-Diskussion).

Klass, Morton (1995): Ordered universes. Approaches to the anthropology of religion. Boulder: Westview Press.

Kleihauer, Maike (1991): Kulturelle Regression bei Jäger- und Sammlerkulturen. Zugl.: Freiburg (Breisgau), Univ., Diss., 1989. Münster, Hamburg: LIT (Ethnologische Studien, 14).

Knußmann, Rainer (1980): Vergleichende Biologie des Menschen. Lehrbuch der Anthropologie und Humangenetik. Stuttgart: Fischer.

Kohl, Karl-Heinz (1993): Ethnologie – die Wissenschaft vom kulturell Fremden. Eine Einführung. München: Beck (C. H. Beck Studium).

Kohl, Karl-Heinz (2003): Die Macht der Dinge. Geschichte und Theorie sakraler Objekte. München: Beck (C. H. Beck Kulturwissenschaft).

Koskinen, Aarne Antti (1953): Missionary Influence as a political factor in the Pacific Islands. Helsinki (Suomalaisen Tiedeakatemian Toimituksia, B, 78,1).

Krauß, Günter (1990): Kefu elak. Traditionelle Medizin in Oku (Kamerun). Göttingen: Ed. Re.

Krebs, Uwe (2004): Erzogen ohne Erziehung? Vom Nutzen impliziter Erziehung und der Bedeutung der Ethnologie für die Erziehungswissenschaft. In: Egli, Werner; Krebs, Uwe (Hg.): Beiträge zur Ethnologie der Kindheit. Erziehungswissenschaftliche und kulturvergleichende Aspekte. Münster: LIT-Verl. (Studien zur Ethnopsychologie und Ethnopsychoanalyse, 5), S. 21-41.

Kroeber, Alfred L.; Kluckhohn, Clyde (1952): Culture. A critical review of concepts and definitions. Cambridge, Mass.: The Museum (Papers of the Peabody Museum of American Archaeology and Ethnology).

Langemann, Christoph (1998): The ferry boat and the passenger, or: The loneliness of the long distance translator. In: Ackermann, Peter (ed.): Diversity, change, fluidity – Japanese perspectives. Bern: Lang (Asiatische Studien, 51,1 : Sondernummer), S. 219-250.

Larson, Bob (1985): Getting along with the Germans. Esslingen München.

Lee, Richard B.; DeVore, Irven de; Nash, Jill (eds.) (1968): Man the hunter. [Symposium on Man the Hunter … April 6-9,1966]. Chicago, Ill.: Aldine.

Lehmann, Friedrich Rudolf (1915): Mana. Eine begriffsgeschichtliche Untersuchung auf ethnologischer Grundlage. Leipzig, Univ., Diss., 1915.

Lehmann, Friedrich Rudolf (1922): Mana. Der Begriff des "außerordentlich Wirkungsvollen" bei Südseevölkern. Leipzig: Spamer (Veröffentlichungen des Staatlich-Sächsischen Forschungsinstitutes für Völkerkunde in Leipzig : Reihe 1, Ethnographie und Ethnologie).

Leighton, A. H. (1980): Kulturwandel und psychische Erkrankungen. In: Pfeiffer, Wolfgang M.; Schoene, Wolfgang (Hg.): Psychopathologie im Kulturvergleich. Stuttgart: Enke (Klinische Psychologie und Psychopathologie, 14), S. 247-256.

Leisi, Ernst (1975): Der Wortinhalt. Seine Struktur im Deutschen und Englischen. 5. Aufl. Heidelberg: Quelle & Meyer (UTB).

Lewis, David Henry (1975): We the navigators. The ancient art of landfinding in the Pacific. 1. paperbound ed. Canberra: Australian National Univ. Press.

Lienhard, Ruth (2002): Restoring relationships. Theological reflections on shame and honor among the Daba and Bana of Cameroon. (Ph.D. dissertation Fuller Theological Seminary). Yaoundé, Cameroon.

Lightfoot-Klein, Hanny (1989): Prisoners of ritual. An odyssey into female genital circumcision in Africa. New York: Haworth Pr. (Haworth series on women, 2).

Lutkehaus, Nancy; Kaufmann, Christian (eds.) (1990): Sepik heritage. Tradition and change in Papua New Guinea. Bathurst: Crawford House Pr.

Lux, Thomas (Hg.) (2003): Kulturelle Dimensionen der Medizin. Ethnomedizin – Medizinethnologie – Medical Anthropology. Berlin: Reimer.

MacCawley, James D. (1981): Everything that linguists have always wanted to know about logic but were ashamed to ask. Oxford: Blackwell.

Mandelbaum, D. G. (1980): Kulturelle Bedingungen und Funktionen des Alkoholkonsums. In: Pfeiffer, Wolfgang M.; Schoene, Wolfgang (Hg.): Psychopathologie im Kulturvergleich. Stuttgart: Enke (Klinische Psychologie und Psychopathologie, 14), S. 116-131.

Marcus, George E. (1994): After the critique of ethnography: Faith, hope, and charity, but the greatest of these is charity. In: Borofsky, Robert (ed.): Assessing cultural anthropology. New York: McGraw-Hill, S. 40-45.

Martin, Laura (1986): Eskimo words for snow. A case study in the genesis and decay of an anthropological example. In: American Anthropologist, Jg. 88, S. 418-423.

Martin, P. S.; Klein, R. G. (ed.) (1984): Quarternary extinctions. Tucson, Arizona.

McCawley, James D. (1974): On identifying the remains of deceased clauses. In: Language Research (Seoul, Korea), Jg. 9/2, S. 73-85 (Also in McCawley 1979:84-95).

McCawley, James D. (1976): Notes from the linguistic underground. New York: Academic Press (Syntax and semantics, 7).

McCawley, James D. (1979): Adverbs, vowels, and other objects of wonder. Chicago: University of Chicago Press.

McCawley, James D. (1982): Thirty million theories of grammar. London: Croom Helm (Croom Helm linguistics series).

McCormack, R. W. B. (1991): Tief in Bayern. Eine Ethnographie. Limitierte Vorzugsausg. Frankfurt am Main: Eichborn (Die andere Bibliothek).

McCormack, R. W. B. (1994): Unter Deutschen. Portrait eines rätselhaften Volkes. Frankfurt am Main: Eichborn.

McGlone, M. S. (1983): Polynesian deforestation of New Zealand: a preliminary synthesis. In: Archaeology in Oceania, Jg. 18, S. 11-25.

Merker, Moritz (1904): Die Masai. Ethnographische Monographie eines ostafrikanischen Semitenvolkes. Berlin: Reimer.

Miner, Horace (1956): Body ritual among the Nacirema. In: American Anthropologist, Jg. 58, S. 503-507.

Minz, Lioba (1992): Krankheit als Niederlage und die Rückkehr zur Stärke. Candomblé als Heilungsprozeß. Freie Univ., Magisterarbeit.-Berlin, 1992. Bonn: Holos (Mundus Reihe Ethnologie, Bd. 56).

Mischung, Roland (2003a): Religionsethnologie. In: Beer, Bettina; Fischer, Hans (Hg.): Ethnologie. Einführung und Überblick. Neufassung, 5. Aufl. Berlin: Reimer (Ethnologische Paperbacks), S. 197-220.

Mühlmann, Wilhelm Emil (1968): Geschichte der Anthropologie. 2., verb. und erw. Aufl. Frankfurt a.M.: Athenäum-Verl.

Müller, Ernst Wilhelm (1981): Der Begriff 'Verwandtschaft' in der modernen Ethnosoziologie. Univ., Habil.-Schr.-Heidelberg, 1967. Berlin: Reimer (Mainzer Ethnologica, 2).

Müller, Ernst Wilhelm (2001): Kultur, Gesellschaft und Ethnologie. Aufsätze 1956-2000. Münster: LIT-Verl. (Mainzer Beiträge zur Afrika-Forschung, 5).

Müller, Klaus E.; Müller, Noela (1997): Der gesprungene Ring. Wie man die Seele gewinnt und verliert. Frankfurt am Main: Lembeck.

Müller, Klaus W. (1988): Elenktik: Gewissen im Kontext. In: Kasdorf, Hans; Müller, Klaus W. (Hg.): Bilanz und Plan. Mission an der Schwelle zum dritten Jahrtausend ; Festschrift für George W. Peters zu seinem 80. Geburtstag. Bad Liebenzell: Verl. der Liebenzeller Mission (Evangelische Missionslehre. Vorträge und Aufsätze, 81), S. 416-454.

Müller, Klaus W. (2010): Das Gewissen in Kultur und Religion. Scham- und Schuldorientierung als empirisches Phänomen des Über-Ich, Ich-Ideal. Lehrbuch Elenktik ; ein Projekt der Forschungsstiftung Kultur und Religion Biebertal. 1. Aufl. Nürnberg: VTR.

Noble, Lowell L. (1975): Naked and not ashamed. An anthropological, biblical, and psychological study of shame. Jackson, Michigan 1975. Jackson, Michigan.

Paul, Sigrid; Bauer, Wolfgang (Hg.) (1984): "Kultur". Begriff und Wort in China und Japan ; Symposion des Forschungskreises für Symbolik, Salzburg vom 25.-27. Juni 1982. Berlin: Reimer (Schriften zur Kultursoziologie, 3).

Pelto, Pertti J. (²1970): Anthropological research. The structure of inquiry. New York: Harper Row.

Petermann, Werner (2004): Die Geschichte der Ethnologie. Wuppertal: Hammer.

Pfeiffer, Wolfgang M.; Schoene, Wolfgang (Hg.) (1980): Psychopathologie im Kulturvergleich. Stuttgart: Enke (Klinische Psychologie und Psychopathologie, 14).

Pfleiderer, Beatrix; Greifeld, Katarina; Bichmann, Wolfgang (1995): Ritual und Heilung. Eine Einführung in die Ethnomedizin. 2., vollst. überarb. und erw. Neuaufl. des Werkes "Krankheit und Kultur". Berlin: Reimer (Ethnologische Paperbacks).

Plattner, Stuart (Calif : Stanford Univ Pr 1989): Economic anthropology. Stanford, Calif.: Stanford Univ. Pr.

Rappaport, Roy A. (1999): Ritual and religion in the making of humanity. Cambridge: Cambridge University Press (Cambridge studies in social and cultural anthropology, 110).

Renner, Egon (1980): Die kognitive Anthropologie. Aufbau und Grundlagen eines ethnologisch-linguistischen Paradigmas. Freie Univ., Diss-Berlin. Berlin: Duncker u. Humblot (Forschungen zur Ethnologie und Sozialpsychologie, 12).

Renner, Egon (1983): Die Grundlinien der kognitiven Forschung. In: Fischer, Hans (Hg.): Ethnologie. Eine Einführung. Berlin: Reimer (Ethnologische Paperbacks), S. 391-425.

Renner, Egon (1983): Ethnologie und Kultur. Der Kulturbegriff als entwicklungsprägender Faktor der ethnologischen Forschung. In: Zeitschrift für Ethnologie, Jg. 108, S. 177-234.

Reuben, David R. (1970): Everything you always wanted to know about sex, but were afraid to ask. London: Allen.

Rist, R. C. (1980): Blitzkrieg Ethnography. On the transformation of a method into a movement. In: Educational Researcher, Jg. 9, S. 8-10.

Ritz, Hans ((1983)): Die Sehnsucht nach der Südsee. Bericht über einen europäischen Mythos. (2. Aufl.). (Göttingen): Muriverlag.

Romanucci-Ross, Lola; Moerman, Daniel E. (eds.) (1983): The anthropology of medicine. From culture to method. South Hadley, Mass.: Bergin & Garvey.

Rösing, Ina (2003): Trance, Besessenheit und Amnesie. Bei den Schamanen der Changpa-Nomaden im ladakhischen Changthang / Ina Rösing. Gnas: Weishaupt.

Rössler, Martin (2003a): Wirtschaftsethnologie. In: Beer, Bettina; Fischer, Hans (Hg.): Ethnologie. Einführung und Überblick. Neufassung, 5. Aufl. Berlin: Reimer (Ethnologische Paperbacks), S. 101-124.

Rössler, Martin (1999): Wirtschaftsethnologie. Eine Einführung. Berlin: Reimer (Ethnologische Paperbacks).

Rudolph, Wolfgang (1968): Der kulturelle Relativismus. Kritische Analyse einer Grundsatzfragen-Diskussion in der amerikanischen Ethnologie. Freie Univ., Habil.-Schr.-Berlin, 1967. Berlin: Duncker & Humblot (Forschungen zur Ethnologie und Sozialpsychologie, 6).

Rudolph, Wolfgang (1971): Kultur, Psyche und Weltbild. In: Trimborn, Hermann (Hg.): Lehrbuch der Völkerkunde. 4., neubearb. Aufl. Stuttgart: Enke, S. 54-71.

Sahlins, Marshall David (1972): Stone age economics. Chicago: Aldine-Atherton.

Salamone, Frank A. : Missionaries and anthropologists: inquiry into their ambivalent relation-ship Missiology 14 1986:55-70 an (1985): Missionaries and anthropologists. An inquiry into their ambivalent relationship. Missiology 14.1986:55-70. In: Missiology, Jg. 14, S. 55-70.

Sapir, Edward (1938): Why cultural anthropology needs the psychiatrist. In: Psychiatry, Jg. 1, S. 7-12.

Scherr, George H. (Hg.) (1989): Journal der unwiederholbaren Experimente. Unwahrscheinliche Untersuchungen & unerfindliche Funde. Frankfurt/Main: Krüger (Band 1).

Scherr, George H. (Hg.) (1989): Journal der unwiederholbaren Experimente. Nie gesuchte Erfindungen & einfallsreiche Patente. Frankfurt am Main: Krüger (Band 2).

Scheunemann, Gerlinde (²1986): Wenn ich "ja" sage, versteht sie "nein". In fremden Kulturen leben. In: Herm, Bruno u. a. (Hg.): Werkbuch Mission. Lesebuch und Orientierungshilfe. Wuppertal, S. 57-70.

Scheurmann, Erich (1977): Der Papalagi. Die Reden des Südseehäuptlings Tuiavii aus Tiavea. Erw. Neuaufl. d. Orig.-Ausg. von 1920 Felsenverl., Buchenbach/Baden; 5.-14. Tsd. Zürich: Tanner + Staehelin.

Schiefenhövel, Wulf; Schuler, Judith (1986): Traditionelle Heilkundige – ärztliche Persönlichkeiten im Vergleich der Kulturen und medizinischen Systeme. Beiträge und Nachträge zur 6. Internationalen Fachkonferenz Ethnomedizin in Erlangen, 30.9.-3.10.1982 = Traditional healers – iatric personalities in different cultures and medical systems. Braunschweig: Vieweg (CurareSonderband, 5).

Schmidt, Wilhelm (1926-1956): Der Ursprung der Gottesidee ; Eine histor.-krit. u. positive Studie. Münster: Aschendorff.

Schmitz, Carl August (1964): Grundformen der Verwandtschaft. Basel: Pharos-Verl. (Basler Beiträge zur Geographie und Ethnologie : Ethnologische Reihe).

Schott, Rüdiger (1971): Aufgaben und Verfahren der Völkerkunde. In: Trimborn, Hermann (Hg.): Lehrbuch der Völkerkunde. 4., neubearb. Aufl. Stuttgart: Enke, S. 1-36.

Schwartz, Theodore; White, Geoffrey Miles; Lutz, Catherine A. (eds.) (1992): New directions in psychological anthropology. Cambridge: Cambridge Univ. Press (Publications of the Society for Psychological Anthropology, 3).

Schweizer, Thomas; Schweizer, Margarete; Kokot, Waltraud, et al. (Hg.) (1993): Handbuch der Ethnologie. Berlin: D. Reimer.

Seitz, Stefan (1977): Die zentralafrikanischen Wildbeuterkulturen. 1. Aufl. Wiesbaden: Steiner (Studien zur Kulturkunde, 45 (Französischer Titel: Pygmées d'Afrique. Paris 1993.)).

Senft, Gunter (2003a): Ethnolinguistik. In: Beer, Bettina; Fischer, Hans (Hg.): Ethnologie. Einführung und Überblick. Neufassung, 5. Aufl. Berlin: Reimer (Ethnologische Paperbacks), S. 254-270.

Sharp, Lauriston (1953): Steel axes for stone-age Australians. In: Human Organisation, Jg. 11, S. 17-22. (also in: Harding/Wallace 1970:385-396).

Société des Océanistes (Hg.) (1984): Sociétés et cultures océaniennes. Ouvrage collect. publ. par la Société des Océanistes (Musée de l'Homme, Paris), en hommage au R. P. Patrick O'Reilly. Paris: Ed. Anthropos (Journal des océanistes, 74/75).

Specht, Jim; White, Peter J. (eds.) (1978): Trade and exchange in Oceania and Australia (Mankind, 11).

Spindler, George Dearborn (1970): Being an anthropologist. Fieldwork in eleven cultures. New York: Holt Rinehart and Winston.

Spiro, Melford E. (1961): Social systems, personality, and functional analysis. In: Kaplan, Bert (ed.): Studying personality cross-culturally. Evanston, Ill.: Row Peterson and Co., S. 93-127.

Spiro, Melford Elliot; Spiro, Audrey G. (1958): Children of the kibbutz. Cambridge, Mass.: Harvard Univ. Press.

Spradley, James P. (1979a): The ethnographic interview. New York: Holt Rinehart & Winston.

Spradley, James P. (1979(b),1980): Participant observation. New York, NY: Holt Rinehart & Winston.

Staewen, Christoph (1991): Kulturelle und psychologische Bedingungen der Zusammenarbeit mit Afrikanern. Ansatzpunkte für eine komplementäre Partnerschaft. München: Weltforum-Verl. (Afrika-Studien).

Stagl, Justin (2003a): Die Entwicklung der Ethnologie. In: Beer, Bettina; Fischer, Hans (Hg.): Ethnologie. Einführung und Überblick. Neufassung, 5.
Aufl. Berlin: Reimer (Ethnologische Paperbacks), S. 34-52.

Stagl, Justin (1981): Kulturanthropologie und Gesellschaft. Eine wissenschaftssoziologische Darstellung der Kulturanthropologie und Ethnologie. 2.,
durchges., verb. und um ein Nachwort verm. Aufl. Berlin: Reimer (Ethnologische Paperbacks).

Stagl, Justin (1983): Politikethnologie. In: Fischer, Hans (Hg.): Ethnologie. Eine
Einführung. Berlin: Reimer (Ethnologische Paperbacks), S. 205-229.

Stein, Gerd (Hg.) (1984a): Die edlen Wilden. Die Verklärung von Indianern,
Negern und Südseeinsulanern auf dem Hintergrund der kolonialen Greuel
vom 16. bis zum 20. Jahrhundert; ethnoliterarische Lesebücher 1. Frankfurt
am Main: Fischer Taschenbuch Verlag.

Stein, Gerd (Hg.) (1984b): Europamüdigkeit und Verwilderungswünsche. Der
Reiz, in amerikanischen Urwäldern, auf Südseeinseln oder im Orient e. zivi-
lisationsfernes Leben zu führen ; Vom 18. zum 20. Jh. Frankfurt am Main:
Fischer-Taschenbuch-Verl. (Fischer-Taschenbücher 3073).

Steyne, Philip M. (1990): Gods of power. (deutsche Ausgabe: Machtvolle Göt-
ter. Eine Untersuchung über Glaube und Gebräuche des Animismus, wie er
von Naturvölkern praktiziert wird, und wie er heute in allen religiösen Bewe-
gungen vorkommt. Bad Liebenzell 1993.). Columbus SC.

Stockitt, Robin (2012): Restoring the shamed. Towards a theology of shame.
Eugene, Or.

Strecker, Ivo A. (1969): Methodische Probleme der ethno-soziologischen Beobachtung und Beschreibung. (Versuch e. Vorbereitung z. Feldforschung).
Univ., Diss.-Göttingen. Göttingen: Univ. Inst. f. Völkerkunde (Arbeiten aus
dem Institut für Völkerkunde der Universität zu Göttingen).

Sullivan, Lawrence E. (ed.) (1989): Healing and restoring. Health and medicine
in the world's religious traditions. New York: Macmillan.

Sun, Longji; Kühner, Hans (1994): Das ummauerte Ich. Die Tiefenstruktur der
chinesischen Mentalität / Sun Longji. [Aus d. Chines. übers. von Stephanie
Claussen … Bearb.,eingel. u. hrsg. von Hans Kühner]. Leipzig: Kiepenheuer.

Sundermeier, Theo (1988 and later): Nur gemeinsam können wir leben. Das
Menschenbild schwarzafrikanischer Religionen. Gütersloh: Gütersloher
Verl.-Haus Mohn (Gütersloher Taschenbücher Siebenstern).

Swain, Tony; Rose, Deborah (Hg.) (1988): Aboriginal Australians and Christian
missions. Ethnographic and historical studies. 1. printing. Bedford Park: Australian Association for the Study of Religions (Special studies in religions).

Swatridge, Colin (1985): Delivering the goods. Education as cargo in Papua New Guinea. Manchester: Manchester University Press.

Swatridge, Colin (1988): Goods and Gods. A follow-up study of "Steel axes for stone-age Australians". In: Swain/Rose 1988:438-451.

Teilhet-Fisk, J. H. (1991): To beat or not to beat, that is the question. A study on acculturation and change in an art-making process and its relation to gender structures. In: Pacific Studies (Lae), Jg. 14, H. 23, S. 41-68.

Thiel, Josef Franz (1977): Grundbegriffe der Ethnologie. Vorlesungen zur Einfuehrung. 2., unveränd. Aufl. St. Augustin: Anthropos-Institut (Collectanea Instituti Anthroposophici).

Thiel, Josef Franz (1984): Religionsethnologie. Grundbegriffe der Religionen schriftloser Völker. Berlin: Reimer (Collectanea Instituti Anthropos, 33).

Thiel, Josef Franz (1986): Was sind Fetische? Frankfurt am Main: Museum für Völkerkunde (Roter Faden zur Ausstellung / Museum für Völkerkunde).

Thomas, John (1984): The Namonuito solution to the "matrilineal puzzle". In: American Ethnologist, Jg. 7, H. 172-177.

Trimborn, Hermann (Hg.) (1971): Lehrbuch der Völkerkunde. 4., neubearb. Aufl. Stuttgart: Enke.

Tylor, Edward Burnett (1871): Primitive culture: researches into the development of mythology, philosophy, religion, language, art and custom. In two volumes. London.

van Gennep, Arnold (1909): Les rites de passage. Étude systématique des rites de la porte et du seuil, de l'hospitalité, de l'adoption, de la grossesse et de l'accouchement, de la naissance, de l'enfance, de la puberté, de l'initiation, de l'ordination, du couronnement, des fiançailles et du mariage, des funérailles, des saisons, etc. / Arnold van Gennep. Paris: Nourry.

Vivelo, Frank Robert (1981): Handbuch der Kulturanthropologie (Cultural anthropology handbook, dt.). Eine grundlegende Einführung. Stuttgart: Klett-Cotta.

Wallace, Ronald L. (1991): The tribal self. An anthropologist reflects on hunting, brain, and behavior. Lanham: University Press of America.

Wassmann, Jürg (2003a): Kognitive Ethnologie. In: Beer, Bettina; Fischer, Hans (Hg.): Ethnologie. Einführung und Überblick. Neufassung, 5. Aufl. Berlin: Reimer (Ethnologische Paperbacks), S. 323-340.

Weniger, Gerd-Christian (1982): Wildbeuter und ihre Umwelt. Ein Beitrag zum Magdalénien Südwestdeutschlands aus ökologischer und ethno-archäologischer Sicht / Gerd-Christian Weniger. Zugl.: Tuebingen, Univ., Diss., 1981. Tuebingen: Archaeologica Venatoria (Archaeologica venatoria, 5).

Whiting, R. (1977): The chrysanthemum and the bat. New York.

Whorf, Benjamin Lee (1963 und später): Sprache, Denken, Wirklichkeit. Beiträge zur Metalinguistik und Sprachphilosophie. Reinbek bei Hamburg: Rowohlt (Rowohlts deutsche Enzyklopädie).

Wienecke, Werner A. (1992): Die Bedeutung der Zeit in Afrika in den traditionellen Religionen und in der missionarischen Verkündigung. Zugl.: Pretoria, Univ. Südafrika, Diss. Frankfurt am Main, Bern, New York, Paris: Lang (Studien zur interkulturellen Geschichte des Christentums).

Wiesemann, Ursula (Hg.) (1992): Verstehen und verstanden werden. Praktisches Handbuch zum Fremdsprachenerwerb. Lahr: Ed. VLM im Verl. d. St.-Johannis-Druckerei (Edition C, 347).

Wiher, Hannes (2003): Shame and guilt. A key to cross-cultural ministry. Univ., Diss. u.d.T.: Wiher, Hannes: Understanding shame and guilt as a key to cross-cultural Christian ministry-Potchefstroom, 2002. Bonn: Verl. für Kultur und Wiss. (Edition Iwg Mission academics, 10).

Williams, Paul V. A. (1979): Primitive religion and healing. A study of folk medicine in North-East Brazil / Paul V. A. Williams. Cambridge: Brewer [et al.] (Mistletoe series).

Williams, Thomas R. (Hg.) (1975): Psychological anthropology. [IX. International Congress of Anthropological and Ethnological Sciences]. The Hague: Mouton [u.a.] (World anthropology).

Wolfram, Herwig (1990): Typen der Ethnogenese unter besonderer Berücksichtigung der Bayern. : Berichte des Symposions der Kommission für Frühmittelalterforschung, 27. bis 30. Oktober 1986, Stift Zwettl, Niederösterreich. Wien: Verl. der Österr. Akad. der Wiss. (Veröffentlichungen der Kommission für Frühmittelalterforschung / Österreichische Akademie der Wissenschaften, 12).

Wolfram, Herwig; Pohl, Walter (1990): Typen der Ethnogenese unter besonderer Berücksichtigung der Bayern. Berichte des Symposions der Kommission für Frühmittelalterforschung, 27. bis 30. Oktober 1986, Stift Zwettl, Niederösterreich. Wien: Verl. der Österr. Akad. der Wiss. (Veröffentlichungen der Kommission für Frühmittelalterforschung / Österreichische Akademie der Wissenschaften, 12).

Worsley, Peter (1973): Die Posaune wird erschallen. "Cargo"-Kulte in Melanesien. 1. Aufl. Frankfurt am Main: Suhrkamp.

Yamamoto, Shichihei (1987): Ursprünge der japanischen Arbeitsethik. In: Barloewen, Constantin von; Werhahn-Mees, Kai (Hg.): Japan und der Westen. Orig.-Ausg., 7.-9. Tsd. 2 Bände. Frankfurt a.M.: Fischer (Fischer-Taschenbücher, 6554), S. 95-129.

Zelizko, J. V.: Kletterfähigkeit der Naturvölker als atavistisches Merkmal der Urzeit. In: Mitteilungen der anthropologschen Gesellschaft in Wien, 66.1935/36.

Zier, Ursula (1987): Die Gewalt der Magie. Krankheit und Heilung in der kolumbianischen Volksmedizin. Berlin: Reimer (Krankheit und Kultur, 3).

Znoj, Heinz P. (1988): Die Evolution der Kulturfähigkeit. Beiträge zu einer Kritik des ethnologischen Kulturbegriffs. Bern: Lang.

Index

Animism
A Cognitive Approach

An Introduction to the Basic Notions Underlying the Concepts of the World and of Man Held by Ethnic Societies, for the Benefit of Those Working Overseas in Development Aid and in the Church

by Lothar Käser

Textbook
to Robert Badenberg's Handbook
The Concept of Man in Non-Western Cultures

In European and other western societies animism is often equated with occultism, spiritism and even with satanism, is evaluated according to European and Christian criteria, and is consequently misunderstood. Such an approach, together with lack of knowledge of the conceptual foundations of animistic thought forms, proves to be a particular impediment when foreigners from European and western cultures come to work in animistically oriented societies to offer development aid, to get involved in NGOs, whether under secular government auspices or the church, as doctors, soldiers, engineers, lecturers, teachers, or in specifically Christian mission. This is because animism not only contains religious elements, but with its particular concept of the world and of man constitutes an all-embracing system of orienting oneself, serving that society as a way of shaping and coping with existence. One has to have some knowledge of this in order to understand the people among whom one is working and for one's work to have successful outcomes.

This textbook does not present animism from a European and western perspective but from that of the people who live it out. The sequence of the individual chapters is arranged in such a way that the reader can learn step by step what animism is, in order finally to understand those characteristic functions that belong to the medium and the shaman in animistic societies.

The author, a professor of ethnology, has considerable experience in this field. He has worked for five years in Oceania and has also undertaken numerous research expeditions in Africa, Asia and South America.

Pb. • pp. 284 • £ 22.50 • $ 37.50 • € 29.95
ISBN 978-3-95776-111-8

VTR Publications • Gogolstr. 33 • 90475 Nürnberg • Germany
info@vtr-online.com • http://www.vtr-online.com

www.ingramcontent.com/pod-product-compliance
Lightning Source LLC
Chambersburg PA
CBHW070608270326
41926CB00013B/2467